MITCHELL
BEAZLEY
WINE
GUIDES

WINES OF
California

STEPHEN BROOK

Wines of California
by Stephen Brook

Edited and designed by Mitchell Beazley, an imprint of Octopus Publishing
Group Ltd, 2-4 Heron Quays, London E14 4JP

A CIP catalogue record for this book is available from the British Library.

ISBN 1 84000 393 6

The author and publishers will be grateful for any information that will assist
them in keeping future editions up to date. Although all reasonable care has
been taken in the preparation of this book, neither the publishers nor the
author can accept responsibility for any consequences arising from the use
thereof or from the information contained therein.

Commissioning Editor: Rebecca Spry
Executive Art Editor: Yasia Williams
Editors: Emma Rice, Jamie Ambrose
Designer: Colin Goody, Peter Gerrish
Index: John Noble
Production: Alix McCulloch

Typeset in Helvetica and Versailles
Printed and bound in China

Contents

Introduction

Wine was being made in California under the auspices of Spanish missionaries in the eighteenth century, but there is no reason to think that this wine was fit for anything other than communion. A commercial wine industry came into being in the mid-nineteenth century, and by century's end, California had a fine reputation for its red wines, the best of which were successfully exported.

The industry was dealt a double blow by phylloxera and then by Prohibition. After the repeal of Prohibition in the 1930s, the wine industry limped along. The craft of making fine wine had been all but lost, wineries were equipped with out-of-date equipment, vineyards were planted with unsuitable varieties geared to the production of mediocre fortified wines. It would take decades, and the forceful intervention of imported winemakers such as André Tchelistcheff, to drag California wine into the modern era.

It was in the 1960s that the extraordinary potential of California began to reveal itself. The wine regions of Europe needed to struggle to produce ripe fruit; in California, in most years, the fruit looked after itself, ripening to perfection in the steady warm sunshine. When, in a famous Paris tasting in 1976, French tasters preferred Californian Cabernet and Chardonnay to the best of Bordeaux and Burgundy, it was a tribute to the joyous hedonism of California grapes. What sun, orange juice, and surfing did for California girls, sunshine and well-drained soils did for California wines.

Within a decade, California winemakers had mastered the art of producing rich, juicy, flavourful wines, bolder and more opulent than their European models. But did they have finesse? The history of the last few decades has been one of refinement. At first, Californian winemakers believed their red wines needed powerful tannins to give them the same longevity as the great wines of Bordeaux. After a while, it dawned on them that a tough, tannic young wine usually ages into a tough, tannic old wine. More recently, talk has been of tannin management, and of picking grapes at full phenolic ripeness rather than merely high sugar levels.

For white wines, too, there was much to learn. Very ripe fruit and lashings of oak could yield rich but ultimately cloying wines from Chardonnay and even Sauvignon Blanc. But the more sophisticated winemakers knew there was more to Chardonnay than obvious fruitiness. They went off to Burgundy to sit at the feet of the masters, and returned to California with the intention of making wines with more complexity, more delicacy, more elegance. And the best of them have succeeded.

Pinot Noir had eluded even the best of California's winemakers, but by the mid-1980s, even this toughest of oenological nuts was beginning to crack. More and more attention was paid to vineyards and site selection, not just for Pinot but for all varieties. The revisitation of phylloxera in the 1980s was, in true American fashion, seen as an opportunity as well as a disaster. Replanting ensured that the right variety was planted in the right spot.

Although California worshipped, and still worships, the twin deities of Cabernet Sauvignon and Chardonnay, plenty of other varieties got a look in: Pinot Noir, Sauvignon Blanc, Merlot, and Zinfandel were all popular, and an increasing number of growers and winemakers became intrigued by other varieties. Winemakers such as Randall Grahm argued persuasively that the Californian climate was better suited to Mediterranean varieties than to the austere Bordeaux red grapes (although it could plausibly be argued that Napa Cabernet is the closest international rival to classed-growth Bordeaux). Throughout California, the acreage planted with varieties such as Syrah, Viognier, and Sangiovese grew and grew, and even oddballs such as Albariño, Arneis, and Trousseau turned up here and there, all offering consumers far greater choice than twenty years ago.

The future looks bright for California. At the cheapest end of the market, it performs no better than Australia, Chile, or the Languedoc, but wines such as Oakville Cabernet, Russian River Pinot Noir, Dry Creek Zinfandel, and Santa Barbara Syrah offer real intensity and diversity. The best wines are not cheap, but they deliver the goods. However, it cannot be denied that many wines are severely overpriced, but a short nationwide economic downturn will probably put an end to the more fatuous antics of the cult wine producers and their acolytes.

For the wine-lover with curiosity, courage, and a reasonable bank balance, California offers greater quality and diversity than ever before. Yet with around 1,000 wineries at work, even the best-informed consumer needs a guiding hand, which this book hopes to provide.

How to Use This Book

The first part of this book takes a thorough look at the different wine regions of California. Although California is widely perceived as focusing exclusively on the international grape varieties such as Cabernet Sauvignon and Chardonnay, there are in fact dozens of different varietal wines being produced today, so there is an extensive section on all these varieties.

A vintage chart is useless, given the size and diversity of California's wine regions, but an attempt has been made to describe the vintages of the last ten years in some detail.

The major part of this guide is devoted to a directory of wineries, arranged according to the wine regions in which they are located. These are assessed on a five-star rating system. In some instances – such as a recent change of ownership, or the lack of any opportunities to taste the wines – no rating is given, as indicated by the initials "NR".

In recent years, most wineries have established websites, and these are a useful source of additional knowledge about them and their wines. All known websites are listed with each entry.

The Region and its Wines

Introduction to the Regions

NAPA VALLEY

Napa Valley is neither the oldest nor the largest of California's wine regions. But it is hard to dispute that it is the state's most prestigious region, producing the majestic Cabernets that have secured a place among the world's best and most costly red wines.

The valley stretches north for some thirty miles from San Pablo Bay to Mount St Helena. At its broadest, it is five miles wide. Although a compact region, Napa Valley is varied in its microclimates. For a start, there is considerable variation between the southern zones and the most northerly ones. The south – that is, Carneros and American Canyon – is markedly cooler, and is far better suited to Burgundian varieties than to Bordeaux varieties, which do not always ripen. The opposite is true of northern Napa, where the daytime heat is more congenial to Cabernet and Zinfandel than to Chardonnay.

Napa Valley is framed to the west by the Mayacamas Mountains and to the east by the Vaca Range. Zones such as Mount Veeder, Spring Mountain, and Diamond Mountain lie on the western slopes at heights of up to 2,200 feet, while Howell Mountain and Atlas Peak lie to the east at similar elevations. Chiles Valley, east of Rutherford, is higher than the valley floor but lower than the mountain zones. These mountain sites yield different styles of wine: the soils are stonier and more impoverished than those on the valley floor, and the height of the vineyards means that they are usually free of the coastal fogs that roll along the valley floor and provide a beneficial cooling effect. They are also above the frost line. These mountain vineyards are often the source of Napa's most rugged and tannic Cabernets.

Until the vine louse, phylloxera, devastated the valley's vineyards for the second time in the 1980s and 1990s, a wide range of grape varieties was planted. Riesling and Muscat often grew alongside Cabernet and Chardonnay. The replanting required after phylloxera allowed growers to eliminate the least suitable varieties, though often the grapes chosen for replanting just happened to be those that fetched the highest prices on the open market. Yet it would be foolish to deny that the Bordeaux varieties and Syrah are far better suited to Napa's climate than grapes such as Riesling. Fortunately, the new vogue for wines from Zinfandel and Petite Sirah should help to preserve the venerable vineyards still planted with those traditional varieties.

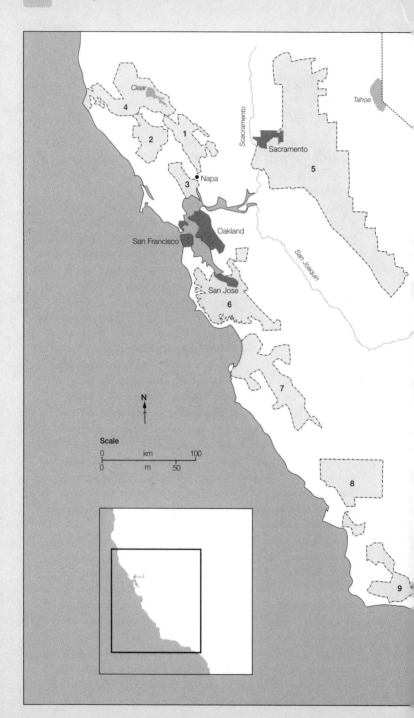

California regions

Mono

Owens

Los Angeles

1. Napa Valley
2. Sonoma County
3. Carneros
4. Mendocino County
5. Sierra Foothills
6. San Francisco Bay
7. Monterey County
8. San Luis Obispo County
9. Santa Barbara County

If there is a historical heartland for Napa Cabernet, it is surely Rutherford, where the early Inglenook and Beaulieu vineyards were planted in the nineteenth century. Nonetheless, Cabernet from Oakville, Yountville, and the Stags Leap District to the south, and from St Helena and Calistoga to the north can be equally fine. Everyone seems to have an understandable affection for the Stags Leap District, which produces the most stylish Cabernets of the valley. The best sites are the alluvial fans on the sides of the valley; vineyards in the valley centre, especially those close to the Napa River, can be too rich in their soil texture. Those from the well-drained benchlands just above Oakville and Rutherford achieve just the right balance of richness, power, opulence, and finesse.

The development of Napa Valley is relatively recent, even though it was a prestigious region in the late nineteenth century. As recently as 1965, there were only about twenty-five wineries in operation. Then Joe Heitz, Robert Mondavi, and others founded or revived wineries, and by the late 1970s there were over fifty. Today there are 232 physical wineries, as well as many other properties, often very small, producing their wines at custom-crush facilities. Nonetheless, acquiring a Napa estate and winery remains the burning ambition for the would-be entrant into the wine business. There may be more excitement and potential in other regions such as Santa Barbara, but Napa remains the collector's Mecca. And this is for a good reason, since no other Californian wine region can point to such a record of success with red Bordeaux varieties.

In addition to Napa Valley itself, the AVAs (official appellations) are Atlas Peak, Chiles Valley, Diamond Mountain, Howell Mountain, Carneros (shared with Sonoma), Mount Veeder, Oakville, Rutherford, Saint Helena, Spring Mountain District, Stags Leap District, Wild Horse Valley, and Yountville.

SONOMA COUNTY

Sonoma County is the most amoeba-like of California's wine regions: constantly dividing and reshaping itself. No doubt this constant redrawing of boundaries has the appeal of a sophisticated parlour game to Sonoma's growers and wineries. The outcome has been a diffusion of AVAs, many of which are overlapping. This is not altogether surprising, as Sonoma is a large county with very diverse microclimates. You can grow just about anything in Sonoma: lean, elegant Chardonnay, complex Pinot Noir, robust Zinfandel, full-bodied Cabernet, spicy Syrah... Sonoma can do it all.

Its history is at least as old as that of Napa Valley, and there were vineyards here from the mid-1850s. Later in the century, many immigrants arrived from Italy and sought to replicate the vineyards of their native land by planting robust red varieties. Their nostalgia is today our legacy, and many ancient, even centenarian vineyards planted with Zinfandel, Petite Sirah, and Carignane still survive as the source of some of Sonoma's most distinctive wines.

Unfortunately, as anyone driving up Highway 101 can see, Sonoma County is succumbing to urban sprawl. Where vineyards once grew on the edges of towns such as Sonoma, Santa Rosa, and Windsor there are now suburban tracts. Furthermore, the big boys have moved into Sonoma. Once a collection of small or medium-sized vineyards with wineries to match, Sonoma has now attracted the attention of the likes of Gallo and Kendall-Jackson, both of which have planted thousands of acres in the county. Nonetheless, the fundamental character of the county has not changed that much.

There are currently around 54,000 acres under vine, with Chardonnay accounting for around one-third of the surface, followed by Cabernet, and then by Merlot and Pinot Noir. In terms of acreage, Alexander Valley is the largest approved viticultural area, or AVA, with 15,000 acres, followed by Sonoma Valley and, level-pegging at 10,000 acres, Dry Creek Valley and Russian River Valley. There are well over 1,000 grape farmers, and 172 "bricks-and-mortar" wineries located here.

The most southerly and coolest region is Carneros, which, as one heads north, leads into Sonoma Valley, one of the county's most versatile regions, where a wide range of grape varieties can be grown successfully. To the west of the valley is the small Sonoma Mountain AVA, home to some fine, if tannic Cabernets. West of Santa Rosa lies the Russian River Valley, a diverse region with some relatively cool spots that have proved exceptional for Pinot Noir. The chilly Green Valley and the Chalk Hill AVAs are in fact subregions within Russian River Valley, and their names are rarely encountered on labels. North of Healdsburg lies the Alexander Valley, a mostly warm region well-suited to Bordeaux red varieties. To the west of Alexander Valley is Dry Creek Valley, best known for some of California's finest Zinfandel. Knights Valley links Sonoma County with Napa; a relatively warm zone, it is home to some extensive Beringer-owned vineyards and to the Peter Michael estate. Finally, there is the Sonoma Coast appellation. This vast region stretches from the border with Marin County in the south to the Mendocino frontier in the north, but those who praise the region are usually referring to the high ridge-lands overlooking the Pacific coastline. These very cool vineyards are capable, except in years when nothing ripens fully, of producing exceptionally intense Burgundian varieties. It has become extremely fashionable, and many chic wine producers have been purchasing land here. Flowers is the best known winery within the region. (The Northern Sonoma AVA was created at the behest of Gallo, and is so large as to be virtually meaningless.)

Being more diffuse than Napa Valley, Sonoma offers good hunting for the wine tourist, with many smaller wineries keen to pour their wines and talk about them. Prices are not quite at extortionate Napa levels, but the fashionable varieties from fashionable wineries are not lagging far behind.

Sonoma County's AVAs are Alexander Valley, Chalk Hill, Dry Creek Valley, Knights Valley, Carneros (shared with Napa), Green Valley, Northern Sonoma, Russian River Valley, Sonoma Coast, Sonoma Mountain, and Sonoma Valley.

CARNEROS

Carneros is an anomaly in that its acreage is shared by two counties: Napa and Sonoma. This is because its climatic and soil conditions pay no attention to administrative boundaries. This is the region, recognized as an AVA in 1983, that is the coolest in both counties, since it is close to San Pablo Bay, and is not only prone to regular invasions of fog but is also notoriously windy, which can puts the brakes on maturation. There had been vineyards here in the third quarter of the nineteenth century, but the usual unholy alliance of phylloxera and Prohibition put an end to grape farming. In the 1940s and 1950s, there was a little new planting at the suggestion of Louis Martini and Beaulieu, but the true revival of Carneros began in the mid-1960s, when significant new plantings at the Sangiacomo, Winery Lake, and other vineyards spurred recognition of the special qualities of Carneros grapes.

Fifty-five per cent of the region lies within Napa, the rest within Sonoma. The soil is a relatively shallow and infertile clay-loam, so the vines do not show excessive vigour. The cool and dry microclimate (rainfall is twice as high in Healdsburg to the north in Sonoma) keeps acidity levels high, and the wines often show an invigorating freshness. Some 9,000 acres are planted, and although many more could be developed, salty soils, a shortage of water for irrigation, and unsuitable microclimates have inhibited further growth. Almost half the vines are Chardonnay, with thirty per cent Pinot Noir. Merlot shows promise, as does Syrah, but Cabernet will only ripen in a few warmer corners. In some years the Bordeaux varieties can show a herbaceous character.

A great deal of research has been undertaken into the character traits of Carneros fruit. In 1987, extensive tastings established that Pinot Noir often shows intense berry (including strawberry) characters, while Chardonnay is often citric, with Muscat-like tones and an occasional appley component. Chardonnay exhibits delicacy but no lack of body or structure. Although Carneros Pinot can have great charm and finesse, it is by no means evident that California's best Pinot Noir is grown here, and many connoisseurs would give the edge to Russian River Valley or the Sonoma Coast. Of course, clonal selection and other factors such as elevation, density of planting, and exposure to strong winds complicate the picture.

Much of the fruit is now dedicated to sparkling-wine production, and it is no coincidence that some of California's leading sparkling-wine facilities are based in Carneros.

MENDOCINO COUNTY

Until fairly recently, Mendocino County, with its stunning Pacific coastline, was better known as a holiday destination than as a vineyard region. Like Sonoma just to the south, it was settled by Italian growers in the 1850s; they chose hillside sites that replicated the slopes of their native land. Many of those old vineyards still survive, and in many cases are still owned by the original settlers' descendants. About one quarter of Mendocino's vines are over fifty years old. It is only in the last decade or so that these old sites have been recognized as a tremendous resource. Before then, these grapes from old-vine Zinfandel, Petite Sirah, Carignane, and other varieties were dispatched south to the large jug-wine companies, where they provided backbone to popular inexpensive blends such as Gallo's Hearty Burgundy and many a white Zinfandel. Even as recently as 1967, the only operating winery in the county was Parducci, followed a year or so later by Fetzer. Even in the 1990s, at least one-third of Mendocino fruit left the county to supply wineries elsewhere.

It was Fetzer which led the other trend that makes Mendocino distinctive: an emphasis on organic, even biodynamic, viticulture. In this respect, Mendocino is far in advance of other wine regions of California and is favoured by the scarcity of mildew and botrytis. Figures now a few years old estimate that the proportion of vineyards cultivated organically to be twenty–five per cent; I suspect that the figure today would be significantly larger.

There is considerable climatic variation in Mendocino, and despite their northerly location, inland districts such as Redwood Valley can be quite warm. Rainfall levels are slightly higher than they are south of the county line. Remember that northern Sonoma is far warmer than southern Sonoma, and the inland valleys of Mendocino have very limited maritime influence. However, the closer one gets to the Pacific shore, the cooler the climate. Anderson Valley in particular can, in some vintages, be so cool that it becomes a real struggle to ripen the grapes. It is for this reason that some of California's top sparkling-wine producers, notably Roederer, have chosen to locate their vineyards here. It is also a good place to grow Riesling and Alsatian varieties, as Navarro has done, although commercial considerations have put the brakes on too heavy an investment in such varieties. Mendocino Ridge is a promising new appellation available only to vineyards located at an elevation of at least 1,200 feet – but at seventy five acres, it is tiny.

Even in the warmer parts of Mendocino, the grapes often retain good tartaric acidity levels, which gives Chardonnay in particular a crisper fruit definition than it would attain in Napa or many parts of Sonoma. It can also benefit varieties such as Viognier. Indeed, Mendocino as a whole is open-minded when it comes to varietal selection. McDowell and Fetzer have led the way in producing Rhône varieties, white as well as red, in commercial quantities, while winemakers such as Greg Graziano have specialized in Italian varieties such as Barbera. Quality can sometimes be patchy, but the wines rarely lack interest and personality.

Mendocino County's AVAs are Anderson Valley, Cole Ranch, McDowell Valley, Mendocino Ridge, Potter Valley, Redwood Valley, and Yorkville Highlands.

SIERRA FOOTHILLS

In the 1850s, prospectors came here in their thousands to pan for gold. In their wake came the usual hangers-on: women, bar operators, grape growers. Within a decade there were around 10,000 acres under vine and some sixty wineries in operation, far surpassing the production of Napa and Sonoma combined. Even after the Gold Rush had ended, the wineries managed to keep going. It was phylloxera and Prohibition that almost wiped them out in succeeding decades. There has been a revival, and the current acreage is around 5,000 and there are fifty wineries. Fortunately, quite a few of the historic old vineyards survived, and one of the glories of the Foothills is its old-vine Zinfandel.

The Foothills, as the name suggests, are marked by the elevation of the vineyards, which lie between the flatlands of the San Francisco Bay and the shining peaks of the Sierra Nevada. The Eldorado AVA only includes vineyards at over 1,400 feet. In fact, many of them are planted at well over 2,000 feet. This high elevation, as well as the thin granitic and volcanic soils, yields wines that are naturally high in tannin. That is why there are many wines that are distinctly rustic; growers and winemakers who know how to attain full ripeness in the grapes and how to tame the tannins can, however, produce superlative wines.

The region falls into three distinct zones. The vineyards of Eldorado County are focused around Placerville in the north, while those of Calaveras County fringe the old mining town of Murphys in the south. The most important zone is Amador County, which lies roughly midway between the two. Within Amador County there are two important subregions: Fiddletown and Shenandoah, both renowned for their Zinfandel.

Zinfandel is the most important variety, but just about everything is grown here, although Bordeaux varieties are not the Foothills' strongest suit. Quite a few wineries have opted to focus on Rhône varieties, and have done so with great success. Others, notably Montevina, have sought to create a niche market for Italian varieties, often with less success. The Foothills is also a good source of sweet wines, either Muscats or port-style wines, which can be impressive.

The popularity of the region with tourists, streaming through on their way to Lake Tahoe and the Sierras, will always be a bonus, and many wineries make a point of associating themselves with the Gold Rush, none more so than Ironstone, with its ever-expanding tourist complex and its astonishing gold exhibits. The Foothills as a whole have rustic charm rather than winemaking sophistication, but that is changing, and a handful of leading wineries have shown just how magnificent a Zinfandel or Syrah can be from this rugged corner of California.

There are also some subregions on the fringes of the Foothills, such as Nevada County, home to a handful of wineries, and North Yuba, where the magnificent terraced vineyards of the Renaissance Winery are located.

The AVAs of the Sierra Foothills are El Dorado, Fiddletown, North Yuba, and Shenandoah Valley.

SAN FRANCISCO BAY

In 1999, a new AVA was created: the San Francisco Bay appellation. It embraces regions to the east of the Bay, such as Livermore and Contra Costa, as well as counties to the south, such as Santa Cruz and Santa Clara. Livermore wineries such as Wente and Concannon were keen on the new appellation, but it's hard to see it catching on in Santa Cruz or Santa Clara, which are quite distant from the Bay.

Nonetheless, the directory will cover broadly the same area, even though there are few unifying factors. Almost all of the regions are – in California terms, at least – fairly ancient, and their history is not, as in Paso Robles or Santa Barbara, one of eager expansion; rather it is one of steady decline. Proximity to San Francisco Bay inevitably means proximity to San Francisco itself. With the Bay area still acting as a magnet to those drawn to the balmy climate, the multicultural society, and the zesty economy, there is a constantly growing demand for housing, and where once there were acres of vineyards, there are instead dreary housing tracts and industrial parks. America's Silicon Valley sizzles on what used to be Santa Clara's and San José's vineyards.

Some wineries do survive in Santa Clara, mostly around Gilroy and Hecker Pass. For the most part, they are still run by the descendants of their Italian founders, and they doze along, catering to a local clientele and rarely aspiring to greatness. Many of the wines are frankly rustic. Santa Cruz Mountains is another matter altogether. Wineries such as Ridge, Mount Eden, and David Bruce are based high up these coastal ranges, drawing on elevated mountain vineyards for much of their fruit. These wines can be among California's most structured and long-lived, but the area under vine is tiny, and some of the vineyards must be considered something of an endangered species.

On the East Bay are the venerable Mourvedre vineyards of Contra Costa County, and a handful of wineries in Livermore, which has some impressive gravelly soils very different to the varied mountain and benchland sites south of the Bay. There are also a handful of wineries around Sacramento in the Lodi region. Detractors of this zone believe it has more in common with the Central Valley (of which, indeed, it forms the uppermost sector) than with the Bay. Lodi is mostly a region of very large commercial vineyards, but good wines are now emerging from here. Overall, this remains a viticulturally conservative area, and the enthusiasm for Rhône or Italian varieties, so prevalent elsewhere, is scarcely exhibited here.

Many of the surviving wineries in the San Francisco Bay AVA are very small, some of them essentially hobby wineries, even if some express high aspirations. These wines are scarcely known even within California, as their case production is very limited and their distribution equally so.

In addition to the catch-all San Francisco Bay AVA, the other AVAs of the region are Ben Lomond Mountain, Lime Kiln Valley, Livermore Valley, Mount Harlan (east of Salinas, and used only by Calera), Pacheco Pass, Paicines, San Benito, Santa Clara Valley, Santa Cruz Mountains, and San Ysidro District.

MONTEREY COUNTY

The Central Coast is a vast area that includes Contra Costa, Monterey, San Luis Obispo, and Santa Barbara counties. Climatically, it is quite distinct from the North Coast regions of Napa, Sonoma, Lake, and Mendocino.

In 1966, there were only five acres of vines in Salinas Valley, the main vineyard region of Monterey County. But the agricultural experts had their eye on the valley, which they suspected would provide ideal conditions for viticulture, as well as offering large expanses suitable for industrial-sized vineyards. By 1975, there were 35,000 acres under vine, a trend encouraged in part by tax shelters offered to investors,

The experts had calculated the suitability of Monterey on the grounds of its coolness and sunniness. Maritime fogs kept the temperature down during the daytime, and low rainfall required irrigation but also allowed growers to control how much water the vines received. What few realized at the time was that the winds roaring down the valley would have a harsh effect on the vines, retarding maturation.

There was a sudden retrenching in the late 1970s. It had now become clear that Cabernet Sauvignon would not ripen properly, except in a few privileged areas. On the other hand, Monterey proved ideal for white varieties, especially Chardonnay. (There used to be a good deal of Riesling, which made delicious wine, but it had limited commercial appeal.) The big wineries moved in to plant vast acreage: Kendall-Jackson tops the chart with its 2,500 acres, Mondavi follows with 1,350, while Hess and Raymond both have over 300. Not to be outdone, in the southern part of Salinas Valley is the mother of all California vineyards: the 8,500-acre San Bernabe, now owned by Delicato Vineyards.

Soon the subregions of Monterey became recognized for their distinctive personalities. Chalone was virtually a monopoly of the Chalone estate, and its high vineyards produced fine Chenin Blanc and Burgundian varieties. The Carmel Valley, although closer to the Pacific than the Salinas Valley, was sheltered and warm, and here indeed was a region where Cabernet could ripen to yield elegant wines. And the Santa Lucia Highlands, usually just above the fog-line, would in time prove the source of exquisite Pinot Noir and fine Syrah, as well as Chardonnay and Riesling.

Given the size of the region, there are relatively few wineries. Some, such as Scheid, Paraiso Springs, Lockwood, and Talbott, are outlets for large vineyard operations. A few are small family or artisanal wineries, and there are a handful of quality-conscious, medium-sized producers such as Chalone. Some of the wineries listed in the directory – notably Mirassou and Lohr – are based in San Jose, but derive almost all their fruit from Monterey County.

In addition to Monterey and the catch-all Central Coast, the AVAs are Arroyo Seco, Carmel Valley, Chalone, Hames Valley, San Lucas, and Santa Lucia Highlands.

SAN LUIS OBISPO COUNTY

This bulky county name is home to a few wine regions, of which the most important is easily Paso Robles. In addition, there is the much more maritime Edna Valley, and the more amorphous Arroyo Grande. Although some vineyards were planted here in 1797 by missionaries, the first commercial winemaking began in the 1880s.

Paso Robles is a large area sheltered from the Pacific by the Santa Lucia Mountains, which should not be confused with the Santa Lucia Highlands located further north, in Monterey County. Paso Robles is bisected by the north-south Highway 101.

To the west of the highway is the appropriately named Westside region. This is a mountain area, with higher rainfall than most of Paso Robles; soils are very varied. The wines tend to have the characteristics found in most "mountain" vineyards: robust tannins and ample structure. The much larger vineyards to the east of Highway 101 are on a plateau. Although all kinds of grape varieties are grown here, they are best known for charming, medium-bodied reds from Cabernet, Zinfandel, Syrah, and other varieties. Daytime temperatures on the plateau can be extremely high, but an elevation of around 1,200 feet keeps night-time temperatures cooler, so Paso Robles wines rarely seem baked.

Edna Valley is almost entirely flat, and its cool climate makes it very well-suited to Chardonnay, which overwhelmingly dominates the 1,400 acres of vineyards. Arroyo Grande also has plenty of Chardonnay, but Pinot Noir gets more of a chance. The soil is lighter in Arroyo Grande than in Edna Valley, and there is less maritime influence. There is also a tiny region called York Mountain, high and cool; it is dominated by red varieties, but Cabernet rarely ripens.

There has been steady growth in the number of wineries in the county. In 1997, there were thirty-six. Today, there are over fifty. They include the very large producers such as Meridian and Arciero, some artisanal, old-fashioned grower/winemakers, and ambitious and sophisticated producers such as Justin and Tablas Creek.

The AVAs are Arroyo Grande Valley, Edna Valley, Paso Robles, and York Mountain.

SANTA BARBARA COUNTY

Like Monterey, Santa Barbara County scarcely existed as a wine region until the 1970s. In 1969, there were a mere eleven acres under vine. Thereafter expansion was rapid, and was mostly restricted to two valleys: Santa Maria and Santa Ynez. There are now about 20,000 acres. Chardonnay dominates, and Pinot Noir is greatly valued, but in the 1990s it became evident that Santa Barbara was also capable of producing delicious Rhône varietals, a trend set to continue.

Santa Maria is the more northerly of the two main regions, an east-west valley some seventeen miles long. Again, as in Monterey, there are many very large vineyards either planted or purchased by the major California wineries, such as Kendall-Jackson and Mondavi, as well as a few

ANDRE TCHELISTCHEFF

This Russian winemaker is rightly revered as the founder of modern Californian winemaking. Born in 1901, he left Russia during the Revolution, and was trained as a wine chemist. In 1937, he was hired by Georges de Latour of Beaulieu to revive his winery after the repeal of Prohibition. This he did, replacing outmoded equipment, controlling fermentation practices, and undertaking changes in the vineyards, too. Tchelistcheff was happy to share his findings and ideas with other winemakers, and an entire generation was influenced by his thoughtful approach. He left Beaulieu in 1973, but continued to work as a consultant in Washington State as well as California. He died at a ripe old age in 1994.

independently owned ranches such as the celebrated Bien Nacido. Many of the best vineyards are on benchland and are well-drained. Rainfall is very low, and the climate decidedly cool. Indeed, in some years Pinot Noir can develop a slight vegetal quality. Natural acidities can be high, and almost all Chardonnay vinified from Santa Maria fruit goes through malolactic fermentation.

Further south is Santa Ynez Valley, which also runs from east to west. Its peculiarity is that with every mile that you move away from the Pacific shore, you gain an additional average degree in temperature. Thus, the western end of the valley is best suited to Burgundian varieties, whereas further east it is warm enough to grow Bordeaux varieties. Not surprisingly, there is a huge varietal range in Santa Ynez.

Many of the original vineyards in Santa Barbara were planted on their own rootstocks and became vulnerable to the outbreaks of phylloxera that occurred here in the 1990s. Many growers took advantage of the situation to replant or restructure their vineyards, bringing them into line with the latest thinking on clonal selection, rootstocks, and trellising systems. This should mean that the future for the county is very bright. Jim Clendenen of Au Bon Climat recalls that some splendid wines were made in the early 1980s, even though much of the plant material was second-rate; now that the viticultural aspect is being sorted out, quality should become even more spectacular.

In 2001 the Santa Rita Hills was elevated to AVA status. This region has 500 acres of vineyards at the western end of the Santa Ynez Valley. This is a cool region with maritime influence.

Existing AVAs are Santa Maria and Santa Ynez Valleys and Santa Rita Hills. Although there has been a burgeoning of wineries in this area during recent years, many of them are very small.

THE REST OF CALIFORNIA

Most of the regions discussed above, with the exception of the Sierra Foothills, are coastal, but it is impossible to ignore the huge inland valleys that are also planted with extensive vineyards. These form the immense 200-mile-long Central Valley, the northern section of which is known as the San Joaquin Valley, which extends southwards from Lodi and the Sacramento Delta through a succession of counties: Yolo, San Joaquin, Stanislaus, Merced, Madera, Fresno, Tulare, Kings, and Kern. About 175,000 acres are planted; most of the vineyards are very large and farmed on an industrial scale to supply the lower end of the market. The region is extremely hot, and expectations for quality are low. High-yielding grape varieties such as French Colombard, Ruby Cabernet, and Burger (never identified as varietals on a label), and even the table grape Thompson Seedless are cultivated here. About seventy per cent of all the wine produced in California comes from the Central Valley, although in future the balance is likely to shift, as large new Central Coast vineyards come into production.

Nonetheless, there are zones, mostly in the north, where good-quality wines can be produced. Lodi has been included in the San Francisco Bay section, but close by are Clarksburg, best known for good Chenin Blanc and Petite Sirah; Solano Green Valley (not to be confused with the district of the same name in Sonoma); and Suisun Valley. Further south, there are good port-style wines and Muscats from Madera in Fresno County. The AVAs are Clarksburg, Diablo Grande, Dunnigan Hills (the fiefdom of RH Phillips), Solano Green Valley, Madera, Merritt Island, and Suisun Valley.

There are some regions south of Santa Barbara, grouped in or around Los Angeles. There was a large wine industry here in the nineteenth century, but it was wiped out by disease. The same thing is happening today, and Pierce's disease, a bacterial infection, has become a major problem. There is a tiny production from Bel Air and Malibu Canyon; the latter now enjoys its own AVA of Malibu-Newton Canyon. Temecula lies between Los Angeles and San Diego, and the acreage, mostly devoted to Chardonnay, has been substantially reduced by Pierce's disease. Further north, around San Bernardino, is Cucamonga Valley, home to some interesting Zinfandel. Vineyards around San Diego in the far south include the San Pasqual Valley. The umbrella AVA here is South Coast, with individual AVAs for Cucamonga Valley, Malibu-Newton Canyon, San Pasqual Valley, and Temecula.

Finally, there is Lake County, located between Napa and Mendocino. This region was revived in the late 1960s; it became best known for its white grapes, notably Sauvignon Blanc, but the number of wineries has dwindled. The Guenoc estate occupies its own AVA. The other AVAs are Benmore Valley and Clear Lake (by far the most important, with over 3,000 acres), and the whole region falls under the vast North Coast appellation.

Grape Varieties

Although there is a common perception that the California wine industry and wine consumer is only interested in two grape varieties – Cabernet Sauvignon and Chardonnay – this is in fact a caricature. A huge range of varieties is grown and vinified in California, although some of them are minuscule in terms of volume. There are a surprising number of wineries throughout California that are focusing almost exclusively on Rhône or Italian varietals.

Albariño This lively Spanish white variety is almost unknown in California, but Qupé produced one in 2000.

Aleatico An Italian red variety used mostly for sweet wines in Tuscany, Elba, and Puglia. Montevina make an acceptable Californian version.

Alicante Bouschet Deeply coloured, this variety was used in the past in California to beef up low-priced jug wines. The acreage has remained steady in recent years at 1,600 acres, and a few wineries, such as Topolos and Wellington in Sonoma, still produce varietal versions.

Arneis Although overall acreage remains tiny, there is growing enthusiasm for this nutty, white Piedmontese variety. Producers include Chimney Rock, Enotria, Seghesio, Viansa, and Wild Horse.

Barbera This underrated Piedmontese red grape was widely planted in California, partly because Italian immigrants knew and understood Barbera, partly because of its abundant yields, and also because its high acidity was not entirely obliterated by the Californian sun. It was a mainstay of cheap jug wines, but some enthusiasts rightly value it for its deliciously vibrant fruit character when yields are kept down. Acreage is in gentle decline, but there are still at least 11,000 acres in California, mostly in the Central Valley. Producers include Biale, Boeger, Bonny Doon, Enotria, Kahn, Louis Martini, Monte Volpe, Montevina, Renwood, Seghesio, and Shenandoah.

Cabernet Franc It is hard to verify, but the Savannah-Chanelle estate in Saratoga claims to have the oldest surviving Cabernet Franc vines in California, theirs having been planted in 1923. In the late 1990s, the variety enjoyed a mild surge in popularity, rising in acreage to 3,500. It had previously been used as a blending variety, but pure versions were relatively rare. As a variety it is vigorous and easy to over-crop. It is certainly enjoying a revival in Santa Barbara, where the relatively cool climate gives a vivid, blueberry-scented wine. The best Cabernet Sauvignon/Cabernet Franc blends include Dalla Valle's Maya, Viader, and Havens' Bourriquot.

Producers of varietal Cabernet Franc include Bedford Thompson, Cosentino, Gainey, Hahn, Ironstone, LinCourt, Longoria, Peju Province, Pride, Reverie, St Francis, Sinskey, Tobin James, Vita Nova, and Yorkville Cellars. Nelson is the one winery that produces only Cabernet Franc.

Cabernet Sauvignon If there is one variety that triumphs in California, it is surely Cabernet Sauvignon. For many years it took second place to Zinfandel in terms of acreage planted, but in 2000, it soared ahead, with 70,000 acres to Zinfandel's 50,000. Quite a few wineries, of which Diamond Creek and Silver Oak are among the best-known examples, have developed a reputation for producing no other wine, and the so-called cult wines, for which the most extravagant prices are paid by collectors, are invariably Cabernets. For many older wine producers, Bordeaux was the model to which they aspired, and it was evident that Napa and Sonoma in particular were very well suited to Cabernet. Some chose to blend in other Bordeaux varieties; others were satisfied with a pure varietal version.

Cabernet was already being planted in California in the 1850s, usually as part of a field blend of Bordeaux varieties used to produce "California Médoc". Phylloxera destroyed most of these vines, and by the time Prohibition was repealed in the 1930s, there were only some 3,200 acres left, all in Rutherford and at Simi in Sonoma. Gradually, however, plantings increased, as it became evident that this was the only international variety with which California had the best and most realistic chance of rivalling the wines of Europe.

Fortunately the variety has proved easy to grow. It enjoys the warmth of California, and fares equally well on rich, alluvial, benchland soils, and on thinner, dry-farmed mountain sites. The latter, such as Sonoma Mountain and Spring Mountain, tend to yield wines with high tannin levels, and it has been a struggle for some producers to tame those tannins. In the early 1980s, many over-tannic wines were produced on the theory that time alone would soften the tannins and give the wines harmony. Often it never happened. In the 1990s, winemakers adopted techniques, such as longer hang-time on the vine or extended maceration in the winery, which have usually proved successful in delivering wines that are more fleshy and rounded and accessible young.

It is arguable that this trend has been taken to extremes, and that many highly rated Cabernets, renowned for their richness and depth of colour, are made from overripe grapes, lack acidity, and will not age well. It is too early to say whether these critics are right.

Cabernet Sauvignon likes warmth, so a handful of regions in California are not well suited to its cultivation. These include the Sonoma coastal ridgetops, Carneros, Russian River Valley, much of Monterey, and most of Santa Barbara. Early attempts to grow Cabernet in these regions resulted in vegetal, green-pepper aromas and flavours that most wine drinkers found off-putting.

It is clear that Cabernet will retain its supremacy because it does indeed give a splendidly rich and complex wine, because it seen as a rival to the legendary wines of Bordeaux itself, and because it is relatively easy to

VARIETAL LABELLING

Until the repeal of Prohibition, California wines were blends under such names as "Claret" or "Chianti". It was the writer Frank Schoonmaker who, in the late 1930s, persuaded wineries to introduce varietal labelling. This was the true birth of Napa Cabernet (from Inglenook) and Sonoma Sylvaner and Napa Pinot Noir (both from Louis Martini). For the first time, consumers could relate grape varieties to the regions in which they were grown.

produce and vinify. Its popularity is growing, and acreage has almost doubled since 1995.

The challenge of the future, as of the past, will be to produce Cabernets that are well balanced and have the capacity to age interestingly in bottle. There has been a retreat from the heavy, extracted styles of the 1970s and early 1980s, but the current trend is to produce Cabernets with lush, fruity flavours and high alcohol. It is clear that these wines have immediate appeal, score extremely well in blind tastings, and give many Cabernet-lovers a great deal of pleasure. But vertical tastings of some of California's top Cabernets and blends, such as Opus One, Diamond Creek, and Insignia, seem to suggest that the most long-lived and complex wines are made in relatively cool years that benefit from a long and even growing season.

Carignane This southern French variety is rarely encountered on its own, but often forms part of "field blends" together with Zinfandel and Petite Sirah. That is because it was planted that way by immigrants in the nineteenth century, and some of those field blends have been retained. It is unlikely that the excessively high-yielding and often coarse Carignane is being replanted, and acreage is slowly but steadily declining. In 2000, there were 7,170 acres. It gives a robust tannic wine with little finesse, but old-vine Carignane can be impressive. It is encountered a good deal in Mendocino and Sonoma, as well as in the Central Valley. Producers of varietal Carignane include Bonny Doon, Cline, Fortino, Pellegrini, Rosenblum, and Shenandoah.

Charbono No one seems sure what Charbono is. Some believe it is related to Dolcetto of Piedmont or Douce Noire of Savoie. Whatever its origin, it yields inky, tannic wines. It certainly has devotees, and this thickly textured, robust wine can be satisfying, if you can picture a good accompaniment for a venison stew on a cold winter's night. Unfortunately, no more than ninety acres (and possibly as few as fifty) remain in production. Wineries releasing Charbono include Duxoup, Fife, Fortino, and Summers.

Chardonnay This is the variety that has been at the head of the California best-seller charts for decades. It's hard to recall that, in 1975, there were no more than 5,000 acres planted. Today, there are 103,000, thanks largely to huge plantings in the 1990s which are only now coming on stream. It thrives in cool regions such as Carneros, the Sonoma Coast, the Russian River Valley, Monterey, Arroyo Grande, and Santa Barbara, but can also give excellent results in slightly warmer regions such as Sonoma Valley and Mendocino.

In a sense there is no such thing as "Chardonnay". Whole monographs could be written on the clonal variations present in California's vineyards, many of fine quality but uncertain origin. Microvinifications have shown that the clones impart very different aromas and flavours to the wine, so the choice of clone can be of paramount importance. Sonoma grower and winemaker Richard Kunde claims to have almost one hundred Chardonnay clones in his extensive vineyards. Moreover, the grape variety is relatively neutral, so it is a gift to the manipulative winemaker, who can use a number of techniques to modify its character. It can be unoaked, massively oaked, lightly sweetened, bone-dry, vinified with natural or cultivated yeasts, and so forth. And despite that essential neutrality, different climatic conditions will also give the wine different personalities. Chardonnays from Napa, excluding the cooler Carneros subregion, can be rather heavy; Chardonnay from Monterey can have a striking, tropical-fruit character.

And if there is some kind of consensus regarding how Cabernet Sauvignon ought to taste, there is none about Chardonnay. This versatility is undoubtedly a positive feature, but it also makes it difficult to generalize about Californian Chardonnay. Moreover, it is subject to the stylistic swings of fad and fashion. In the 1970s, many Chardonnays were heavily oaked; impressive but fatiguing. In the 1980s, such wines were criticized as being difficult to consume with food, so a new, leaner, fitter style was invented. Eventually this was taken to extremes, and the wines became more and more featureless.

ANYTHING BUT CHARDONNAY?

It's often said that consumers are tiring of Chardonnay, which in America has become synonymous with white wine, and are looking for new varieties, new flavours. If only it were true. More and more Chardonnay is being planted, which may lead to lower prices, but won't encourage diversification. There is keen interest among winemakers, wine writers, and some sommeliers in varieties such as Viognier, Roussanne, Arneis, and Pinot Gris, but the overall sales of these relatively unfamiliar wines remain small. This is a shame, as some of the most exciting white wines in California are being produced from such grapes.

At the same time, there was much discussion about whether California Chardonnay should be encouraged to go through malolactic fermentation, which would lower its malic acidity and give it additional roundness and, it was claimed, complexity. Wineries of the old school, such as Mayacamas and Forman, blocked the malolactic fermentation as a means of conserving acidity and freshness, but most winemakers followed the Burgundian model of encouraging malolactic. Fears that low-acidity Chardonnays would not age well may prove well founded, but since most California Chardonnay is consumed within three years, the question is largely academic.

In the late 1990s, the heavy-artillery school of Chardonnay was back in fashion: picking at ultimate ripeness regardless of acidity levels, whole-cluster pressing, lees-stirring, and minimal handling, which sometimes resulted in unfiltered wines that were cloudy. But this was the stylistic goal to which many of the most fashionable winemakers aspired, urged on by the American press, which believes, in the words of James Laube, that "California Chardonnay, with all its diversity and complexity, is the most consistently excellent wine in the world today" – a claim that might cause a few non–American eyebrows to be raised.

In 1999, a British magazine mounted a blind tasting of California Chardonnays that were assessed simultaneously by a local team in London and an American team of experts in New York. There was a clear difference in the results. The Americans favoured the lush, buttery, oaky, high-alcohol wines, the British preferred the leaner, more elegant styles, so there does seem to be a big difference in national taste. The Napa wine producer Jayson Pahlmeyer, whose powerful Chardonnay is made under the supervision of "wine goddess" Helen Turley, refers to his wine with approbation as "industrial-strength Chardonnay", which is the very characteristic that makes the wine unpalatable to many European tasters.

Style wars apart, it is futile to deny that much California Chardonnay is well-made, flavourful, and gives immense pleasure to millions. It rarely has the mineral complexity of its principal role model, white Burgundy, but in its place it offers lush fruit, varying degrees of oakiness, and, in the best examples, a refreshing citric zest to give a lift to the always-abundant fruitiness.

The difficulty for ambitious Chardonnay producers is that they do, whatever they may say to the contrary, aspire to match or even surpass the great white wines of Burgundy, but must do so in a climate and *terroir* very different to those of France. The rocky, limestone soils of Burgundy are hard to replicate in California, so instead, the winemakers have focused on microclimates, opting more and more for cool regions such as Monterey and the uplands of the Sonoma Coast, where acidity can most easily be conserved and where the growing season is prolonged. If California

Chardonnays rarely attain the complexity of great Burgundy, they often offer instead a wealth of concentration, purity of flavour, and varying degrees of power and finesse. The top wines from Kistler, Landmark, Ramey, Peter Michael, Au Bon Climat, and others may not be truly Burgundian, but there can be no doubt that they are magnificent expressions of the Chardonnay grape.

Chenin Blanc In its native habitat, the Loire Valley, Chenin Blanc exhibits an acidity that often needs to be balanced against a little residual sugar to tame the wine's over-assertiveness. That very acidity proved a godsend in the hot regions of California's Central Valley, which is why the variety was valued, as well as the fact that it generated high yields. Very little Chenin was released as a varietal wine, as its primary use was to give white blends vigour and some aromatic complexity.

The inexorable rise of Chardonnay has been bad news for Chenin, and plantings have been almost halved since the mid-1980s, although some 19,400 acres remain under vine. As in the Loire, there is no single style that finds favour. Nonetheless, it is often vinified as an off-dry wine, so as to provide an alternative for some of the old-fashioned wine-drinkers who often find Chardonnay too dry. Unfortunately, most such wines soon become cloying: Pine Ridge's bizarre Chenin–Viognier blend is an example.

A handful of wineries bravely persist in making dry Chenin, and this can be an excellent wine with food. Chappellet makes an outstanding version, as do Ventana and Adelaida, although not everyone will be comfortable with the latter's very high alcohol. Chalone makes a famous and honeyed dry Chenin from very old vines, but quantities are small.

Cortese This north Italian variety is rarely encountered in California, although Mount Palomar in Temecula claims to have been the first grower to plant it.

Counoise Originating in southern France, this red grape has a surprising number of devotees. One of the few varietal versions was made by Eberle as a rosé until 2000, when he stopped production; it is also grown at Tablas Creek in San Luis Obispo County.

Dolcetto This Piedmontese red variety yields dark-coloured, supple, plummy wines for early drinking, although it can sometimes be tannic. Although it is encountered in California, it rarely resembles its Italian model. One of the best examples comes from Enotria in Mendocino. Others are produced by Bargetto, Wild Hog, Mosby, and Viansa, but some of these – notably the Viansa wine – can be strikingly thin for Dolcetto.

Fiano This fine southern Italian white grape is almost nonexistent in California. The one occasionally encountered example, from Podere dell'Olivos in Santa Barbara, is excellent.

Flora This is a bizarre cross between Gewurztraminer and Semillon that results in perfumed wines with a soft structure. It has not proved popular with growers or consumers, and fifty acres, at most, survive. Schramsberg still uses it as a component in its off–dry *crémant* sparkling wine.

Freisa In Piedmont, Freisa is vinified either as a light summer red, with a slight frizzante prickle, or, less commonly, as a full-bodied red. So it's not surprising that California has not really got to grips with Freisa. Montevina does produce a version, and it is occasionally found from Mosby and Podere dell'Olivos in Santa Barbara.

French Colombard Until the 1990s, the acreage of this variety (known in France as Colombard) exceeded that of Chardonnay. Forty two thousand acres survive, so it has to be a major component in many wines. It was planted, mostly in the Central Valley, for predictable reasons: high yields, good acidity, a fruity floral quality, and an absence of ageing potential. In the past, Parducci and, improbably, Chalone made varietal versions, but I have never encountered one.

Gamay This popular French variety, the mainstay of Beaujolais and the Maconnais, has had a complex history in California. It began in the early twentieth century, when cuttings called "Gamay Beaujolais" were planted in Santa Clara, while other cuttings, usually labelled "Gamay Noir" or "Napa Gamay", were adopted in Napa. It later turned out the two similarly named varieties were in fact different. Ampelographical research subsequently revealed that the Napa version was similar to the French variety, but the Gamay Beaujolais was some kind of clonal variation of Pinot Noir. It was ruled that Gamay Beaujolais would be phased out once existing plantings died out.

To confuse matters further, it has been decided that Napa Gamay should hitherto be referred to as Valdiguié, and some pleasantly fruity wines have been released under that barely pronounceable name by Gallo Sonoma, Beringer, Hop Kiln, and Lohr.

Gewurztraminer Gewurztraminer is a demanding variety, requiring a good deal of warmth but not too much. It can easily come across as heavy and lumpish, and, if picked too early to avoid those traps, it can be bland and characterless, lacking the characteristic rose-petal and lychee aroma that distinguish the variety. Not surprisingly, acreage has halved since the mid-1980s to around 1,550 acres, but is at least holding steady.

This gradual decline is a shame, given that California Gewurztraminer can be very good, and makes a far better match with spicy food than the ubiquitous Chardonnay. Moreover, a lot of consumers like the wine, as I have often observed in tasting rooms, where a Chardonnay may be admired, but it's the Gewurztraminer that is often bought. The problem is that growers cannot obtain a good enough price to justify replanting this variety, and even existing plantations are often grafted over to more profitable varieties.

Mendocino is a good hunting ground for Gewurztraminer; Navarro, Lazy Creek, Fetzer, Handley, and Husch all make good examples. There are a handful of versions from Sonoma, notably DeLoach, Alderbrook, and Mill Creek, and Ravenswood produce a good late-harvest Gewurztraminer. In the south there are fine examples from Ventana, Fogarty, Babcock, Bedford Thompson, and Firestone. Ten years ago, the list would have been much longer, but many wineries have simply given up on Gewurztraminer.

Grenache The workhorse grape of southern France and northern Spain does not have a particularly good track record in California. Acreage has remained steady at around 11,400, but most of it is in the Central Valley, where it is used as a blending variety. Patches of old-vine Grenache remain in Gilroy and the North Coast, and Rhône Rangers such as Randall Grahm of Bonny Doon have been swift to latch on to it. Other wineries, notably Phelps, use Grenache to make a firm, fruity rosé. There are decent red Grenache wines from Shenandoah in the Foothills, but the only examples that come close to rivalling a fine Châteauneuf or Priorat are from Alban in Arroyo Grande and T-Vine in Napa.

Grey Riesling This variety was put into wide circulation by Wente, as it was planted in Livermore in the 1860s. It bears no relation to Riesling, but is either a variety from the Cognac region or Trousseau Gris. It gives a simple fruity wine that can be very enjoyable, but, with no more than 100 acres surviving, is probably heading for extinction.

Grignolino Joe Heitz waved the flag for this Piedmontese red variety, which he found already planted in the first vineyards he bought in Napa Valley in 1961. Heitz has continued to produce two wines: a rosé and a surprisingly good port-style wine. Scarcely one hundred acres remain in California.

Lagrein This is a popular variety in the South Tyrol in northern Italy. The only example in California appears to be from Picchetti in Santa Cruz.

Malbec This Bordeaux variety is not easy to grow, and in California, Petit Verdot is valued more as a blending grape. However, Arrowood makes an excellent wine from Malbec.

Malvasia Bianca The main Californian homes for this variety are the Central Valley and Monterey, where it used by producers such as Wild Horse and Morgan to make a light, aromatic wine. But its principal use remains as a blending variety for inexpensive whites, such as some of the Gallo wines and Bonny Doon's Big House White. It is also made as a fortified wine. 2,500 acres are planted.

Marsanne Of the trio of white Rhône varieties, Marsanne is surely the dullest. Even in the northern Rhône, with the singular exception of the remarkable wines of Hermitage, it hardly scintillates. It has enjoyed a modest popularity in California because, of the three, it is the easiest to grow. Fetzer makes a decent version in Mendocino, and other good North Coast examples come from Phelps and Wellington, though none rises to any great heights. Examples from Santa Barbara include Qupé, Beckmen, and Andrew Murray.

Merlot Merlot has been the great red-grape success story of the past decade. In 1986, there were fewer than 3,000 acres planted; in 2000, there were 50,000 in production. The first varietal Merlots were made in the late 1960s, and some distinguished examples were made by Duckhorn, Newton, Cuvaison, Beringer, St Francis, and Matanzas Creek. In 1972, there were only four wineries offering Merlot; by 1991, there were 225.

As a thin-skinned variety with dense clusters, Merlot is, however, prone to rot, but on the other hand it can give high yields. At first, only a bit was planted, in imitation of St-Émilion and Pomerol, on flat clay soils, but they did not always give outstanding fruit, at least not in Californian conditions. Poor drainage was the gravest problem. Gradually the variety began to planted on relatively cool slopes. It does well in Carneros and Santa Barbara, but most of the acreage is in the Central Valley, which is not an ideal habitat. The picking date is essential: picked too early, it can be thin; picked too late, it can be jammy and raisiny.

Some of the wineries listed above have shown that Merlot is certainly capable of producing rich, flavourful red wine, more supple than Cabernet, with considerable ageing potential, but there are signs that the fashion for the wine may have peaked. Even enthusiasts for the variety, such as Duckhorn, find that it rarely works well as a pure varietal wine, but benefits from blending in some Cabernet to give it more structure. Any slip in popularity is almost certainly a consequence of the rush to plant Merlot just about anywhere to meet the anticipated demand; the result was a lot of insipid wine. However, it is likely to remain popular because it can be grown in most parts of California, and good examples come from throughout the North Coast as well as from the Central Coast and Lodi.

SPARKLING WINES

Compared to the chilly slopes of the Champagne region, California is rather too warm to produce top sparkling wines. But producers, often subsidiaries of Champagne houses such as Taittinger, have been swift to identify the best regions in which to grow grapes with the required acidity and flavour. Carneros and Anderson Valley in Mendocino have emerged as the best bets. The top producers: Roederer, "J" Wine Company, Domaine Carneros, Artesa, Gloria Ferrer, Jepson, Mumm Napa, S Anderson, Domaine Chandon, Schramsberg, Iron Horse, and Handley.

Since most American, and indeed, European, drinkers do not or cannot age their wines in bottle, Merlot would seem to be a more logical choice of "favourite red variety" than the tougher, more tannic Cabernet Sauvignon. It is for precisely these reasons that Merlot has enjoyed its remarkable success in California. When it's not overcropped and when it's picked ripe, Merlot has an immediate fleshy, succulent appeal that is not to be despised. The lack of truly great examples may have more to do with the deficiencies of the variety in California's growing conditions than with any failure to come to grips with the demands of the grape. In the great majority of cases, a good Merlot tasted alongside a good Cabernet will fail to win the day.

Mission This is the variety that the Spanish brought to California in the eighteenth century, and is thought to be the same as Pais of Chile and the Criolla Chica of Argentina. It gives a pale red wine that is prone to oxidation. Its sole virtue was a commercial one: it produced very high yields. Not surprisingly, Mission has virtually disappeared, but there are a few outposts in the Sierra Foothills. It seems to fare best as a lightly sweet wine. Deaver had some vines dating back to 1855, but they had to be pulled out in 1997. Only Nine Gables, Sobon, and Story still produce wine from Mission.

Mourvedre This variety is responsible for the renown of Bandol in Provence. It is known in Spain, Australia, and in parts of California as Mataro. Curiously, the oldest vines in California are older than those in Bandol. These celebrated vines are at the Oakley Vineyard in Contra Costa County, and they supply wineries such as Cline, Edmunds St John, Jade Mountain, and Ridge. Half the 400 acres of Mourvedre are located in this county.

Mourvedre yields a rich, red, tangy wine, which develops smoky, leathery overtones with age. Sadly, it is in decline. It needs both steady heat and maritime influence to ripen properly, and it may be a fluke that the Oakley

---

FORTIFIED WINES

These have a bad image in the United States, being associated with images of down-and-outs stumbling along clutching bottle-shaped brown paper bags. But there are some pleasant Muscats from Napa and the Sierra Foothills and above all from Andrew Quady in the Central Valley, and some excellent port-style wines. Some, such as those from St Amant, Mondavi Woodbridge, and Renwood, are made from some of the traditional Portuguese varieties planted in the Douro Valley; others are made from Zinfandel, Petite Sirah (producers include Clos Pegase and Imagery), or even, as at Shafer, from Cabernet Sauvignon (and DeLoach makes one from all three). When they avoid excessive jamminess, these wines can be delicious.

and other vineyards, mostly in the Sacramento Delta, were successfully
planted with the variety. It is hard to know where else the variety could
be planted with high expectations.

Muscat The two principal Muscat varieties are Muscat of Alexandria and
Muscat Blanc (often known as Muscat Canelli or Muscat Frontignan).
The former is planted on 5,000 acres in the Central Valley, where it can
add aroma and body to some white-wine blends. Muscat Canelli is more
distinguished in California, where it is planted in many parts of the state.
Good examples come from Pecota in Napa and from Eberle in Paso Robles,
and many wineries with an Italian heritage in Sonoma also produce Muscat
Canelli. It is invariably vinified as a sweet or lightly fortified dessert wine. It
is difficult to make well, as excessive sweetness and low acidity can result in
a cloying beverage.

Nebbiolo This is the grape from which the great wines of Barolo and
Barbaresco are made. It is very tricky to grow. There are significant clonal
variations, and even when grown in ideal sites it emerges as a tannic,
high-acidity, high-alcohol wine that can be difficult to balance. Early efforts
to work with Nebbiolo in California were fairly disastrous. Martin Brothers
in Paso Robles produced it for many years, and still do so under the new
name of Martin & Weyrich. It is not a distinguished wine. The only truly
fine examples I have encountered are those from Bonny Doon and
Renwood, and Podere dell'Olivos is another significant producer. Only
196 acres have been planted.

Negrette A relatively obscure French variety from the Frontannais, it is grown
in Cienega Valley and vinified only by DeRose and Wild Horse.

Petit Verdot When it's good, it's very, very good, and when it's bad… Petit
Verdot, a red variety from Bordeaux used solely for blending, is much prized
in the Médoc when it ripens properly. In warm California it does ripen more
regularly, but it gives irregular crops. It fetches a very high price in Napa
Valley, so it is clearly prized by producers of Bordeaux blends. Most wineries
follow the Bordeaux model by limiting its contribution to no more than five
per cent, but a few blends tend to use significantly more: these include
Acronicus from Vita Nova, Mosaic from De Lorimier, and Trésor from
Ferrari-Carano. Plantings stand at around 300 acres.

Petite Sirah This variety has been around in California since the nineteenth
century, but its exact identity has, until recently, been a mystery. One thing
is certain: it is not the same as Syrah, but may well have acquired its name
from being labelled as "Hermitage" when cuttings were first imported to
California. In the late 1990s, Professor Carole Meredith of the University of
California at Davis conducted a DNA analysis of Petite Sirah vines. They
turned out to be not one variety, but a handful, including Durif, Peloursin,
and Aubun, and about a dozen others that simply could not be identified.

Petite Sirah yields a very dark, tannic wine, and some bottlings from the 1970s were scarcely altered twenty years later. It often appears in blends with Zinfandel or Carignane, having been planted alongside them in field blends. After a period when Petite Sirah was scorned for its rusticity, there has been a revival. Properly vinified it can give a splendid, full-bodied wine, and more sophisticated tannin management has tamed its aggression.

Producers such as Ridge, Stags' Leap Winery, and Concannon had a good reputation for the wine for decades. More recently, it has been revived by David Bruce, Fife, Edmeades, Lolonis, Rosenblum, and Turley. In terms of acreage, Petite Sirah was dwindling until the mid-1990s, when a slight increase in planting occurred. At present, there are 3,680 acres in production, mostly in the North Coast, but also in Livermore and the Central Valley.

Pinot Blanc Although a few wineries, notably Martin Ray and Chalone, had produced Pinot Blanc for many years, it was not a variety that attracted much attention in California. Some of it lacked distinction, and it later turned out that many of the vines identified as Pinot Blanc were in fact the Muscadet grape, Melon. Fritz in Sonoma had the courage to label one of its wines as Melon, even though the wine doesn't taste remotely like Muscadet.

Indeed, it's quite hard to say of what or how Pinot Blanc should taste. Richard Arrowood, a leading producer of varietal Pinot Blanc, sees it as a dense wine with honey and orange aromas; other growers and producers find more citric, appley flavours. It generally yields a wine low in acidity, so it rarely benefits from ageing. The fact that it appears to be a cousin of Chardonnay without ever attaining the nobility of a great Chardonnay will surely always work against the wine and prevent it from becoming widely popular.

There are about 1,000 acres in production, most of them in Monterey, but much Pinot Blanc is used for sparkling wine production. Good varietal Pinot Blanc is now produced by Au Bon Climat, Arrowood, Byron, Domaine St Gregory, Gehrs, LinCourt, Lockwood, J.Lohr, Pavona, Ventana, and Wild Horse.

Pinot Gris This Burgundian variety, more commonly encountered in Alsace, has a double personality. In Alsace, it is transformed into a rich, musky, fleshy white; in northeast Italy, as Pinot Grigio, it is cropped at high levels and tends to yield a fresh but neutral style. This double act is reflected in California. Some growers, especially those with an Italian heritage such as Viansa, Luna, Monte Volpe, and Seghesio, opted for a style reminiscent of Pinot Grigio. But many versions don't seem to have strong personality. Although wineries such as Navarro, Swan, Long, Benessere, Montevina, Flora Springs, Kahn, and Bedford Thompson produce sound versions, few of them can match the best Pinot Gris from Oregon, where the variety has proved a resounding success. Acreage is slowly increasing, and in 2000 stood at 1,600.

BARGAIN PINOT NOIR

Pinot Noir is sensitive to yield and that makes it expensive to cultivate – so cheap Pinot Noir is a contradiction in terms. Nonetheless, there are some sensibly priced Pinots from California that can give a great deal of pleasure without reaching the sublime heights of which Pinot is capable. These include Beaulieu, Fetzer, Husch, Meridian, Navarro, Ramsay, Saintsbury "Garnet", Steele, and Wild Horse.

Pinot Noir Until about fifteen years ago, Pinot Noir had a long but not particularly happy history in California. The most distinguished early example was made at Beaulieu in 1946, and the winemaker, André Tchelistcheff, credited the wine's splendour to the vines planted in 1902 from cuttings imported from Burgundy. But this low-yielding clone vanished long ago. Burgundy clones were also planted by Martin Ray in the Santa Cruz Mountains in 1942, but the surviving vines are now too old to produce much of a crop. Viticulturalists have sought to preserve some of the older "heirloom" clones, but almost all Pinot Noir vines now being planted are Dijon clones from Burgundy, which seem to be producing very satisfactory results.

As is well known, this is an ultra-sensitive grape, finicky about where it is planted and how heavily it is cropped, and fragile enough to lose all its character during fermentation. It's a cool-climate grape, yet it needs to ripen fully if thin, vegetal flavours are to be avoided. It is also thin-skinned and prone to spring frosts and to rot; it lacks colour, which to many American drinkers is still an indication of quality and richness in a wine, leading some winemakers to extract more from the skins than they are programmed to deliver.

American admirers of Pinot Noir had made pilgrimages to Burgundy and come back with what they believed was the "secret" of great Pinot Noir. For some, such as Josh Jensen of Calera, that secret resided in the limestone soils of Burgundy, which he sought, with some success, to replicate in California. For others, it had to do with ageing the wine properly in French barrels. Clonal selection has also proved crucial, and growers worked hard to isolate or import the most promising clones.

It soon became apparent, however, that site was crucial. Planted in warm spots such as the valley floor in Napa, it lost its character, whereas in the cooler regions of Carneros, Russian River Valley, Monterey, or Santa Maria Valley, it retained its delicate traits. In the 1980s, winemakers such as Ted Lemon and Joseph Davis had worked in Burgundy and observed how the wines were made, and their low yields and a "hands-off" approach were widely adopted. Before then, it had been common to treat Pinot as though it were Cabernet, by going for maximum fruit extraction – fine for Cabernet, disastrous for Pinot. The new school of winemakers had a lighter touch. *Pigeage*, or punching down the cap during fermentation, became commonplace, and, if at all possible, the wine was bottled without fining or filtration so as to retain as much of the fruit and perfume as possible.

There are now some 19,000 acres of Pinot Noir, so the variety has become a major player in California, even if a substantial proportion of that acreage is used for sparkling wine. Few experts can agree on the very best sites for Pinot Noir. For my money, Carneros is the least spectacular of the regions mentioned above, and most of the memorable Pinots I have encountered from California have come from Russian River Valley or the new vineyards on the ridges above the Sonoma Coast. Sometimes Santa Barbara County Pinot can have a slightly vegetal quality, and the proliferation of large commercial vineyards in Monterey and Santa Barbara means that yields are often higher than they should be. In general, California Pinot Noir is not as long-lived as red Burgundy. With few exceptions, the wines have less tannin and structure, and there is no Californian equivalent – yet – of Richebourg.

The number of excellent producers is growing each year, so it is somewhat invidious to single out individual wineries for mention. However, those in the top rank must surely include Arcadian, Au Bon Climat, Dehlinger, Farrell, Flowers, Kistler, Littorai, Rochioli, Testarossa, and Williams & Selyem. In some vintages, or from certain reserve bottlings, the following can sometimes rival the preceding list: David Bruce, Calera, Chalone, La Crema, Etude, Foxen, Hanzell, Hartford Court, Mondavi, Mount Eden, Rutz, Saintsbury, Sanford, Sinskey, Talley, and Torres. Many producers in the Central Coast and Santa Barbara often produce small *cuvées* from fruit purchased from leading vineyards, but these bottlings can be inconsistent. So can Pinot Noir from Mendocino, where it is quite common in Anderson Valley, but maddeningly irregular in quality.

Pinotage Precisely why anyone in America would want to grow this South African cross of mixed repute is something of a mystery. The only two versions I know are from Rubissow-Sargent and "J" in Sonoma.

Refosco This red variety from northeast Italy is rare in California but is produced by Montevina.

Riesling There used to be a sizeable acreage of Riesling in California, but it is declining quite rapidly. In 1986, there were 8,500 acres; today there are no more than 2,000. In part this is because a lot of Riesling was planted in the wrong place, such as Napa Valley. But there have been regions where it has been grown with great success: Anderson Valley, parts of Sonoma, and in Monterey, where roughly half the surviving acreage is located. Regrettably, it is a wine that is out of fashion and, in California, stylistically indistinct.

Dry Rieslings exist but are rare; most are vinified in an off-dry style, which has a poor image, even though some of these wines can be delicious.

Randall Grahm of Bonny Doon is a fervent admirer of Riesling, and has declared: "Riesling is perceived to be a nerdy variety, but in fact, it's the hippest grape we have." Even so, he sources most of his grapes from outside California in the Pacific Northwest. Fetzer and Lohr are among the largest producers, and Navarro in Anderson Valley makes an exceptional version. Other good examples come from Ventana, Greenwood Ridge, and, in Santa Barbara, from Firestone, Gainey, Koehler, and Fess Parker.

In Germany, botrytized late-harvest Riesling is highly prized and extremely costly. A few producers in California have copied the style with surprising success. In the 1970s, Richard Arrowood at Château St Jean made some spectacular Trockenbeerenauslese-style Rieslings. Because the cost of production was very high, the wine was pricey, too, and only small quantities were produced. Jekel in Monterey, Firestone in Santa Barbara, and Phelps in Napa also made delicious sweet Rieslings, but they have mostly abandoned the style, although a handful of producers, such as Navarro and Greenwood Ridge, continue to produce it.

The bad news is that estates such as Heller, Babcock, and Paraiso Springs have given up on Riesling and grafted over existing vines to other varieties. Quite simply, the price is too low.

Roussanne When you mention the name of this splendid southern-French grape variety to a Californian producer, it sometimes brings a blush to the cheek. This is why. In the mid-1990s, it became apparent that a number of delicious Roussannes were being produced in California. It's not an easy variety to grow: it is susceptible to disease and yields are naturally low. Nonetheless, the results from a number of producers were dazzling. I was one of many who admired gorgeously perfumed, full-bodied wines from a range of growers from Mendocino to Santa Barbara.

Then it turned out that the wines we had all been admiring were not made from Roussanne at all, but from Viognier. Randall Grahm of Bonny Doon had brought in some cuttings of what he thought was Roussanne, and these were propagated and constituted the plant material of over half the plantings of "Roussanne." A lot of owners of wineries, including Zaca Mesa, Wild Horse, Cline, Andrew Murray, Mer et Soleil, and others, were left with egg on their faces when they realized their admired Roussannes were nothing of the sort. Chuck Wagner of Caymus and Mer et Soleil went so far as to sue the nursery, which in turn sued Grahm. Fortunately, an out-of-court settlement was agreed.

Authentic Roussanne was planted by Alban in Arroyo Grande and by Tablas Creek in Paso Robles. Good examples are also made by Domaine de Terre Rouge, Truchard, and Fetzer.

BEST SANGIOVESE PRODUCERS

This is a tricky variety to get right, as the vine is over-prolific and acidity levels can be uncomfortably high. The leading producers are Ferrari-Carano, Noceto, Pepi, Plumpjack, Rabbit Ridge, Seghesio, Shafer, Swanson, and Staglin.

Sangiovese This is the major indigenous red grape of Tuscany and the mainstay of Chianti. It was only to be expected that some Italian enthusiast would want to try it out in California. There was one problem: clonal selection. It has taken the Tuscans the best part of twenty years to sort out the mistake they made in the 1970s, when poor-quality, overproductive clones of Sangiovese were planted.

Naturally, one of the pioneers of California Sangiovese – none other than Piero Antinori from Florence – was not going to make that mistake, and he took care that the clones he planted at his Atlas Peak estate in Napa were of high quality. Unfortunately, the wine was far from exceptional and it has mostly stayed that way. This probably has more to do with location than clone. A winemaker who planted a clone in Redwood Valley in Mendocino found that he had small clusters which gave good wine, whereas the same clone planted in Alexander Valley produced large clusters that resulted in more insipid wine. The other important factor with Sangiovese is yield: this is a vine that loves to grow, and the best way to control this vigour is to plant it on soils that will discourage its prolific nature.

Nor were winemakers clear about how to vinify Sangiovese. Some subjected it to hefty oak-ageing, which was a mistake except for the most concentrated examples. The trouble was that much Sangiovese was dilute and pallid. By now winemakers have a better feel for the variety, and there are a growing number of excellent examples.

What may be the oldest Sangiovese in California is at the Seghesio property in Sonoma, which was probably planted in 1910, although it was not formally identified until 1989. As recently as 1990 there were only 186 acres, but by 2000 there were 3,300. It has thrived throughout the North Coast and in the Sierra Foothills. It has been a late arrival in Santa Barbara, but various growers there have obtained the excellent Brunello clone, which is now being planted.

There are dozens of good examples, although many are made in small quantities. In Napa Valley, look for Pepi, Swanson, Atlas Peak Reserve, Biale, Benessere, Cosentino, Staglin, Dalla Valle, Flora Springs, Krug, Plumpjack, Shafer, and Showket; in Sonoma: Seghesio, Ferrari-Carano, Iron Horse, Trentadue; in Mendocino: Fetzer, Monte Volpe, and Gabrielli. In the

Foothills, Noceto produces nothing but Sangiovese, and in Santa Barbara, there are good wines from Babcock and Vandale.

Sauvignon Blanc There is ample evidence that Sauvignon Blanc doesn't much like California, and that Californians don't much like Sauvignon Blanc. The hallmark of the grape is its fresh acidity. In the Loire Valley and New Zealand, that can sometimes be too much of a good thing, and even in the warmer Bordeaux region simpler examples always have a citric zest. A few California producers have tried to produce Sauvignon in a Sancerre style, which means unoaked and high in acidity. Togni made a good example in the 1980s but nobody liked it much, though he made it primarily to have a wine to drink with oysters at home.

Instead, most winemakers treated Sauvignon as though it were a slightly downmarket version of Chardonnay, higher-yielding and capable of being sold at a cheaper price. This remains the standard Sauvignon, rich in melon and fig flavours that are more reminiscent of Semillon than Sauvignon. A very few producers took it seriously, and tried to make a wine reminiscent of a top Graves, such as Haut-Brion or Domaine de Chevalier. That involved a lot of expense: barrel-fermentation in top-quality oak, for a start. Producers such as Newton found that they were having to sell at a loss, and understandably gave up.

Nonetheless, there has always been a market for Sauvignon in California, and acreage has remained steady at about 13,500 for a decade. It was being produced by Wente in Livermore Valley in the 1930s, both in dry and sweet styles modeled on Sauternes. The real breakthrough came in 1967, when Robert Mondavi launched his still-popular Fumé Blanc, supposedly based on Pouilly-Fumé. There was, however, one major difference. Pouilly-Fumé is rarely oaked; Mondavi's wine most certainly was. Dozens of producers soon followed where he led: Murphy-Goode, DeLoach, Iron Horse, Dry Creek, Babcock, Carmenet, Matanzas Creek, and Kenwood.

If there was no consensus about how to make the wine, there wasn't any about how to grow the vines, either. A prolific variety, it threw out a lot of vegetation that sometimes hampered access of the bunches to sunlight. The consequence was underripe fruit that had a marked, and deservedly unpopular, vegetal quality reminiscent of asparagus. The Californians, as ever, were quick to learn about canopy management, and different trellising systems were adopted that have more or less cured that problem.

There are also debates about clonal selection. Without going into too much detail, it is worth mentioning that many wineries prize the so-called Musqué clone, which thrives in the Ventana vineyard in Monterey. This clone is bought by, among others, Cain. Sauvignon grows just about everywhere, and seems to do well in unfashionable regions such as Mendocino and Lake County. Flora Springs still makes a palatable

Sauvignon that never goes anywhere near a barrique; also in Napa Valley, Mason has become something of a Sauvignon specialist. A few upmarket high-priced versions are attempting to create once again a niche for Graves-style Sauvignon. These include Cain, Rudd, Araujo, and Selene. A very few late-harvest Sauvignons are still being produced, notably by Chalk Hill.

Scheurebe In 1974, German-born Walter Schug persuaded Joseph Phelps to cultivate this crossing, developed in 1916, of Riesling and Sylvaner. He made some very good sweet wines from the variety. Schug left Phelps to set up his own winery, but his successor, Craig Williams, has kept the faith by producing Eisrebe, a kind of icewine from Scheurebe. It is a wine I can live without.

Semillon Semillon is in decline, and only 1,430 acres remain. This may not be a bad thing, since it is too vigorous a vine for most parts of California. It is also a low–acidity grape that mysteriously ages well, which can make it useful as a blending component with Sauvignon Blanc, but on its own, it can be a flat and dull wine. Bernard Portet of Clos du Val betrays his Bordelais origins by confessing he prefers Semillon to Chardonnay, and he makes one of the better versions in Napa Valley. Duckhorn's Decoy is also a worthwhile Semillon.

Over the years, some wineries have made excellent sweet wines, Sauternes-style, from the variety. Phelps is one of them, but most others, including Chalk Hill and Château St Jean, have, alas, phased out the style.

Sylvaner A workhorse grape variety popular in Alsace and Germany, Sylvaner had quite a following in California until about twenty years ago. By the early 1980s, about 1,000 acres remained, mostly in the Central Coast. At the very most, some one hundred acres now survive, almost all in Monterey and Santa Barbara. Rancho Sisquoc in Santa Maria valley still produces the wine under the synonym of Franken Riesling.

Symphony This is a cross between Muscat of Alexandria and Grenache Gris, developed in the 1940s by Dr Harold Olmo at the University of California but first planted in the early 1980s. This statement invites the question: why did he bother? Some like the heavy scent and feel it is a good accompaniment to spicy oriental food. Its main producer, Château de Baun, has gone out of business, but the wine is still made by Ironstone and Baywood.

Syrah This great French variety was virtually unknown in California in the 1980s. In 1986, there were only about 120 acres planted, and this acreage rose to a staggering 12,700 by the end of the century. The few older vineyards had always made excellent wine. The oldest Syrah in California is at McDowell in Mendocino; planted in 1948, it is still the source of delicious wine. In the 1930s, the University of California brought over the so-called Montpellier clone from France, and this was planted by the Christian Brothers in 1959, but the good monks only used it as a blending wine. This

CALIFORNIA'S BEST SYRAHS

Syrah succeeds in producing delicious wines in all parts of California, so everyone who is keen to try vinifying the variety can have a go. Given that it is a fairly recent addition to the roster of varieties, the success rate is extraordinary. The leading producers are Babcock, Bonny Doon, Curtis, Eberle, Jaffurs, Havens, Jade Mountain, McDowell, Andrew Murray, Ojai, Phelps, Qupé, Sierra Vista, Swanson, Terre Rouge, Testarossa, and Truchard.

clone (virused, according to some) was the source of cuttings planted by Phelps in the 1970s; the wine was excellent, and I drank a good deal of it myself.

In the meantime, Gary Eberle, hired to plant extensive vineyards in Paso Robles for Estrella River Vineyards, insisted on planting Syrah, and used the so-called Chapoutier clone. This was the basis for plantings at Ojai, Qupé, Sierra Vista, and other estates. Eberle himself estimates that eighty per cent of all Syrah plantings in California are derived from the Chapoutier clone. And there were other clones that have been traced through various vineyards. Australian winemakers, such as Daryl Groom at Geyser Peak in Sonoma, have introduced Shiraz rather than Syrah. Meanwhile, in Paso Robles, the Perrin brothers of Château de Beaucastel propagated their native clones of Syrah at the Tablas Creek estate and nursery. *Chacun à son goût.*

Although the plant material under the umbrella name of Syrah is clearly diverse, the resulting wines have proved first-rate. At first it was thought that Syrah liked heat, but it soon became clear that in locations such as Alexander Valley, it was too hot for the variety, and the grape showed more complexity and more black-pepper character when grown in cooler climates. At present, it is showing its considerable potential in Carneros, Monterey, and Santa Barbara. It favours rocky soils over alluvial valley soils.

Phelps, Eberle, Qupé, and Preston were among the pioneers of Syrah in California, but it is fast becoming ubiquitous. And so it should. It's a forgiving variety, it has a delicious and complex fruit quality, it marries well with the powerful oak influence that many Californian winemakers favour, and it succeeds in a variety of styles.

Tempranillo The popular Spanish grape is curiously underrepresented in California, although Baywood produces a perfectly pleasant example from vineyards in Yolo County, and Truchard has released one. Bryan Babcock has Tempranillo in his Santa Barbara vineyards.

Tocai Friulano A white variety popular in northeastern Italy, and adopted successfully by Jim Clendenen at Il Podere dell'Olivos, and by Greg Graziano at Monte Volpe. Montevina and La Famiglia also produce it.

Trousseau Grown in Cienega Valley, this truly obscure variety is vinified with enthusiasm by Ken Volk at Wild Horse.

Trebbiano Dull at the best of times, it is hard to see why anyone would espouse this Tuscan white variety, but Ivan Tamas produces a wine from fruit grown in Livermore.

Viognier This beautifully perfumed white variety is native to the Northern Rhône, where it exasperates those who grow it with its susceptibility to disease and poor fruit set. But it seems to flourish in the dry, warm California air, and delivers far better yields than in its home territory. Seventeen hundred acres have been planted, almost all of them in the 1990s. Its cause has been taken up with enthusiasm by a handful of producers, notably Calera and La Jota, but it has taken off with difficulty, perhaps because many consumers find its name hard to pronounce.

Yet there are other reasons for its sluggish commercial performance. For many years, winemakers didn't know what to do with it. Many treated it like a wayward kind of Chardonnay and threw it into new oak; others picked it when far too ripe, so that the wine emerged as over-alcoholic. And many wines were simply overpriced and encountered justified consumer resistance.

Nonetheless, some splendid Viogniers are now being produced in California. Fetzer manages to create a lovely wine in large volumes, and there is one made from organically grown grapes from its spin-off Bonterra brand. Craig Williams at Phelps has always shown a sure hand with Viognier, as has John Alban at his winery. In addition, vineyards in the Central Coast sells Viognier to a myriad of small producers.

But it's not an easy wine to get right. The hallmark of Viognier is its exquisite honeysuckle scent, and it has to be vinified with care if that aroma is to be preserved. Also, Viognier needs to be very ripe, and that inevitably means, in California, that the wine will have high alcohol. This is no problem, unless you can actually taste the alcohol, which all too often is the case. Many winemakers admit that they need to use "spinning cone" technology in order to remove alcohol from the finished wine.

A good deal of Viognier is planted in Mendocino, where the leading producers, other than Fetzer, are Claudia Springs, Jepson, and McDowell. In Napa there are good examples from Beringer, Darioush, Pride, and Miner; in Sonoma, from Preston, Kunde, Arrowood, and Cline; in the Sierra Foothills, from Sobon and Terre Rouge; in Monterey, from Chalone (since 1999); in San Luis Obispo from Alban and Eberle; and in Santa Barbara, from Curtis, Andrew Murray, and Sunstone.

Viognier seems to be on a roll, but many grape farmers, especially in Mendocino, are wearying of the variety, and its acreage may actually decrease in the years ahead, which would be a great shame.

Zinfandel The origins of the closest thing California has to an indigenous variety remain tangled. Genetically, Zinfandel seems to be the same variety as the southern Italian Primitivo, but there is no record of Primitivo having been grown in California until the very late nineteenth century, by which time Zinfandel had been established, at least along the East Coast of America, since the 1830s. It is even possible that Primitivo was planted in Italy by returning Italian immigrants, who had taken Zinfandel cuttings home with them.

Whatever its true history, Zinfandel remains a remarkable grape variety because of its versatility. It likes heat and doesn't seem bothered by poor soils, so that it flourished on the mountain slopes of Sonoma, Napa, Mendocino, and the Sierra Foothills, where it was usually dry-farmed. It can give very high yields, but conscientious growers try to keep those under control, and very old vines exercise natural self-discipline. Partly to feed the demand for White Zinfandel, acreage has been increasing through the 1990s and now stands at 50,200.

At its frequent best, Zinfandel yields a rich, bright, powerful red wine, with a strong, primary fruit character backed by moderate tannins. Its viticultural drawback is that it ripens unevenly. On the same bunch it is common to find green, unripe berries and raisining berries almost side by side. Growers tend to pick as late as possible to ensure that there is minimal representation of unripe berries. The drawback of this is that it is often picked in an overripe condition, resulting in porty, jammy wines with high alcohol. Some consumers like that style; others detest it. It certainly isn't exactly food-friendly.

For decades, Zinfandel provided cheap and drinkable jug wines, so minor deficiencies such as overripeness or underripeness did not matter much. Consumers began to realize that Zinfandel was a serious wine when a handful of enthusiastic winemakers sought out venerable vineyards and

---

ZINFANDEL

A few producers are so entranced by this variety that they routinely produce a number of bottlings, many of them from individual vineyards, and in some cases they make Zinfandel only. These include Biale, DeLoach, Hartford Court, Ravenswood, Ridge, Rosenblum, Saucelito Canyon, Seghesio, Storybrook Cellars, and Turley.

bottled single-vineyard wines separately. At one time, Ridge was bottling a couple of dozen of different Zinfandels; Swan and Ravenswood did likewise. In the Sierra Foothills, wineries such as Montevina produced powerful wines from Zinfandel vines well over a century old.

Different sites certainly do give different characteristics to Zinfandel. Amador County Zinfandel from the Foothills can be hefty, pruney, and porty; from Paso Robles, Zinfandel is softer and more charming. Its quintessential expression seems to emerge from Dry Creek Valley, where the wines have a strong berry character and a firm core of fruit. And there are dozens of splendid sites planted with old Zinfandel throughout Napa, Sonoma, and Mendocino.

At the same time, there was far more Zinfandel planted than could be used for red table wines, given that Zinfandel could never aspire to the cachet of Cabernet or Pinot Noir. Someone had the bright idea of vinifying it as a rosé with a dollop of residual sugar. This new style, evolved in the mid-1970s, was dubbed White Zinfandel, although it was pink. No one can agree on who invented the wine. Sutter Home was the first winery to make a vast commercial success of the style, but winemakers such as David Bruce had made the style earlier.

Ironically, the phenomenal success of this dire concoction was to prove the saving of Zinfandel vineyards that might otherwise have been grubbed up on the grounds of old age, low yields, and low prices. Today, the two styles coexist happily. A third style came into being in the late 1960s, but has faded away. Late-harvest Zinfandel was first produced by Mayacamas in Napa when grapes were left too long on the vine. The result resembled a fine Italian Recioto, but many wines in this style were either too alcoholic or too sweet for most palates, and it became apparent they also tended to fall apart after a few years in bottle, unlike vintage port, with which the wine was sometimes compared.

ZINFANDEL: A QUESTION OF PARENTAGE

Zinfandel arrived on the East Coast of the United States in the 1820s and later went west. But only in recent years has DNA "fingerprinting" brought us closer to understanding the identity of this splendid grape. Zinfandel, it transpires, is identical to the Italian Primitivo of Puglia. But Zinfandel existed in the US before it was being planted in Puglia! Others assert that Zinfandel is the same as the Croatian Plavac Mali. More research established that this was not the case, but that Zinfandel is either a parent of Plavac Mali, or that Plavac Mali is a parent of Zinfandel. So the mystery has yet to be solved.

In the 1990s, a new fad developed: old-vine Zinfandel picked at extreme levels of ripeness. Pioneered by Turley, these were wines of great intensity but sometimes alarming levels of alcohol. The American wine press admired these wines enormously, and not only did they become sought-after and expensive, but other wineries began to ape the style. Nobody gave much thought about when a dry red wine with seventeen degrees of alcohol would actually be consumed.

It is inevitable, given the uneven ripening of Zinfandel and the need to pick late, that the wine will often have an alcohol level of around fifteen degrees, even a touch more. If the wine is well-balanced and has ample fruit, this does not matter. The deliberate cultivation of high-alcohol styles seems perverse. The outstanding producers – Ridge, Edmeades, Seghesio, Ravenswood, Hartford Court, Nalle, Rafanelli, Rosenblum, Storybook Mountain, Peachy Canyon, and many others – usually succeed in making rich, ripe, full-bodied Zinfandel that emphasizes exuberant fruit rather than naked power.

Rules and Regulations

Compared to most European wine regions, California remains mostly unregulated. There are no restrictions on which grape varieties may be planted in any zone, nor are yields regulated. This has been a sensible approach, since, until quite recently, most Californian wine regions were uncharted territory. No one knew for sure, for example, what would grow best in Monterey County. The hunch was that Cabernet Sauvignon would prove ideal; experience proved everyone wrong, and today Chardonnay thrives in Cabernet's place. So trial and error play a huge role in the evolution of Californian viticulture. There are regulations on plant material to ensure that no virused vines appear in Californian vineyards. In the past, many cuttings were smuggled in from Europe, a practice greatly frowned upon by the authorities. (For an account of what happened when a well-meaning winemaker smuggled in some vines, *see* "Roussanne" in the "Grape Varieties" section.)

In Europe, appellations are tied to criteria that are supposed to guarantee a minimal quality level, such as restrictions on yield, stipulations on minimum vine density, and a list of permitted grape varieties. There are appellations in California, but it is important to note that they are merely geographical entities, and carry no implications about quality. Wineries and grape farmers may petition the Bureau of Alcohol, Tobacco and Firearms (BATF), which regulates such matters, to have an appellation created. There follows a lengthy process of consultation to establish whether there is popular support for the appellation, and to define its boundaries. If the new appellation (or Approved Viticultural Area, usually abbreviated to AVA) is approved, the decree will only define such matters as geographical boundaries and elevation.

When the AVA is closely defined, it serves a useful purpose. Thus Carneros or Anderson Valley have distinctive microclimates, and a wine from either is likely to have certain characteristics. Other AVAs are so broad that they are all but useless."North Coast" can include wines from four major counties: Napa, Sonoma, Mendocino, and Lake. Other AVAs – Guenoc or York Mountain, for example – are the fiefdoms of a single winery. Yet other AVAs contain a few dozen acres of vineyards but no wineries at all, so they might as well not exist. Moreover, the fact that many AVAs overlap (*see* Sonoma County) can only confuse the consumer.

If the AVA regulations are confusing, the regulations pertaining to labelling can be positively misleading. A wine with a single variety identified on the label need contain no more than seventy-five per cent of wine from that variety. Thus it would be legal for a Chardonnay to contain twenty–three per cent Chenin Blanc or Semillon. For a wine such as Cabernet Sauvignon, traditionally blended with other Bordeaux varieties,

WHAT IS BRIX?

American wine producers use Brix as a system of measuring grape sugar (and thus potential alcohol), just as the French use Baumé and the Germans use Oechsle. Sometimes wine labels will state Brix levels at harvesting, and, in the case of sweet wines, residual sugar in terms of Brix. It is difficult to convert Brix into final alcohol by volume, as the latter depends on the efficiency or otherwise of the yeasts during fermentation. A useful rule of thumb is to multiply the Brix by 0.56 to calculate alcohol levels. Thus, twenty-five Brix is equivalent to fourteen per cent, and five Brix of residual sugar is roughly seventy grams per litre.

there is a certain logic to this rule. For wines usually presented as pure varietal in character, there is too much leeway for surreptitious blending of inferior varieties. A grower in the Central Coast sells Syrah to a Napa winery known solely for its Burgundian varieties; either the Napa proprietor is making a little Syrah for home consumption, or he is using it to beef up his Pinot Noir. This is legal, but is it defensible?

If a county is named on the label, only seventy-five per cent of the grapes need come from that county. Thus, a Sonoma County Sauvignon Blanc could contain a substantial proportion of inferior fruit from the Central Valley. If the wine is labelled as coming from a specific AVA, then eighty-five per cent of the wine must come from that district. This means that a Howell Mountain Cabernet Sauvignon can legally contain fourteen per cent of Cabernet from another region. However, if a single vineyard is named on the label, then ninety-five per cent of the wine must come from that vineyard. A wine identified as being from a particular vintage must contain ninety-five per cent of wine from the year specified.

The term "estate-bottled" is not as clear-cut as might be supposed. It means that the vineyards are either owned or controlled in terms of farming and harvesting by the winery. However, if the winery is in a different area from the winery, then the term cannot be used. Thus, Wente owns substantial vineyards in the Central Coast and exercises full control over them, but because the Wente winery is in Livermore, it cannot use the term "estate-bottled" on the label of its Monterey wines if it wishes to use the specific Arroyo Seco appellation, but it is allowed to use the much larger Central Coast appellation. This is because the rules require that, for the term "estate-bottled" or "estate-grown" to be used, the vineyard and winery must be in the same appellation.

However, a brand name such as Beringer's Founder's Estate seems to be permitted, even though the wine is not "estate-grown."

MERITAGE

The vexed question of what to call Bordeaux blends from California was resolved by organizing a contest in 1988. Six thousand entries were submitted, including such fine names as "Claret Cake" and "Tutti Cali Frutti". Unfortunately, these entries were rejected in favour of the innocuous "Meritage", submitted by Neil Edgar. Not every winery warmed to the term, and many continued to retain proprietary names for these blends. Others objected to forking out $500 as a registration fee in order to use the term.

Californians wrestled for many years with the problem of how to identify a Bordeaux blend. In the late 1980s, a contest was held to come up with a new generic name for such blends, and the winning entry was the ungainly "Meritage". The rules for Meritage stipulate that any wine thus labelled as must be made from two or more of the following: Cabernet Sauvignon, Cabernet Franc, Merlot, Malbec, Petit Verdot, St Macaire, Gros Verdot, and Carmenère. (White Meritage was a blend of Sauvignon Blanc and Semillon.) Production must be limited to no more than 25,000 cases from any vintage. Although some wineries continue to use the term, many others prefer to use a proprietary name such as Insignia (Phelps) or Isosceles (Justin).

How to Read the Label

California wine labels should present no problems to purchasers. The information you would expect to find is: the name of the producer; the grape variety (or the name of the wine, if it is a proprietary brand such as Insignia); the vintage; the degree of alcohol by volume (not very reliable, as the rules tolerate considerable leeway); the appellation, together with any single vineyard name that may be applicable; and government health warnings, such as the magic words "Contains Sulfites" and the American surgeon-general's deliberations on the health risks involved in wine consumption.

Additional information is sometimes provided, often on a back label: number of bottles produced; the precise composition of the wine in terms of grape varieties or vineyard sites blended, residual sugar (where applicable); the producer's address and website; a description of the wine; and so forth.

Vintage Reports

Vintage assessments, including these below, should be treated with caution. Climatic conditions in California are far from uniform, and even within regions there can be significant differences between, say, Alexander Valley and Russian River Valley in Sonoma. The notes below focus primarily on the North Coast, but assessments of other regions have been included, too. There is a tendency in the American press to rate vintages as a whole, which can be seriously misleading. This is comparable to rating Europe as though it were a single wine region. The skills of growers and winemakers, the size of the crops and the willingness to reduce them by green-harvesting, and the decision when to harvest are all crucial factors that contribute to wine quality, and they have little to do with vintage conditions.

2000

If not the epic millennial vintage many producers may have been longing for, 2000 nonetheless may well prove very good. The winter was cool on the North Coast, and budbreak normal. The growing season was mild with cool evenings, except for a very hot spell in June. Sparkling wine producers were happy with the quality of the fruit they were picking from early August: it was clean and healthy. However, there was rain in late August, with more to come in mid-September and October, together with another very hot spell in late September. Such dramatic changes throughout the growing season must have left the North Coast vines bewildered, but they still managed to produce some very good wines, especially from early ripening Chardonnay, Sauvignon Blanc, Pinot Noir, and Merlot.

On the other hand, not all the Chardonnay ripened fully. Cabernet was more problematic, especially since there was more cool damp weather in late October. Those who had green-harvested generally had no problem attaining full maturity eventually. Growers in Calistoga and on Howell Mountain were more seriously affected by the wet weather. Zinfandel fared better than Cabernet in general. Overall, sugar levels were on the modest side, which should give elegant red wines rather than alcoholic blockbusters. Crop size was normal for reds, higher than average for whites. Winemakers are convinced that for red wines this is the best vintage since 1997.

In Sonoma, growers with Burgundian varieties enjoyed an easy growing season, despite several heat spikes, with the harvest over by early October. Chardonnay was very ripe and high in sugar, except in Russian River Valley, and Sauvignon was excellent, too, but Cabernet ripened with greater difficulty because of the late rains. Other red varieties escaped more or less unscathed, although some dry-farmed vineyards did suffer from the heat spikes. So Zinfandel is uneven and wide-ranging in quality; there were some

Zinfandels in Sonoma and elsewhere with stuck fermentations and some residual sugar. Overall in Sonoma, the vintage should be as good as 1999, if not as great as 1997.

In Mendocino, a mild winter and warm summer kept fruit healthy. A heat spell in September caused Zinfandel some problems, but the wines seem to be shaping up well, with both high sugars and high acidity. Chardonnay, Syrah, and Merlot are excellent, and Pinot Noir from Anderson Valley very concentrated.

In the Sierra Foothills, producers were very happy with the quality, which they believed excelled 1999 and could rival 1991 or 1994. However, there was considerable uneven ripening among Zinfandel, largely because of the uneven weather with heat spikes in July, and cooler weather in later August. Rainy spells during the harvest did not affect fruit quality, and there was no rot. The yield was high, so many growers thinned bunches or bled tanks during fermentation to obtain greater concentration. In Eldorado County quantities were affected by frost in May, which did considerable damage.

Good quality was reported in the San Francisco Bay region, including the Santa Cruz Mountains. In the Central Coast, the weather was variable, and some Chardonnay in the cooler regions lacked full ripeness. Monterey had better yields than 1998 or 1999, and whites were excellent. Cabernet could be disappointing in the Central Coast, as cool autumnal weather slowed down maturation.

In Santa Barbara, quality was very high. The growing season was decidedly cool, but it warmed up in September, which caused some vines to shut down and others to speed up maturation. Whites were picked in early October and there was some late rain before the reds were picked. Growers with excessive yields had serious problems with ripening. Nonetheless, quality overall was fine.

1999

This year brought probably the coolest and longest growing season anyone could recall in California. The spring was the coldest of the decade. It was a small crop, too, with yields down between ten and twenty-five per cent. Fortunately a late September heatwave assisted ripening, and some varieties were picked in a rush but in perfect weather conditions. The cool weather earlier kept acidity levels high, and in the North Coast the vintage is proving exceptional for whites. Pinot Noir, too, is intense and flavourful, and Zinfandel distinctly superior to 1998.

The Foothills had a trouble-free growing season and harvest, and any weak wines can be attributed to overcropping. Acidity levels were high, so the wines should have ample freshness.

DO CALIFORNIA WINES AGE?

With very few exceptions (Stony Hill, Mayacamas), Chardonnay and Sauvignon Blanc are styled to be drunk young. Indeed, it is hard to think of any California white wines, other than the occasional Riesling or Marsanne, that might actually improve after five years. Most experts recommend drinking red wines within the first eight years or so, but a well-structured Cabernet or Merlot can age for ten or fifteen years without difficulty. Pinot Noir rarely improves with age in California, and Zinfandel can either be enjoyed young for its exuberant fruitiness, or, in the case of outstanding and well-balanced wines, kept for up to fifteen years – but it's risky. The current trend towards picking overripe Cabernet and Merlot with lush fruit but very low acidity is worrying; it seems likely that most of these wines will tire after just a few years in bottle.

Monterey shivered in June and the summer was cool here, too, but the vintage was saved by an Indian summer. There was a small but good crop of Chardonnay and Pinot Noir.

The season was even more protracted in Santa Barbara, where heavy rain in early November delayed harvesting for some varieties until mid-November. There was some uneven ripening, and sugar levels were lower than usual.

1998

The spring in the North Coast was cold and wet, which delayed flowering and led to the prospect of a late harvest. There were heat spikes in July, but steady warm weather in August helped ripening. In Napa, heavy rain returned in late September and this caused some vineyard managers to panic and start picking. Those who waited were rewarded with a fine, warm October and full maturation. Nonetheless, not all Cabernet was picked as ripe as it should have been. Zinfandel from the North Coast was marked by noticeable tannins and high acidity.

After the equally poor start to the year in Sonoma, growers were dismayed by heavy incursions of fog just when harvesting was beginning, and this was accompanied by cool, damp weather. Again, those who had the courage to wait were greeted by warm weather in October and the prospect of full maturation. Whites are probably more lean than in easier vintages, but that may be no bad thing. The difficult conditions affected the Sierra Foothills, too, and rain marred the quality of the vintage.

In the Central Coast, conditions were better, and some producers in San Luis Obispo reported the best Pinot Noir since 1994.

In Santa Barbara, the vintage was far better than in the North Coast, with excellent Chardonnay picked after a long growing season. Syrah was good too, although Pinot Noir was better in 1999 as many Pinot vines never ripened properly. Overall, this is a vintage for white wines rather than reds in Santa Barbara.

The 1998 vintage has been attacked as mediocre by many wine critics, and it is true that the wines lack the flesh and opulence of greater years. But there are many perfectly satisfactory wines for early or medium-term drinking. And conscientious producers, who reined in their vines during the growing season, made some excellent wines.

1997

This was a precocious year, with early budbreak promising an early harvest. In the North Coast, there was rain in August, followed by humid weather that did provoke rot in vineyards that were not well-managed. The harvest began in late August (except for grapes destined for sparkling wines, which were picked as early as the end of July) but continued into mid-October. After a short rainy spell in September, the weather in Napa turned dry and breezy, so there was no rot. The problem with the vintage was the enormous crop; across California, the crop was thirty-two per cent higher than the previous year. Chardonnay in particular was abundant. The relative coolness of the summer produced some exceptional Cabernet. There was some rot among Zinfandel in coastal vineyards, but by and large this has proved a fine vintage for Zinfandel. Because of the enormous crop, especially of Chardonnay, some wineries ran short of tank space and risked overripeness by leaving some fruit on the vine for longer than was needed.

Conditions were similar in Sonoma, and both the growing season and the harvest were without mishap. In some of the cooler regions, including Russian River Valley and Carneros, the summer rains provoked rot in Chardonnay but not Pinot Noir. On the other hand, rot was sporadic rather than widespread, and some vineyards were unaffected. Many growers were able to complete picking by early October. The crop was very large but quality was impeccable, and vinification posed no problems. Pinot Noir was extremely ripe but retained good acidity.

The Foothills enjoyed excellent weather, with little of the rain that fell in the North Coast. Some producers reported their best-ever vintage. The near-drought conditions helped keep yields at sensible levels, especially in dry-farmed vineyards.

The rain that fell in the North Coast gave most of Monterey and the Central Coast a miss. Here, too, the harvest was abundant and the best growers bunch-thinned.

In Santa Barbara, yields were normal and the growing season was long. Some rain gave rise to rot, but damage was slight. The only problem here was the tendency of different grape varieties to ripen simultaneously.

Overall, grape growers and winemakers were wildly excited by the vintage, many reporting it the best in their experience. Critics were more circumspect, especially those who rightly worried about the extremely high yields in the North Coast. However, now that the wines have been in bottle for some time, it is apparent that the vintage is a very fine one, on a par with 1994.

1996

Napa enjoyed an unusually warm winter with ample rainfall. Budbreak was early. The spring was cool and there was some rain in May that affected the flowering for Chardonnay, Sauvignon Blanc, and Cabernet Sauvignon. This meant that in some vineyards the crop was reduced by up to forty per cent, though most were not affected that badly. After a cool June, the summer warmed up until late August, when there was another cool spell. Conditions during harvesting were dry. Whites developed well, although the crop overall was about twenty per cent down. The disappointments were among the reds, some of which were thin and lacked flesh and tannic backbone.

Sonoma, too, had problems during flowering because of rain. Temperatures seemed more steady and warmer than in Napa, and the harvest was quite early and took place in warm conditions. But, as in Napa, yields were lower. Much Pinot Noir was soft and charming but lacked structure and was best drunk young.

Mendocino had the same problems during flowering as the rest of the North Coast, so the crop was reduced by around fifteen per cent. But the summer was unusually hot, so the grapes ripened easily. Zinfandel had its usual problems of uneven ripening, and throughout the North Coast the Zinfandels were less complex and full-bodied than usual.

In the Santa Cruz Mountains, climatic conditions were similar to the North Coast and the crop was small. But tannin levels in Cabernet were exceptionally high.

The Central Coast and Santa Barbara enjoyed better conditions than the North Coast and did not experience a loss of crop due to poor flowering. Temperatures were high, especially in Paso Robles and Santa Barbara. After a long growing season the harvest was swift and straightforward. Rhône-style and other reds were of exceptional quality in Santa Barbara.

1995

The year got off to a poor start in Napa and Sonoma, with a wet winter and damp, cool spring. Problems at flowering were responsible for a reduction in crop size of up to twenty per cent. In May, the weather improved, and the summer was steady and warm, even resulting in some dehydration towards the end of September. Late flowering led to a late harvest, but an Indian summer helped bring the grapes to full ripeness. The whites proved elegant with good acidity; the reds were supple and destined for medium-term drinking.

Mendocino was burdened with very wet weather in May and June, and it did not warm up properly until August and September. But quality turned out to be good, with much successful Zinfandel here and elsewhere in the North Coast.

In the Sierra Foothills, 1995 was a superb year. South of the bay, the crop size was also small. The weather was cooler in the Santa Cruz Mountains than in the North Coast, with an unusually moderate autumn. In Monterey, the crop was down by as much as seventy-five per cent, and poor flowering also reduced the crop in Santa Barbara, where two-thirds of the usual crop was lost.

1994

The spring in Napa was long and cool; rain in May inhibited berry growth, and berries and clusters remained small, which was to prove beneficial for quality. Nor was the summer especially hot. Nights were unusually cool, which helped the grapes to maintain good acidity levels. However, the temperatures throughout the summer were steady, other than a spell of heat in early August, so ripening was even. There was some rain in Mendocino in September, but not enough to cause concern. The growing season in the North Coast was prolonged, and some Cabernet was still being picked in November; there was unusually fine balance between sugar levels and acidity, resulting in very stylish wines and some of the best Pinot Noir ever seen from Carneros and the Russian River Valley. Merlot and Cabernet were also exceptional throughout the North Coast. Zinfandel was more variable, but the best were ripe and rich and powerful; a few suffered from overripeness. The crop size was normal, but some vineyards benefitted nonetheless from bunch-thinning.

Overall, this is a lovely vintage, especially for reds, in the North Coast, with delicious Cabernets and Merlots and opulent Zinfandels, certainly the best vintage since 1991. Pinot Noir was exceptional, and some growers considered 1994 the best vintage ever for the variety. The small berries and clusters provided wines that were deep in colour, concentrated in flavour, and yet not too tannic. Whites, especially Chardonnay, were more problematic, especially where overcropped vineyards allowed the spread of rot.

Conditions were not nearly so favourable in the Central Coast, where there was a good deal of rain, and San Luis Obispo and Santa Barbara experienced considerable rot, especially among Chardonnay. Monterey fared slightly better. More rain fell in October, but by then most of the grapes, fortunately, were already picked. Only late-ripening varieties suffered. Despite these problems, overall quality was high, and there was fine Pinot Noir from Santa Barbara.

1993

In Napa, the spring was warm, but wind and rain arrived in May just in time to mess up the flowering. From the start, it was evident that the vintage would be short by around thirty per cent. The summer was erratic, with prolonged cool spells followed by periods of considerable heat, especially in August and September. Harvesting took place from late August to late September, again with fluctuating temperatures. In some vineyards, grapes attained high sugar levels before they were physiologically ripe, and this led to some unbalanced wines if the grapes were picked too soon. An Indian summer rewarded those who chose to wait and allow the fine autumnal weather to bring the Cabernet especially to full ripeness. Despite these problems, quality was good if uneven, although many of the reds may not prove especially long-lived, as acidities were low, even though there were some quite tannic wines. Indeed, a few leading properties such as Dominus chose not to bottle any Cabernet under their principal labels, which has damaged the reputation of a perfectly pleasant vintage. Cabernet, Merlot, and Pinot Noir were good if lacking in intensity, and Zinfandel produced some delicious wines.

In Sonoma, too, the crop was reduced by poor weather at flowering, but the grapes ripened well during a protracted growing season, so quality was good, although the wines lack structure. Generalizations are risky, but overall, Sonoma seems to have fared slightly better than Napa, with some good Pinot Noir from the Russian River Valley. Quality was good in the Foothills, too.

The Central Coast and Santa Barbara were largely spared the wet weather that bedevilled the flowering further north. Yield was normal and quality much more even. Chardonnay was fruity and forward, and much Pinot Noir of exceptional quality.

1992

After a wet winter, the spring in the North Coast was cool, so flowering was prolonged and uneven. After a wet June, the summer was warm and dry. High temperatures prompted many to harvest early, with much Sauvignon Blanc picked in August, but other growers chose to wait, as the cool nights posed no danger to grapes left hanging on the vine. Quality was even, but the large crop meant there was some dilution, and many wines lacked some phenolic ripeness and displayed quite high tannins, which have taken years to soften. Chardonnay and Pinot Noir fared well, especially in Carneros.

The harvest in Sonoma was unusually early, with good quality across the board, and forward, somewhat ungainly wines. Much Zinfandel was overripe and jammy, with lowish acidity, but Chardonnay had good acidity. Mendocino experienced a very hot summer and an early harvest.

Overall, this was an awkward vintage in the North Coast, certainly of good quality, but somehow lacking in harmony; all the elements required to sustain excellent wine were present but in differing proportions. Thus, some wines suffered from an excess of tannin or acidity or alcohol.

1991

Very wet weather in March gave rise to some anxiety in Napa, but during flowering the weather was perfect. With the exception of a very hot spell in July, the summer temperatures were moderate, giving a prolonged growing season. Some estates did not harvest Cabernet until the end of October, when the Indian summer came to an end with stormy weather. The red wines were classic, with deep colour, fine concentration, and firm acidity. Nor were they marred by overripeness. Pinot Noir did well, too, but some Chardonnay can lack acidity. It was a large harvest, the biggest crop since 1982, and conscientious growers thinned their crop, which helped the grapes to ripen despite the cool summer. In a few vineyards, Cabernet and Merlot did not ripen fully, either because of a cool microclimate or because of overcropping, and a handful of wines are green. But these are the exceptions.

The cool weather also led to a late harvest in Sonoma; the wines were excellent and abundant. This was a fine year for Zinfandel, both in the North Coast and in the Sierra Foothills.

This long, cool growing season was replicated in all the principal regions of the state, although heavy rain fell towards the end of the season in parts of the Central Coast. Nonetheless, Chardonnay was ripe with good acidity, and Pinot Noir from Santa Barbara was intense and elegant.

There is much debate as to whether 1990 or 1991 is the superior vintage, especially for Cabernet. It is impossible to provide a definitive answer, given the variations within California, but it is clear that both vintages are first-rate.

1990

Spring rains in Napa and the North Coast led to a fairly difficult flowering, and some varieties – mostly Cabernet, Merlot, and Sauvignon Blanc – had a reduced crop. The summer that followed was hot, and grapes for sparkling wines were picked as early as the second week in August. The dry, warm weather continued through to harvesting, which took place in mild conditions. All Chardonnay was picked in the North Coast by the end of

September. Despite the warm conditions, acidity levels were mostly good, sometimes a touch low. There was fine Pinot Noir from Carneros, and the Cabernet was certainly the best since 1985.

Zinfandel from Sonoma, especially from the Dry Creek Valley, was outstanding, with unusually good balance. The harvest in the Central Coast was interrupted by heavy rain, especially in Santa Barbara, but much of the crop was in and damage was not great. The wines are rich and balanced. Only in the Foothills was 1990 a lacklustre year. Nonetheless, quality throughout California was more even than in the rival vintage of 1991.

Earlier vintages of exceptional quality for red wines are: 1987, 1985, 1980, 1978, and 1974.

Directory of Wineries

This directory lists all major wine producers in California. It should be noted that many wineries own few or no vineyards, and that most wineries purchase a substantial proportion of their grape requirements. This makes it difficult to "place" some wineries within regions. Mondavi, for example, owns vineyards throughout the state, yet because the company is so closely associated with Napa Valley, it is listed as a Napa winery.

In other cases, I have listed wineries in the final "Other Wineries" section, because they lack such an identity. This can apply equally to major players such as Gallo and to tiny *négociant* wineries such as Littorai.

"No visits" should not be interpreted too literally. Many wineries have no retail facilities, but will welcome visitors by appointment. In contrast, many micro-wineries produce their wines at leased facilities, so in such cases there is no winery to visit.

Napa Valley

All telephone and fax numbers have a dialling code of 707 unless otherwise indicated.

Abreu ☆☆☆☆

2366 Madrona Avenue, St Helena, CA 94573.

Tel: 963 7487. Fax: 963 5104.

10 acres. 600 cases. No visits.

Napa Valley's best-known viticulturalist and vineyard developer produces a small amount of sumptuous and high-priced new-oaked Cabernet from the Madrona Ranch.

S Anderson ☆☆☆

1473 Yountville Crossroad, Yountville, CA 94599.

Tel: 944 8542. Fax: 944 8020. 4bubbly.com

68 acres. 13,000 cases. Tasting room.

From vineyards in Yountville and Carneros, the Anderson family makes flavourful vintage-dated sparkling wines of fine quality. Unfortunately, they represent only one-third of production, the growing remainder consisting of Cabernet (Chambers Vineyard), Merlot, and Chardonnay. Most of the sparkling wines are made in a full-bodied, rich style, with a minimum period of four years on their yeasts, and in the case of Reserve wines, around six years.

Araujo ☆☆☆☆☆

2155 Pickett Rd, Calistoga, CA 94515.

Tel: 942 6061. Fax: 942 6471. araujoestatewines.com

41 acres. 4,000 cases. No visits.

Bart and Daphne Araujo bought this exceptional vineyard in the early 1990s. Before that it had been known as the Eisele Vineyard, the source of stunning Cabernets from Ridge and Phelps. The Araujos added Sauvignon Blanc, Viognier, and Syrah.

The wines are made by Françoise Pechon, and are of outstanding and consistent quality, especially the Cabernet and Syrah. They have a strong Calistoga character, with flavours of chocolate and black olives, as well as blackcurrant and cedar. Although the Cabernet has deservedly attracted the most attention, the Syrah is magnificent, too, one of the best examples emerging from Napa Valley.

Atlas Peak ☆☆→☆☆☆

3700 Soda Canyon Rd, Napa, CA 94581.

Tel: 252 7971. Fax: 252 7974. atlaspeak.com

500 acres. 35,000 cases. No visits.

This mountain site was developed in the early 1980s by William Hill, who sold it to a number of investors, including Antinori of Tuscany. There were high hopes for Atlas Peak as a producer of fine Sangiovese, but success has proved elusive.

Since 1993, Antinori has been the majority shareholder. The regular Sangiovese bottling lacks excitement, but the Reserve is of good quality. There is also a Bordeaux/Sangiovese blend called Consenso, and a Merlot.

Bacio Divino ☆☆☆

PO Box 432, St Helena, CA 94573.

Tel/fax: 942 8101. baciodivino.com

No vineyards. 1,000 cases. No visits.

This is the private label of Claus Janzen, who works for Caymus (*qv*). Since 1993, he has been making small quantities of this supple, voluptuous Napa blend of Cabernet, Sangiovese, and Petite Sirah. It's saved from blandness by the lift of the Sangiovese on the finish and its engaging, concentrated flavours.

Barnett ☆☆☆→☆☆☆☆

4070 Spring Mountain Rd, St Helena, CA 94574.

Tel: 963 7075. Fax: 963 3724. barnettvineyards.com

14 acres. 2,500 cases. No visits.

Cabernet and Merlot come from a low-yielding terraced vineyard planted high on Spring Mountain in 1983. In some years the Barnetts also release tiny quantities of Cabernet from their Rattlesnake Vineyard, and a Chardonnay from purchased fruit. Charles Hendricks is the winemaker.

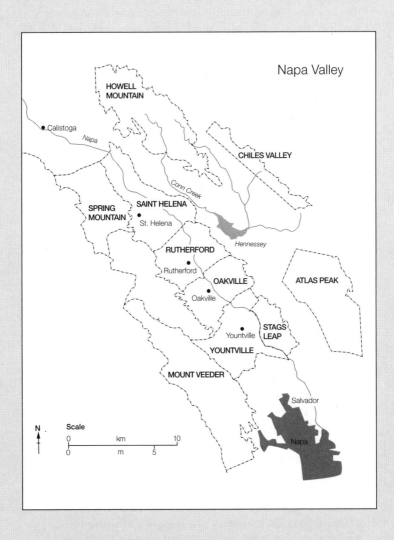

Beaulieu Vineyards ☆→☆☆☆☆

1960 St Helena Highway, Rutherford, CA 94573.
Tel: 967 5230. Fax: 967 9149. bvwines.com
1,200 acres. 1,400,000 cases. Tasting room.

This legendary property was founded by French immigrant Georges de Latour in 1899, and under its equally legendary winemaker André Tchelistcheff produced some magnificent Cabernets in the 1950s and 1960s. In 1969, the estate and winery was bought by the Heublein company, and quality plummeted as production was swiftly expanded. Today, Beaulieu is owned by another corporate giant, Diageo.

Quality improved substantially in the 1990s. The lacklustre Beau Tour range was replaced by a "Coastal" range. A Signet Collection Series was introduced to focus on limited-production wines such as Rhône blends and a Sangiovese. Reserve wines were improved; to the celebrated Private Reserve Cabernet were added Pinot Noir and Chardonnay from Carneros, and a Bordeaux blend called Tapestry. In the late 1990s, Beaulieu released Cabernets made from clones planted in its most historic vineyards, showing that it was far from neglecting its heritage.

At the basic level the wines are sound if unexciting, but the more expensive ranges deliver wines of considerable character and quality. These are well worth investigating and can often be sampled at the tasting room.

Benessere ☆

101 Big Tree Rd, St Helena, CA 94574.
Tel: 963 5853. Fax: 963 9546. benesserevineyards.com
42 acres. 4,000 cases. Tasting room.

Founded in 1996, Benessere specializes in Sangiovese, although other wines such as Merlot and Zinfandel are also produced. The Sangiovese is easily the most interesting wine in the range, but both Pinot Grigio and Zinfandel also show considerable promise.

Beringer ☆☆→☆☆☆☆☆

2000 Main St, St Helena, CA 94574.
Tel: 963 4812. Fax: 963 1735. beringerblass.com
2,500 acres. 3.6 million cases. Tasting room.

This historic winery was built in the 1880s by the German-born Frederick Beringer. The family sold the property in the 1970s, since when it has been owned by a succession of corporations, of which the latest is the Australian Mildara-Blass group. Through all these changes, chief winemaker Ed Sbragia, has been in charge, so the wines have remained consistent. Beringer is fortunate in owning a great deal of acreage, although it also buys in fruit for wines such as its popular White Zinfandel.

The basic range is known in some markets as Founder's Estate and carries the California appellation. Despite being large-volume wines, they are made in a rich, oaky style, which is a Beringer (or Sbragia) hallmark. The next range up in quality is the Appellation Collection, with Chardonnay, Sauvignon Blanc, and Viognier from Napa, and Zinfandel and Pinot Noir from the North Coast. The top wines are the Bordeaux blends known as Alluvium, and the Private Reserves. For some tastes, the Private Reserve Chardonnay is overblown, but the Cabernet and the Howell Mountain Merlot are magnificent wines with excellent ageing capability.

Sbragia's predecessor, Myron Nightingale, pioneered a botrytized wine made from Sauvignon and Semillon grapes artificially induced with botrytis in a humidified chamber. This curious wine is still produced and is named Nightingale in the inventor's honour.

Biale ☆☆☆☆

2040 Brown St, Napa, CA 94559. Tel: 257 7555. Fax: 257 0105.
8 acres. 4,000 cases. No visits.

Aldo Biale's father emigrated from Genoa and planted Aldo's Vineyard on the outskirts of Napa in 1937. It remains the source of one of Biale's nine Zinfandel bottlings, the others being made from outstanding old Zinfandel vineyards throughout Napa and Sonoma. Small quantities of Petite Sirah, Sangiovese, and Barbera are also made. The Zinfandels are richly fruity and well-balanced, making Biale one of the most consistent Zinfandel producers in the state.

Blankiet *NR*

Yountville, Napa. Fax: 915 581 5120. blankiet.com
16 acres. 250 cases. No visits.

This new winery, focusing on a Cabernet-Merlot blend from an excellent site near Dominus in Yountville, has not yet released its first vintage, the 1999. But with California's celebrity winemaker Helen Turley vinifying the blend, it will attract much attention and no doubt be of good quality – and very expensive.

Brown Estate ☆☆☆

3233 Sage Canyon Rd, St Helena, CA 94574. Tel: 963 2435. Fax: 963 0179.
50 acres. 2,000 cases. No visits.

Founded by Jamaican doctor Bassett Brown in 1981, this estate in Chiles Valley is run by his children. Grapes are sold to other wineries such as Grgich, but Brown also produces delicious and supple Zinfandel.

Bryant Family Vineyard ☆☆☆☆☆

PO Box 332, Calistoga, CA 94515. Tel: 314 613 3640. Fax: 314 231 4859.
10 acres. 1,100 cases. No visits.

Don and Barbara Bryant, who live in St Louis, Missouri, entrust the winemaking of their property in the eastern hills to Helen Turley. She has transformed the Bryant Cabernet into one of California's cult wines, and it sells at auction for over $1,000 a bottle. The 1994 was majestic and profound.

Buehler ☆☆

1820 Greenfield Road, St Helena, CA 94574.

Tel: 963 2155. buehlervineyards.com

65 acres. 45,000 cases. No visits.

Corporate executive John Buehler bought this property near Conn Valley in 1972 as a tax shelter, and only began producing his own wines in 1978. There is a wide range of wines, including a second label (California Series) made from purchased grapes.

Burgess Cellars ☆☆☆

1108 Deer Park Rd, St Helena, CA 94574.

Tel: 963 4766. Fax: 963 8774. burgesscellars.com

120 acres. 30,000 cases. Tasting room.

Founded in 1972, Burgess owns vineyards on Howell Mountain, and a Chardonnay vineyard in Yountville. The estate is best known for its red wines, especially its vibrant Zinfandel, which is consistently delicious. The second label is Bell Canyon.

Cain ☆☆☆☆

3800 Langtry Rd, St Helena, CA 94574.

Tel: 963 1616. Fax: 963 7952. cainfive.com

84 acres. 20,000 cases. No visits.

There are few California vineyards more spectacular than those planted by Cain on terraces some 2,000 feet up on Spring Mountain. The best grapes are used for the estate's Bordeaux blend, Cain Five, a powerful, extracted wine of very high quality. Winemaker Chris Howell has had extensive international experience, and is active in improving the vineyards as well as monitoring the wine.

Since 1993, a more accessible wine has been added, Cain Cuvée, and there is also a voluptuous Sauvignon Blanc called Cain Musqué, produced from grapes grown in Monterey.

Cakebread ☆☆☆→☆☆☆☆

8300 St Helena Highway, Rutherford, CA 94573.

Tel: 963 5221. Fax: 963 1067. cakebread.com

82 acres. 85,000 cases. Tasting room.

Still very much a family-operated winery with a loyal following, Cakebread has been producing excellent wines for almost three decades. The Sauvignon Blanc is one of the best in Napa, spicy and elegant, but the best wines are the Cabernet and Merlot. The basic Napa Cabernet is rich and oaky, and surprisingly expensive. Even better are the parcel selections such as the Rutherford Reserve, the Three Sisters Cabernet from the eastern hills, and the Benchland Select from the western benchlands, which offer a fascinating view of the *terroirs* of Napa Valley. The wines are of high quality, but are expensive for a large-volume Napa winery.

CULT WINES

A combination of high quality Cabernet Sauvignon from Napa Valley, the sanction of a celebrity winemaker, and sheer scarcity has helped create "cult wines" from a few producers. That these rare wines (often produced in quantities of no more than 400 cases per year) keep turning up at auction suggests they are collected more than drunk. They have the status of fashion accessories more than bottles of wine to be imbibed and enjoyed. That said, some of them really are superb. Recent auction records establish that the most "collectible" wines are Screaming Eagle, Colgin, Bryant Family, Dalla Valle "Maya", Harlan, and Grace Family – all Cabernets, of course.

Cardinale ☆☆☆☆

7600 St Helena Hwy, Oakville. See Pepi. cardinale.com
210 acres. 4,000 cases. No visits.

Owned by Jess Jackson, this label draws on his mountain vineyards in Napa and Sonoma to produce a rich, Cabernet-dominated Cabernet-Merlot blend. Recent vintages have been very impressive, if overpriced.

Caymus ☆☆☆

8700 Conn Creek Rd, Rutherford, CA 94573.
Tel: 963 4204. Fax: 963 5958. caymus.com
64 acres. 55,000 cases. No visits.

Twenty years ago, Caymus, like most Napa wineries, produced a large range of wines, but by the mid-1980s it had become best known for its lush Cabernets. The most celebrated wine, the Special Selection, is produced from estate grapes grown in Rutherford; the wine is aged for over two years in new and older barriques. It is intended to be drinkable on release. Although highly acclaimed by the American press, the Special Selection can nonetheless lack freshness and vigour. Winemaker Chuck Wagner also makes a full-bodied Napa Sauvignon that can lack typicity, and a very oaky white blend known as Conundrum that is marred by a touch of sweetness. In general, the Caymus range offers immediate gratification rather than long-term satisfaction. On the other hand, the lush, forward style of these wines has enormous appeal to the winery's large band of loyal admirers.

Domaine Chandon ☆☆☆

1 California Drive, Yountville, CA 94599.
Tel: 944 2280. Fax: 944 1123. domainechandon.com
1,100 acres. 375,000 cases. Tasting room.

Domaine Chandon was the first French-owned sparkling wine producer in California, and has been a success story from the start, offering a range of rich but often stylish wines at sensible prices. The best-known wine is the Brut Cuvée, which draws on fruit from Napa and Sonoma. Other sparkling wines include Shadow Creek, a *blanc de noirs*, and the Pinot-dominated Reserve Cuvée, which is aged on the yeasts for four years. There are also super-premium wines such as Etoile, a blend of older vintages. In 2001, winemaker Dawnine Dyer, who had been here since 1976, retired and was replaced by Wayne Donaldson. It is too early to say whether this augurs a change of style.

Chappellet ☆☆

1581 Sage Canyon Rd, St Helena, CA 94574.
Tel: 963 7136. Fax: 963 7445. chappellet.com
120 acres. 25,000 cases. No visits.

Donn Chappellet planted his vineyard high on Pritchard Hill on the eastern side of the valley in 1967. In the past the wines were tough and angular, especially the very tannic Cabernet, and they are still wines that benefit from bottle-age. It is worth looking out for Chappellet's firm, dry Chenin Blanc, and he occasionally produces a high-priced sweet Chenin. The second label is Pritchard Hill.

Chateau Montelena ☆☆☆→☆☆☆☆☆

1429 Tubbs Lane, Calistoga, CA 94515.
Tel: 942 5105. Fax: 942 4221. montelena.com
100 acres. 30,000 cases. Tasting room.

This was one of Napa Valley's best-known wineries during the 1890s, but it foundered during Prohibition. It was revived by lawyer James Barrett, whose son Bo has been winemaker since 1981, when he replaced two of Napa's most revered winemakers, Mike Grgich and Jerry Luper. It was Grgich who made the 1973 Chardonnay that triumphed at the Paris tasting which pitted Napa wines against the finest from France.

Today, the Chardonnay is made in an atypical style for Napa, with no malolactic fermentation and very little new oak. It is invigorating, if austere, but far less impressive than the Cabernet Sauvignon, which is a California classic: ripe, intense, noble, and long-lived. There is a second Cabernet-based wine, Calistoga Cuvée, made from locally purchased grapes, and an attractive alternative to the now costly Cabernet. There is also a good Zinfandel. Unlike many Napa estates where winemakers come and go, Montelena has shown remarkable consistency for almost three decades. Prices have risen in recent years, but they remain reasonable given the quality of the wines.

Chateau Potelle ☆☆

3875 Mount Veeder Rd, Napa, CA 94558.
Tel: 255 9440. Fax: 255 9444. chateaupotelle.com
300 acres. 30,000 cases. Tasting room.

Jean-Noel and Marketta Fourmeaux du Sartel came to Napa from France to study the wine industry for the French government – and stayed. Although based high on Mount Veeder, their vineyards are more dispersed: Bordeaux varieties are planted on the Silverado Trail; Chardonnay and Cabernet on Mount Veeder; and Zinfandel and Syrah in Paso Robles; plus, they use grapes that are bought in from Carneros and Sonoma. As one would expect, the range of wines is varied; the Reserve bottlings carry the mysterious initials "VGS". Winemaking is ambitious, using only natural yeasts and a good dose of new oak, yet quality has been inconsistent, suggesting a lack of focus.

Chateau Woltner ☆☆

150 White Cottage Rd, South Angwin, CA 94508. Tel: 963 1744. Fax: 965 2446.
55 acres. 12,000 cases. Tasting room.

The Woltner family came here after they sold their majority interest in Château La Mission Haut-Brion in Bordeaux. With enormous ambition, they planted all-Chardonnay vineyards high on Howell Mountain. They released a range of high-priced, single-vineyard wines, which did not go through malolactic fermentation; their austere style did not win them popularity. Supposedly made for the long haul, they rarely revealed their alleged promise. By 2000, the Woltners realized that Howell Mountain was not ideal *terroir* for Chardonnay and sold the property to Ladera Vineyards.

Chimney Rock ☆☆☆

53550 Silverado Trail, Napa, CA 94558.
Tel: 257 2641. Fax: 257 2036. chimneyrock.com
132 acres. 22,000 cases. Tasting room.

Hotelier Sheldon "Hack" Wilson planted his vineyards on a former golf course, and built his winery in 1989, since when Douglas Fletcher has been the winemaker here. The focus is on Bordeaux varieties, plus Chardonnay bought in from Carneros. The vineyards had to be replanted after phylloxera, and in 2000, a year before Wilson's death, half the company was bought by the Terlato Wine Group. Thus the future direction of the estate is uncertain, although Fletcher remains at the helm, producing elegant red wines.

Clos du Val ☆☆☆

5330 Silverado Trail, Napa, CA 94558.
Tel: 259 2225. Fax: 252 6125. closduval.com
300 acres. 75,000 cases. Tasting room.

Bordelais brothers Bernard and Dominique Portet went their separate ways in the early 1970s. Dominique founded the Taltarni estate in Australia; Bernard came to Stags Leap and created Clos du Val. The French influence is very apparent in the wines, which are well-structured and intended to be aged. The Cabernet and Zinfandel often succeed better than the Pinot Noir and Chardonnay, but overall quality is high. Nor does Bernard Portet rest on his laurels: he occasionally makes a robust Semillon and, since 1994, a Sangiovese. Yet it's hard not to feel that quality ought to be rather higher.

Clos Pegase ☆☆☆

1060 Dunaweal Lane, Calistoga, CA 94515.
Tel: 942 4981. Fax: 942 4993. clospegase.com
350 acres. 50,000 cases. Tasting room.

Lebanese-born businessman and art collector Jan Shrem caused a furore when he commissioned Princeton architect Michael Graves to build a large new winery near Calistoga, and some of the neighbours tried to put a stop to it. Detractors liken it to a crematorium; admirers, including myself, marvel at the Minoan-style stateliness and elegance of the structure. The wines have never been quite as impressive as the winery, and there has been quite a turnover of winemakers, the incumbent since 1996 being Steven Rogstad.

Pegase's largest vineyard is named after Shrem's Japanese wife, Mitsuko, and is in Carneros; it is the source of good Chardonnay and Merlot, and even some Cabernet. There is a honeyed Sauvignon Blanc made from Monterey grapes, and a charming Vin Gris from Merlot. The Reserve wines can be impressive, although some of the older vintages have not aged well. Clos Pegase is well worth visiting for its fine display of modern paintings and sculpture, which Jan Shrem has generously dispersed throughout the property.

Colgin *NR*

7830 St Helena Highway, Oakville, CA 94574. Tel: 524 4445.
8 acres. 600 cases. No visits.

This boutique winery is renowned for its ultra-expensive Cabernet Sauvignon, grown at the base of Howell Mountain. The first release was in 1992 and the wines, which were made by Helen Turley until 1999, were highly acclaimed. The wine is aged in one hundred per cent new oak.

Corison ☆☆☆☆

PO Box 427, Oakville, CA 94574. Tel: 963 0826. Fax: 963 4906. corison.com
8.5 acres. 3,500 cases. No visits.

Cathy Corison made her name as a winemaker working for Freemark Abbey and Chappellet. In the late 1980s, she started producing her own wines from purchased Cabernet grapes, ageing them in fifty per cent new barriques. In 1996, she released an additional wine from the Kronos Vineyard near Rutherford. These are lovely Cabernets, typically Napa in their richness, but certainly not lacking finesse.

Cosentino ☆☆

7415 St Helena Highway, Yountville, CA 94599.
Tel: 944 1220. Fax: 944 1254. cosentinowinery.com
64 acres. 25,000 cases. Tasting room.

Mitch Cosentino's welcoming tasting room is situated along the main highway. It opened in 1990 and is popular with tourists, who are offered a sometimes bewildering range of wines. Grapes are purchased from all over the North Coast, and in the late 1990s, Cosentino purchased another property in Chiles Valley. Despite Cosentino's exuberant approach to marketing, these are serious wines, but there are too many of them, and there is little consistency. He is best known for Bordeaux blends, Cabernet Franc, and Zinfandel.

Robert Craig Wine Cellars ☆☆☆☆

830 School St, Napa, CA 94559.
Tel: 252 2250. Fax: 252 2639. robertcraigwine.com
20 acres. 9,000 cases. No visits.

The focus of this winery is on three rich and concentrated Cabernet blends: one from Mount Veeder, one from Howell Mountain, and the voluptuous Affinity, which is composed of grapes taken from valley-floor vineyards.

Crichton Hall ☆→☆☆

1150 Darms Lane, Napa, CA 94558. Tel: 224 4200. Fax: 224 4218.
17 acres. 5,000 cases. No visits.

Founded in 1983 by a British investment banker and his American wife, this winery has specialized in Burgundian-style Chardonnay and also produces some Pinot Noir and Merlot from mostly Carneros fruit.

Cuvaison ☆☆☆

4550 Silverado Trail, Calistoga, CA 94515.
Tel: 942 6266. Fax: 942 5732. cuvaison.com
450 acres. 63,000 cases. Tasting room.

Cuvaison's tasting room is near Calistoga, but most of its vineyards are in Carneros. In 1999, it bought the Brandlin Ranch on Mount Veeder. Owned by immensely rich Swiss industrialists, Cuvaison has long specialized in Chardonnay, which accounts for two-thirds of production. The winemaker since 1982 has been John Thacher, and Michel Rolland is a consultant here. The regular bottlings are sound, if a touch bland, but there are some excellent reserve wines. The Merlot, aged in two-thirds new oak, can also be exceptional.

Dalla Valle ☆☆☆☆☆

7776 Silverado Trail, Napa, CA 94558. Tel: 944 2676. Fax: 944 8411.
25 acres. 4,000 cases. No visits.

Italian-born founder Gustav Dalla Valle died in 1995, and the hillside property is now run by his Japanese widow, Naoko. Initial releases of Cabernet Sauvignon and the Bordeaux blend (Cabernet Sauvignon and Cabernet Franc) called Maya were monumentally tannic, but the wines became marginally more accessible in the late 1990s, when Mia Klein took over the winemaking. There is also a good Sangiovese called Pietre Rosse. The Bordeaux-style wines in particular need ageing, which may be part of their appeal to collectors, who are prepared to pay very high prices, especially for Maya.

Darioush ☆☆☆→☆☆☆☆

4240 Silverado Trail, Napa, CA 94558.

Tel: 257 2345. Fax: 257 3132. darioushwinery.com

40 acres. 6,500 cases. Tasting room.

Iranian-born supermarket tycoon Darioush Khaledi bought the former Altamura property in southern Napa in 1997. At present, it resembles a building site, but by 2004 a palatial, Iranian-style winery will be up and running.

Initial releases of Chardonnay, Viognier, Cabernet, Shiraz, and Merlot show great promise, and no expense is being spared to make the best possible wine. Rather confusingly, the second label is known as Estate, while the top bottling is the Signature label. Steve Devitt is the winemaker.

Diamond Creek ☆☆☆☆→☆☆☆☆☆

1500 Diamond Mountain Rd, Calistoga, CA 94515.

Tel: 942 6926. Fax: 942 6936. diamondcreekvineyards.com

21 acres. 3,000 cases. No visits.

Al Brounstein, a former sales representative for Sebastiani, bought this unpromising parcel of overgrown hillsides in 1968. After he cleared the land, he realized there were three different soil types, so he produced different wines from each: Volcanic Hill, Red Rock Terrace, and Gravelly Meadow. He later added the minute Lake Vineyard, which doesn't always ripen fully.

Anyone who doubts that there is *terroir* character in Napa Valley should look at these beautifully landscaped vineyards and taste the wines. There have been years when the wines have been too tannic and austere, but since the 1990s, Diamond Creek has been back on top form, releasing classically structured wines that need ten years or more to reach fully drinkability. At the age of eighty, Al Brounstein's pace and energy have been slowed, very slightly, by Parkinson's Disease, but his charm and wit should not obscure the remarkable achievement in creating and maintaining this estate in the first place. The wines are expensive.

SWEET WINES

Sadly, late-harvest sweet wines are no more fashionable in California than in many other parts of the world, so wines with the intensity of a great Sauternes or Beerenauslese are rare. Fortunately, a few producers persist with the style, using mostly Riesling, but also other grapes such as Sauvignon Blanc and Viognier. Producers include Arrowood, Beringer, Far Niente "Dolce", Freemark Abbey, Jekel, Long, Navarro, Renaissance, and Swanson.

Dominus ☆☆☆☆

PO Box 3327, Yountville, CA 94599.
Tel: 944 8954. Fax: 944 0547. dominusestate.com
124 acres. 8,000 cases. No visits.

Is it an aircraft hangar? Or the headquarters of the villain in the latest James Bond movie? The dark, shed-like Dominus winery, encased in caged rock to facilitate ventilation, is not a welcoming structure. Nor, at first, was the wine. Christian Moueix, of the eponymous Libourne *négociant* house, and his winemaker Jean-Claude Berrouet, tried to apply Bordelais principles to the fruit from this historic vineyard, which had once been the source of top Inglenook Cabernet. The Dominus wines turned out to be tough and almost harsh. Not slow to correct his errors, Moueix adapted viticultural practices to the microclimate and soil conditions of Yountville, and the wines became much better balanced. Vintages such as 1991 and 1994 have been outstanding here.

Duckhorn ☆☆☆☆

1000 Lodi Lane, St Helena, CA 94574.
Tel: 963 7108. Fax: 963 7595. duckhornvineyards.com
183 acres in Napa. 60,000 cases. Tasting room.

Although a versatile and adventurous producer, Dan Duckhorn is best known for his excellent Merlots, which he was releasing long before the varietal became fashionable. Along with the Cabernets, these are big, powerful wines in a full-throttled, Napa Valley style, although the fruit comes from various locations. A wine called Paraduxx, first made in 1994, has proved very successful: a vigorous blend of Zinfandel, Cabernet, and Merlot. Duckhorn has also bought acreage in Mendocino, and more recently on Howell Mountain, so there will undoubtedly be more new wines to look forward to. Long-term winemaker Tim Rinaldi left in 2001 and has been replaced by Mark Beringer. Duckhorn also produce Pinot Noir from Goldeneye (*qv*) in Mendocino.

Dunn ☆☆☆☆☆

805 White Cottage Rd, Angwin, CA 94508. Tel: 965 3642. Fax: 965 3805.
25 acres. 4,000 cases. No visits.

Randy Dunn was the winemaker at Caymus who was responsible for creating the Special Selection Cabernet Sauvignon. He could have had a tremendous career as a winemaker for top Napa producers, but preferred to cherish his independence and go his own way. Since 1979, he has produced two Cabernets: one from various parts of Napa, the other solely from Howell Mountain. The latter is usually rated more highly, but the Napa bottling is less tannic and sometimes more appealing. Yields are very low and flavour intensity amazingly high. The tannins are somewhat tamed by an ageing period in French oak of well over two years. These are dense, profound, Napa Cabernets for the long haul.

Elyse ☆☆☆

2100 Hoffman Lane, Napa, CA 94558.
Tel: 944 2900. Fax: 945 0301. elysewinery.com
4 acres. 8,000 cases. Tasting room.

Ray Coursen takes a casual approach to winemaking, and since he owns virtually no vineyards, his range can vary according to the fruit he is able to purchase. Although once accused of making wines "by neglect", Coursen can turn out some delicious wines, especially Zinfandel. The range of Zinfandels includes one from Howell Mountain – the impressive Morisoli Vineyard – and a blend of eight vineyards known as "Coeur du Val." There is also an old-vine blend called Nero Misto, made from Petite Sirah, Zinfandel, and Alicante. Not subtle, but delicious.

Etude ☆☆☆→☆☆☆☆

PO Box 3382, Napa, CA 94558. Tel: 257 5300. Fax: 257 6022.
No vineyards. 8,000 cases. No visits.

Tony Soter's name may not be well known outside Napa, but he is the winemaker responsible for Spottswoode, Moraga, Viader, and many other prestigious estates. Etude is his own label, using only purchased fruit from vineyards that he in effect leases and farms himself. Soter's strength lies with robust Pinot Noir, but there are good wines, too, from Pinot Blanc and Pinot Gris. In 2001 the company was bought by Beringer Blass.

Evensen Vineyards ☆☆

8254 St Helena Highway, Oakville, CA 94562. Tel: 944 3296.
5 acres. 1,000 cases. No visits.

Richard Evensen planted his vineyard in 1966 and made the unusual decision to focus on Gewurztraminer, although some of the vines have been replaced by Chardonnay. In some years, Evensen succeeds well with this tricky variety.

La Famiglia di Robert Mondavi ☆☆

See Mondavi.
40 acres. 40,000 cases. Tasting room.

Made mostly from purchased grapes, this label is developed to market Italian varieties produced in a light, clean style.

Far Niente ☆☆☆→☆☆☆☆

1 Acacia Drive, Oakville, CA 94562.
Tel: 944 2861. Fax: 944 2312. farniente.com
235 acres. 45,000 cases. No visits.

Gil Nickel, an Oklahoma nurseryman, bought this magnificent stone winery in 1979; it was originally built in the 1880s but abandoned during Prohibition. The winemaker, Dirk Hampson, has been with Far Niente since 1983, and has focused production on three wines: a toasty Chardonnay that does not go through malolactic fermentation, a sumptuous new-oaked

Cabernet, and a Sauternes-style wine, "Dolce", which is aged for three years, also in new barriques. Quality is high, but not always high enough to justify the prices demanded.

Flora Springs ☆☆☆

1978 West Zinfandel Lane, St Helena, CA 94574. Tel: 967 8032. Fax: 963 7518.
600 acres. 35,000 cases. Tasting room on St Helena Highway.

Jerome Komes is the former president of the Bechtel corporation, and he bought an abandoned winery in Napa Valley in 1977. At the same time, he acquired extensive vineyards; most of the grapes grown are sold to other wineries. Nonetheless, Flora Springs releases a large range of wines, which have been made for two decades by Ken Deis. The white wines, however, usually lack concentration and excitement. The reds are distinctly better: fine Cabernet reserves from Rutherford vineyards, charming, chocolatey Merlot, and a fleshy blend – one-third each of Cabernet Franc, Cabernet Sauvignon, and Merlot – called Trilogy. The Sangiovese is attractive, and the winery is planning a Super-Tuscan-style wine to be called Poggio del Papa, a blend of Sangiovese, Cabernet, and Merlot.

Today the winery is run by Jerome Komes's son John, who amuses himself in exceptional years by producing his own wine under the Toad Hall label. In 1997, for example, he made an unusual blend of Malbec and Cabernet Sauvignon. The Toad Hall wines are sold at the tasting room.

Folie à Deux ☆☆

3070 St Helena Highway, St Helena, CA 94574.
Tel: 963 1160. Fax: 963 9223. folieadeux.com
7 acres. 30,000 cases. Tasting room.

At this informal winery north of St Helena, Napa Valley meets the Sierra Foothills. The founders, the Dizmangs, divorced in 1995 and sold the winery. The new regime brought in Scott Harvey as winemaker; he had previously worked at Renwood and was a fan of old-vine Foothills Zinfandels, many of which he continues to produce for his new masters. Less impressive are the other wines in the range, such as the dry Chenin, the light Merlot, the simple Sangiovese. But the Zinfandels are worth seeking out. Look for the single-vineyard Zinfandels from D'Agostini, Harvey, Eschen, and Bowman, and the barrel selection known as La Grande Folie.

Ric Forman ☆☆☆☆

1501 Big Rock Rd, St Helena, CA 94574. Tel: 963 0234. Fax: 963 5384.
80 acres. 4,000 cases. No visits.

The unassuming Ric Forman was the original winemaker at Sterling, and founded his own winery in 1983. He has vineyards in Rutherford and Howell Mountain, but sells most of the fruit. Forman mostly makes Chardonnay and Cabernet Sauvignon, though in 1994 he added a Merlot. The Chardonnay is a welcome relic from the oenological past: bone-dry, appley, made without malolactic fermentation, and aged in fifty per cent new oak. It's a reined-in style that needs bottle-age to show its distinguished best. The Cabernet is as close as Napa gets to a claret-style wine, and this, too, benefits from age.

Franciscan ☆☆☆

1178 Galleron Rd, Rutherford, CA 94573.
Tel: 963 7111. Fax: 963 7867. franciscan.com
520 acres. 600,000 cases. Tasting room.

Franciscan, founded in 1971, has been through endless changes of ownership. In 1999, the vast Canandaigua group (now known as Constellation) bought up Franciscan and some of its sister wineries, which included Mount Veeder (*qv*), Quintessa (*qv*). and Estancia (*qv*). In the 1990s, under the leadership of Agustin Huneeus, Franciscan established itself as an excellent producer of mid-priced, large-volume wines. Whether this reputation will survive the new ownership remains to be seen; an encouraging sign is that Huneeus is still associated with the winery.

Franciscan has superbly located vineyards in Oakville and Rutherford. The most interesting wines are the Cuvée Sauvage Chardonnay, made with natural yeasts and aged in eighty-five per cent new barriques, and the Bordeaux blend called Magnificat. Most of the wines are aged in French and American oak and are excellent value.

Franus ☆☆☆

2055 Hoffman Lane, Yountville, CA 94558. Tel: 945 0542. Fax: 945 0931.
No vineyards. 7,500 cases. No visits.

Peter Franus was the winemaker at Mount Veeder winery until 1993, when he set up his own operation. He buys in all his grapes: Zinfandel from Brandlin Ranch on Mount Veeder and from the Planchon Vineyard in Contra Costa County, which was planted in 1902. These are delicious wines, with intensity of fruit and little trace of portiness. There is also a magisterial Cabernet.

Freemark Abbey ☆☆☆

3022 St Helena Highway, St Helena, CA 94574.
Tel: 963 9694. Fax: 963 0554. freemarkabbey.com
300 acres. 46,000 cases. Tasting room.

This Napa Valley institution was founded by a partnership that included several grape farmers who acquired the abandoned old winery in 1967. In the 1970s and 1980s, Freemark Abbey produced some splendid Cabernets, especially from the Bosché and Sycamore Vineyards, and former winemaker Jerry Luper was a pioneer of German-style, botrytized Rieslings, which he called "Edelwein"; it is still produced, but only in rare years when botrytis strikes. The Chardonnays, made without malolactic fermentation, were crisp rather than fat. By 2001, the partners, dwindling in numbers and energy, sold the property to the Legacy Estates Group. It is too early to say what effect this will have on quality or production strategy.

Frog's Leap ☆☆☆→·☆☆☆☆

8815 Conn Creek Rd, Rutherford, CA 94573.
Tel: 963 4704. Fax: 963 0242.
137 acres. 55,000 cases. Tasting room.

Frog's Leap originated as an easygoing partnership between John Williams and Larry Turley. The wines were stylish and delicious, and the marketing was done with wit and high good humour. In 1994, the partnership split up (*see* Turley). John Williams moved to a splendid site in Rutherford, with a large red barn. Here he continues to turn out elegant Sauvignon Blanc, Cabernet Sauvignon, and Zinfandel, and in the late 1990s a fine blend of Cabernet Sauvignon and Cabernet Franc simply called Rutherford.

Williams is keen on organic viticulture and vinifying with indigenous yeasts. From the start, he has aimed for elegance and balance rather than power and extraction, and the result is a fine range of wines that work wonderfully well with food. Ironically, the winery has often been underestimated because of Williams' refusal to go for rich, powerful styles. Nor, in the eyes of some of his detractors, is humour compatible with excellence in winemaking. Nonetheless, anyone who can produce a wine called "Leapfrogmilch" deserves support!

Grace Family Vineyards *NR*

1210 Rockland Rd, St Helena, CA 94574.
Tel: 963 0808. Fax: 963 5271.
3 acres. 800 cases. No visits.

One of the best-known boutique wineries, Grace acquired its reputation after its wines, usually released in magnums, attained high prices at Napa charity auctions. The wine is pure Cabernet, aged in new French oak, and made by Heidi Peterson Barrett.

Graeser ☆☆☆

255 Petrified Forest Rd, Calistoga, CA 94515. Tel: 942 4437.
9 acres. 4,000 cases. No visits.

Dick Graeser has planted Bordeaux varieties at his vineyard which is situated east of Calistoga. The soils are rich and this is clearly reflected in the style of wines. Chardonnay and Semillon are also produced, but from purchased grapes.

Green & Red ☆☆☆

3208 Chiles Valley Rd, St Helena, CA 94574.
Tel: 965 2346. Fax: 965 1241.
26 acres. 6,000 cases. No visits.

With relatively cool vineyards planted at 1,000 to 1,500 feet above the valley floor, Green & Red turns out intense Zinfandel and Chardonnay that have been growing in renown in the late 1990s.

Grgich Hills Cellars ☆☆☆→☆☆☆☆

1829 St Helena Highway, Rutherford, CA 94573.
Tel: 963 2784. Fax: 963 8725. grgich.com
250 acres. 30,000 cases. Tasting room.

Mike Grgich came to California from Croatia in 1958 and worked with Andre Tchelistcheff at Beaulieu and at Chateau Montelena before setting up his own winery in 1977. Grgich has always preferred a non-interventionist style of winemaking, and draws on a variety of grape sources. His Chardonnay is often outstanding, the Cabernets rich and oaky (one of which is made from Yountville fruit), and the Zinfandel can be excellent, too, if less consistent. There is a spicy Fumé Blanc and a creamy late harvest wine called Vjoletta, named after his daughter.

Groth ☆☆☆

750 Oakville Cross Rd, Oakville, CA 94562.
Tel: 944 0290. Fax: 944 8932. grothwines.com
165 acres. 50,000 cases. Tasting room.

The Groth winery occupies a new mansion that would be more appropriate to a Houston suburb than the verdant Napa Valley, and its flashiness sometimes seems reflected in the wines, which are oaky and boldly flavoured.

A perfect score from Robert Parker for its 1985 Cabernet Reserve made Groth's reputation, but subsequent vintages of both Cabernet and Chardonnay have been erratic in quality.

Hagafen Cellars ☆☆

4160 Silverado Trail, Napa, CA 94558.
Tel: 252 0781. Fax: 252 4562. hagafen.com
No vineyards. 7,000 cases. Tasting room.

Since 1980, Ernie Weir has specialized in the production of kosher wines from mostly white varieties such as Riesling and Chardonnay, but in 2001 Sauvignon Blanc and Syrah were added to the range. Quality is sound but unexciting.

Harlan Estate ☆☆☆☆☆

PO Box 352, Oakville, CA 94562.
Tel: 944 1441. Fax: 944 1444. harlanestate.com
26 acres. 2,500 cases. No visits.

Bill Harlan is a successful businessman who transformed the Meadowood country club into a leading Napa resort, and he founded Merryvale winery (*qv*). He started producing wines from his own property in 1987, focusing on Cabernet Sauvignon and Merlot.

The vineyards are organically farmed, and yields are very low; the wines are aged for two to three years in new barriques. The 1994 Cabernet was close to perfection.

KOSHER WINES

Until twenty years ago, kosher wine was red and sickly sweet, and many Jews still prefer this style for ritual purposes. But many Orthodox Jews, required to drink kosher, also want to drink well. A few kosher wineries exist in California; they follow strict procedures to ensure that only Orthodox Jews have direct contact with the wines during the production process. Hagafen, in Napa Valley, is the oldest kosher winery, but Gan Eden in Sonoma is well-established, too. St Supéry in Rutherford also releases kosher wines under the Mount Madrona label.

Harrison Vineyards ☆☆☆☆

1527 Sage Canyon Rd, St Helena, CA 94574.
Tel: 963 8271. Fax: 963 4552. harrisonvineyards.com
17 acres. 3,000 cases. No visits.

The Harrisons' first releases were from the unpromising 1989 vintage, but they really got going after their winery was completed in 1994. The range includes a full-bodied, oaky Chardonnay, a polished, concentrated Cabernet, and a slightly overblown Zinfandel.

Hartwell Vineyards ☆☆☆☆

5795 Silverado Trail, Napa, CA 94558.
Tel: 255 4269. Fax: 255 4289. hartwellvineyards.com
20 acres. 1,500 cases. No visits.

Bob Hartwell's tiny Stags Leap District vineyard produces a greatly sought-after pure Cabernet, as well as, since 1999, a Merlot. The Cabernet, now made by Celia Masyczek, is aged for twenty-one months in new barriques.

Havens ☆☆☆

2055 Hoffman Lane, Napa, CA 94558. Tel: 945 0921. Fax: 945 0931.
12 acres. 16,000 cases. No visits.

Michael Havens, a former professor of English, established his winery in 1984, buying grapes from leading vineyards in various parts of Napa Valley. The largest production is of Merlot, which, like the Syrah, is sourced from Carneros. Bourriquot is a blend of two-thirds Cabernet Franc and one-third Merlot.

Heitz ☆→☆☆☆☆

436 St Helena Highway, St Helena, CA 94574.
Tel: 963 3542. Fax: 963 7454. heitzcellar.com
350 acres. 40,000 cases. Tasting room.

Joe Heitz, who died in 2000, was one of the great personalities of Napa Valley. Not especially interested in grape-growing, he had the good fortune to buy fruit from outstanding vineyards such as Martha's Vineyard and Bella

Oaks. From them he made intense, eucalyptus-scented Cabernets of considerable longevity. He also made Chardonnays that were lean and charmless, and some pretty wines from the rare Grignolino variety. For some years, the wines have been made by Joe's son, David. By the late 1980s, it was clear that there were bacterial problems with many of the wines. The Heitzes were reluctant to make changes in their winery, and their reputation suffered. However, by the late 1990s many of the problems appeared to have been overcome, and the Cabernets are showing better and cleaner fruit.

Hess ☆☆☆

4411 Redwood Rd, Napa, CA 94558.
Tel: 255 1144. Fax: 253 1682. hesscollection.com
700 acres. 90,000 cases. Tasting room.

Swiss tycoon Donald Hess came to California in 1978 and bought property on Mount Veeder, including the former Christian Brothers winery that was so large it could also accommodate much of Hess's art collection. The first wines were made in 1983. Chardonnay and Cabernet Sauvignon dominate production. The second label, rather confusingly named Hess Select, is produced from grapes sourced from various parts of California, including Hess's large vineyards in Monterey. Overall, the wines are very well-made and offer good value.

Howell Mountain Vineyards ☆☆☆→☆☆☆☆

PO Box 521, St Helena, CA 94574.
Tel: 967 9676. Fax: 963 3920. howellmountain.com
80 acres. 2,500 cases. No visits.

This recent venture combines the resources of two leading vineyard owners, with Ted Lemon hired to make the wines. The range is dominated by imposing, tannic Zinfandels.

Jade Mountain ☆☆☆

2750 Los Amigas Rd, Napa, CA 94559.
Tel: 226 9997. Fax: 226 1685. chalonewinegroup.com
18 acres. 8,000 cases. No visits.

Since the mid-1980s, Douglas Danielak has been producing excellent wines from Rhône varietals, using grapes grown on Mount Veeder, as well as old-vine Mourvedre leased in the Sacramento delta. As well as a Mount Veeder Syrah, there are flavourful blends such as Provencale (from Syrah and Mourvedre) and Jumeaux (Mourvedre and Cabernet Sauvignon). In 2000, the brand name and inventory were sold to the Chalone group.

La Jota ☆☆☆☆ (until 2000)

1102 Las Posadas Rd, Angwin, CA 94508. Tel: 965 3020. Fax: 965 0324.
34 acres. 4,000 cases. No visits.

In 2001, Bill Smith sold this well-regarded winery to Markham (*qv*). Smith had specialized in Howell Mountain Cabernet, and was a pioneer of California Viognier. Now he intends to concentrate his efforts on Pinot Noir from Sonoma Coast vineyards under his WH Smith label. The future of La Jota is unclear.

Judd's Hill ☆☆☆

647 Greenfield Rd, St Helena, CA 94574.

Tel: 963 9093. Fax: 963 1147.

14 acres. 4,000 cases. No visits.

Art Finkelstein made a great success of the Whitehall Lane winery in the 1980s, but the business grew too large for his comfort, so in 1988 he sold it and retreated to his country ranch in the eastern hills, where he replanted his vineyards.

Finkelstein also buys in fruit to produce his Napa Cabernet, whereas his own vines are used for the Estate Cabernet. Yields are low, and the style is vigorous and well-balanced.

Robert Keenan ☆☆

3660 Spring Mountain Rd, St Helena, CA 94574.

Tel: 963 9177. Fax: 963 8209. keenanwinery.com

50 acres. 10,000 cases. Tasting room.

Insurance broker Robert Keenan planted these vineyards up on Spring Mountain in the mid-1970s. Pierce's disease has affected the vineyards and the Chardonnay was replanted in 1995.

Keenan is best known for his Merlot. All the reds are made in a slightly astringent style that is somewhat charmless. The first release of the Napa Zinfandel in 1999 was uncharacteristically lush and fruity.

Charles Krug ☆☆→☆☆☆

2800 Main Street, St Helena, CA 94574.

Tel: 967 2200. Fax: 967 2291. charleskrug.com

1,200 acres. 900,000 cases. Tasting room.

This is one of the oldest wine estates in Napa Valley, and the winery dates from 1861. It closed at Prohibition. In 1943, Cesare Mondavi bought the property, which he ran with his two sons Peter and Robert. The two brothers clashed so badly that in 1966, Robert left to found his own winery in Oakville. Peter remained at Krug, and the property is still run by him and his sons.

Peter Mondavi was a fine technician and pioneered techniques such as cold fermentation and sterile filtration. Krug offers a wide range of varietals at relatively low prices. Yet quality is sound and consistent, and occasional Reserve bottlings have been of excellent quality in the 1990s. The Napa Vista range is also produced by the winery. Charles Krug also produces a range of inexpensive wines under the CK Mondavi label with the California appellation. Most of the fruit for this range comes from their Yolo County vineyards.

Lail Vineyards ☆☆☆→☆☆☆☆

PO Box 249, Rutherford, CA 94573. Tel: 963 3329. Fax: 963 7519. lailvineyards.com
6 acres. 1,200 cases. No visits.

Robin Lail would be running the great Inglenook estate, were it still in the hands of the Daniel family. Instead, she owns vineyards, divided between Cabernet and Merlot, that allows her winemaker, Philippe Melka, to make very fine wine named after her father: "J Daniel."

Laird Family Estates ☆☆☆

5055 Solano Ave, Napa, CA 94558.
Tel: 257 0360. Fax: 224 7249. lairdfamilyestate.com
2,000 acres. 3,500 cases. Tasting room.

Ken and Gail Laird are grape growers with forty-one separate Napa vineyards. Beginning with the 1999 vintage, they have started to release a few estate-grown wines, although the overwhelming majority of their fruit is still sold to other wineries. The first releases were Chardonnays, from Napa and Carneros: rich, spicy wines with a high price tag. From 2001, the winemaker will be Christina Benz, formerly at Murphy-Goode in Sonoma. Future releases will include Cabernets and a Merlot.

Lewis Cellars ☆☆☆→☆☆☆☆

524 El Cerrito Ave, Hillsborough, CA 94010.
Tel: 866 529 4637. Fax: 415 454 7758. lewiscellars.com
No vineyards. 7,000 cases. No visits.

Former racing driver Randy Lewis buys in Cabernet and Merlot from parts of Napa, and his Chardonnay comes mostly from Sonoma. The Russian River Valley Chardonnay is lush but not too heavy, and the top red is the magnificent Cabernet Reserve.

Livingston-Moffett ☆☆☆

1895 Cabernet Lane, St Helena, CA 94574.
Tel: 963 2120. Fax: 963 9385. livingstonwines.com
10 acres. 6,000 cases. No visits.

John and Diane Livingston sold their Cabernet grapes from their Rutherford acreage to other wineries until 1984, when they started to produce wines under their own label. John Kongsgaard is the winemaker, and in addition to the Moffett Vineyard Cabernet there is a Stanley's Selection made from bought-in Napa Cabernet. Small amounts of Chardonnay and Syrah are also released.

Lokoya ☆☆☆

7600 St Helena Highway, Oakville, CA 94562. Tel: 945 1391. Fax: 944 5628. lokoya.com
20 acres. 1,500 cases. No visits.

This is one of the upmarket Kendall-Jackson labels. Lokoya is dedicated to Cabernets from subregions within Napa, such as Rutherford, Diamond Mountain, and Howell Mountain. Since 2000, Marco DiGiulio has been the winemaker. The style is bold, oaky, and alcoholic, and prices are very high.

Long ☆☆☆

1533 Sage Canyon Rd, St Helena, CA 94574. Tel: 963 2496. Fax: 963 2907.
21 acres. 5,000 cases. No visits.

Bob Long's vineyards, beautifully set in an amphitheatre on Pritchard Hill, began as a weekend retreat that was soon planted with Riesling and Chardonnay, and then other varieties. Surprisingly little-known outside California, these are elegant wines that can show real distinction: the Riesling is charming, the Sauvignon Blanc fresh and lively, as is the Pinot Gris, whereas the Chardonnay is more toasty. Some Sangiovese, like the Sauvignon, is made from purchased fruit, and a tannic Cabernet completes the range.

Luna Vineyards ☆☆

2921 Silverado Trail, Napa, CA 94558.
Tel: 255 5474. Fax: 255 6385. lunavineyards.com
44 acres. 30,000 cases. No visits.

Based near Napa, this is a partnership that includes Mike Moone, formerly a Beringer executive, and winemaker John Kongsgaard. In 1995, they bought the former St Andrew's property, and replanted its Chardonnay vineyards with Pinot Gris. Their specialties are Pinot Gris, Sangiovese, and Merlot. Results thus far have been less than impressive.

Markham ☆☆→☆☆☆

2812 St Helena Highway, St Helena, CA 94574.
Tel: 963 5292. Fax: 963 4616. markhamvineyards.com
350 acres. 150,000 cases. Tasting room.

Founded by Bruce Markham in 1978, this winery soon established a reputation for its Merlot and Cabernet. Indeed, it was one of the first Napa wineries to take Merlot seriously before it became fashionable. Markham was sold to a Japanese company in 1988, but standards have been maintained.

The range is a straightforward collection of basic varietals, aged in French and American oak. This is a large commercial winery that releases a consistently sound, if rarely exciting, range. The second label is called Glass Mountain: 150,000 cases of wine from purchased grapes. The winemaker is Michael Beaulac, who has also taken over responsibility for the recently acquired La Jota property (*qv*) on Howell Mountain.

Louis M Martini ☆

254 St Helena Highway, St Helena, CA 94574.
Tel: 963 2736. Fax: 963 8750. louismartini.com
600 acres. 150,000 cases. Tasting room.

In 1922, Louis Martini founded a winery in San Joaquin Valley, and moved operations to Napa Valley in 1933; at the same time he began to acquire some excellent vineyards. Control of the winery has remained within the family to this day, and various generations have made significant contributions to the industry. Louis Martini pioneered a sweet Moscato *frizzante* of great charm; his son initiated mechanical harvesting; and the first Carneros Pinot Noir was vinified by the winery in 1952.

The best wines were almost always the Special Selection and Private Reserve Cabernet Sauvignons, which aged well, but most other wines were often unremarkable and sometimes dilute. Competition within Napa Valley is too intense for the unremarkable to be good enough, and Martini have slipped far behind. The occasional wine in the "Heritage" range can be of interest.

Mason Cellars ☆☆☆

7830 St Helena Highway, Oakville, CA 94562.
Tel: 9844 1710. Fax: 944 1293. masoncellars.com
No vineyards. 20,000 cases. No visits.

Since 1993, Randy Mason has been producing one of the few outstanding Sauvignon Blancs from Napa Valley. There's a Merlot, too, and in 2002 he will add a Cabernet to the range.

Mayacamas ☆☆☆

1155 Lokoya Rd, Napa, CA 94558. Tel: 224 4030. Fax: 224 3979. mayacamas.com
50 acres. 5,000 cases. No visits.

Bob Travers, a banker from San Francisco, bought this historic mountain property in 1968; he restored the vineyards and hired Bob Sessions, now of Hanzell (*qv*), as his initial winemaker. In the 1970s, Mayacamas produced some remarkable wines: long-lived Cabernet and Chardonnay, and one of the first late harvest Zinfandels with phenomenally high alcohol (they proved delicious young but did not age well). Travers is happy to exist in a kind of time warp, and the style of his wines has scarcely changed in three decades. The Cabernet remains lean and claret-like, a far cry from the rich, jammy blockbusters commonly encountered 2,000 feet down on the valley floor. The Chardonnay, too, is lean and flinty. Opinions are sharply divided about the quality: some people love these wines for their strong personality and food-friendliness, others find them too austere to give much pleasure. I incline towards the former view, but sympathize with the latter!

Merryvale ☆☆☆☆

1000 Main St, St Helena, CA 94574.
Tel: 963 2225. Fax: 963 4441. merryvale.com
No vineyards. 80,000 cases. Tasting room.

This St Helena winery has been around since the 1930s, but in its present incarnation it was founded in 1983 by Bill Harlan (*qv*) and partners; in 1992, Jack Schlatter of Switzerland took a fifty per cent share. The owners were astute in their choice of winemakers: Bob Levy until 1998 and subsequently Steve Test; Michel Rolland has been a consultant since 1989. The basic range is known as Classic, then there are the Reserve wines aged in barriques; at the top of the range are the Prestige wines: Silhouette Chardonnay and the Bordeaux blend known as Profile. Despite the fairly high volumes, the wines are made with scrupulous care: whole-cluster pressing for Chardonnay; natural yeast fermentation for the reds, and minimal filtration. Profile is probably the best wine: a sumptuous, new-oaked blend, sleek, and – like all the Merryvale wines – showing tremendous finesse. This is a winery that has been going from strength to strength.

Miner Family Vineyards ☆☆→☆☆☆☆

7850 Silverado Trail, Oakville, CA 94562.
Tel: 945 1260. Fax: 945 1280. minerwines.com
85 acres. 12,000 cases. Tasting room.

One of the flashier new wineries along the Silverado Trail, this owes its existence to software millions. Much of the fruit comes from Oakville Ranch, a vineyard and winery also owned by the Miners. Chardonnay, Viognier, and Cabernet Sauvignon are from Napa Valley, but grapes for Sangiovese and Pinot Noir are bought in from other parts of California. This makes it hard to assess the new winery, but the overall style is opulent and oaky. Prices are high, but the Napa wines in particular are very good.

Robert Mondavi ☆☆→☆☆☆☆

7801 St Helena Highway, Oakville, CA 94562.
Tel: 226 1395. Fax: 963 4003. robertmondavi.com
1,600 acres (Napa). 1.7 million cases. Tasting room.

Now in his late eighties, Bob Mondavi still comes into his office daily, although he no longer has responsibility for the day-to-day running of the winery he founded in 1966. Mondavi today is a venerated patriarch of the wine world, but his early years were fraught with difficulty. He left the family business while in his early fifties in order to found his own winery, and was financially stretched until a court case between him and his brother Peter was settled in Bob's favour.

Robert Mondavi is a man who has never rested on his laurels; he is constantly striving to learn and improve. He created the Fumé Blanc style of oaked Sauvignon that soon became the Californian norm for this variety.

TOP RED MERITAGE WINES FROM NAPA

Affinity (Robert Craig), Alluvium (Beringer), Andrus Reserve (Pine Ridge), Cain Five (Cain), Cardinale, Dominus, Insignia (Phelps), Maya (Dalla Valle), Opus One, Pahlmeyer Red, Profile (Merryvale), Quintessa, Rubicon, Trilogy (Flora Springs), Viader, Von Strasser Reserve.

His winery has conducted exhaustive research programmes, notably into oak-ageing, the results of which he has shared with other producers. He has also been at the forefront of viticultural innovation, and has countered neo-Prohibitionism with a forceful emphasis on wine education.

Although Mondavi is associated with Napa Valley wines, these represent a small proportion of the winery's output, as the company has expanded greatly, and not only within California. The case production of Napa wines is around 350,000 cases, supplemented by 1.3 million under the Mondavi Coastal label and around 6.5 million at Mondavi Woodbridge (see "Other Wineries"). In addition, Mondavi has acquired Byron (qv) and Arrowood (qv) wineries, and has an equal share in Opus One (qv).

With so much activity, it is not surprising that quality at the Napa winery has, ever so slightly, slipped. The regular bottlings lack excitement, but there are still excellent reserve wines, notably the Pinot Noir and Cabernet. Subregional bottlings such as the Oakville Cabernet can also be exceptional.

Tim Mondavi stresses that he, like his father, is keen to make wines that are impeccable with food, emphasizing elegance rather than power. This, he suspects, is why some American critics have been less than enthusiastic about recent releases. The company's indisputable commitment to quality is evident from the construction of a new $28-million winery equipped with costly wooden fermentation tanks.

Monticello ☆☆

4242 Big Ranch Rd, Napa, CA 94558. Tel: 253 2802. Fax: 253 1019.
125 acres. 20,000 cases. Tasting room.

Jay Corley, a businessman from Los Angeles, founded this Oak Knoll winery in 1980. The best wines are the Corley Reserves and the impressive barrel-fermented sparkling wine called Domaine Montreaux, which is aged for seven years on the yeast. However, the red wines are excessively lean.

Mount Veeder ☆☆☆→☆☆☆☆

PO Box 407, Rutherford, CA 94573. Tel: 963 7112. Fax: 963 7867. franciscan.com
60 acres. 10,000 cases. No visits.

This winery, founded in 1973, made some impressive Cabernets in the 1980s under Peter Franus (qv), until it was sold to Franciscan (qv) in 1989. Franciscan expanded the vineyards and eliminated varieties such as Chardonnay. The best wine is the outstanding Mount Veeder Reserve, a powerful, structured Bordeaux blend, aged for twenty-one months in oak.

Mumm ☆☆☆

8445 Silverado Trail, Rutherford, CA 94573. Tel: 942 3434. Fax: 942 3469.
112 acres. 230,000 cases. Tasting room.

Part of the Seagram empire until the company's sale to Diageo, Mumm has always had access to vineyards owned by sister company Sterling (qv), as well as vineyards in cooler sites within Carneros. Quality has always been sound, sometimes excellent. The best-selling *cuvée* is Cuvée Napa, which likes some other wines in the range, contains some Pinot Gris. The top wines are aged three to four years on the yeast. The flagship *cuvée* is called DVX, a late-released vintage wine made half from Pinot Noir, half from Chardonnay, with a small proportion of the must fermented in oak barrels.

Newlan ☆☆→☆☆☆

5225 Solano Ave, Napa, CA 94558.
Tel: 257 2399. Fax: 252 6510. newlanwine.com
30 acres. 12,000 cases. Tasting room.

Founded as a vineyard by Bruce Newlan in 1967 and as a winery in 1981, this is one of the few producers in southern Napa to have made a success of Cabernet Sauvignon. There is also some Chardonnay and Pinot Noir, and a Zinfandel made from bought-in fruit. These are big, serious wines, generously oaked but occasionally over-tannic.

Newton ☆☆☆☆

2555 Madrona Avenue, St Helena, CA 94574. Tel: 963 9000. Fax: 963 5408.
190 acres. 50,000 cases. No visits.

Peter Newton, the British-born co-founder of Sterling, sold up in 1977 and bought extensive acreage on Spring Mountain, which he and his wife, Su Hua, transformed into arguably Napa's most exquisitely landscaped vineyards. There have been many changes of winemaker, yet quality has remained high and consistent. Newton was a pioneer of Napa Merlot in the 1980s and made delicious Graves-style Sauvignon Blanc, which was phased out because of the unviable cost of production. Today, Newton focuses on Chardonnay and Cabernet Sauvignon, all aged in French oak. The Red Label designation is used for purchased fruit.

Neyers ☆☆→☆☆☆

PO Box 10218, St Helena, CA 94574. Tel: 963 8840. Fax: 963 8894.
80 acres. 20,000 cases. No visits.

Bruce Neyers is a research chemist who founded this winery in 1980. Ehren Jordan, who is also the winemaker at Turley (*qv*), sources most grapes from top vineyards in Napa, Carneros, and Sonoma Coast. These assertive, sometimes over-powered wines are made in small quantities and are expensive.

Nichelini ☆☆

2950 Sage Canyon Rd, St Helena, CA 94574.
Tel: 963 0717. Fax: 963 3262. nicheliniwinery.com
100 acres. 2,000 cases. Tasting room (weekends only).

A family-operated winery founded in 1890, Nichelini is located in Chiles Valley. The wines, which include Petite Sirah, Cabernet, and Merlot, are made by a Nichelini descendant, Greg Boeger, who has his own winery (*qv*) in the Sierra Foothills. The most impressive wine is the old-vine Zinfandel.

Nickel & Nickel ☆☆☆

PO Box 7, Oakville, CA 94562. Tel: 944 2861. Fax: 944 2312.

42 acres. 3,500 cases. No visits.

Gil Nickel of Far Niente (*qv*) has also acquired a parcel of vineyards (planted with Bordeaux varieties and Syrah) in Oakville close to Mondavi. Initial releases were from purchased grapes from Napa and Sonoma, but eventually there will be a winery here, and the range will focus on estate-grown fruit.

Niebaum-Coppola ☆☆→☆☆☆☆

1991 St Helena Highway, Rutherford, CA 94573.

Tel: 968 1161. Fax: 967 4178. niebaum-coppola.com

195 acres. 200,000 cases. Tasting room.

In 1975, film director Francis Ford Coppola bought the mansion that once belonged to Napa Valley pioneer Gustave Niebaum, as well as vineyards that had been components of the celebrated Private Reserve Cabernets from Beaulieu (*qv*). He capped this purchase twenty years later when he bought and renovated the Inglenook Winery. Coppola made his reputation as a wine producer with Rubicon: a dense, tannic Bordeaux blend that used to be aged for many years in cask and bottle before release. More recently, the wines have been released younger and they are indeed more accessible than the blockbusters of the 1980s. In 1999, he created a sister wine for Rubicon in the form of a white blend called Blancaneaux.

Other estate wines include a Merlot and Viognier, and a Zinfandel under the Edizione Pennino label. The more modestly priced Diamond Series is made from purchased grapes, as is the inexpensive Francis Coppola Presents range. These non-estate lines are sound but unexciting, but the estate wines, which are made in a rich, oaky, sumptuous style, are first-rate.

Oakford Vineyards *NR*

1575 Oakville Grade Rd, Oakville, CA 94562.

Tel: 945 0445. Fax: 945 0140. oakfordvineyards.com

40 acres. 1,000 cases. No visits.

This small operation in Oakville, founded in 1988, focuses on a high-priced pure Cabernet aged in French and American oak. There was a change of ownership in 1998, when Carol Wilson bought the property.

Oakville Ranch Vineyards ☆☆☆

7850 Silverado Trail, Oakville, CA 94562.

Tel: 944 9500. Fax: 945 1280. minerwines.com

80 acres. 4,000 cases. Tasting room.

The family who owns Miner Vineyards (*qv*) also own this property, which indeed supplies some grapes to Miner. The wines are Chardonnay, Cabernet, Merlot, and Robert's Blend, which is dominated by Cabernet Franc. The Cabernet is very oaky but graceful.

Opus One ☆☆☆☆☆

7900 St Helena Highway, Oakville, CA 94562.
Tel: 944 9442. Fax: 944 2753. opusonewines.com
104 acres. 30,000 cases. Tasting room.

Throughout the 1970s, Baron Philippe de Rothschild of Mouton-Rothschild and Robert Mondavi pondered how to work together, and in 1979 they founded a property, Opus One, devoted to a single wine: a Napa interpretation of a classic Bordeaux blend aged in new oak. Vineyards with close-density planting were created, and a dazzling new winery with a ravishing barrel cellar was commissioned and built. It took a decade for the Opus winery to come on stream, which may be why the quality improved in the 1990s. Opus One is sleek, concentrated, elegant, and distinguished, but some may baulk at the price.

Pahlmeyer ☆☆→☆☆☆☆☆

PO Box 2410, Napa, CA 94558. Tel: 255 2321. Fax: 255 6786. pahlmeyer.com
112 acres. 4,500 cases. No visits.

Genial lawyer Jayson Pahlmeyer aims high. From 1986, his first winemaker was Randy Dunn, replaced in 1992 by Helen Turley and in 1999 by Erin Green. The current releases – Chardonnay, Merlot, and the Proprietary Red – reflect their penchant for high-powered, high-alcohol wines. Throughout the 1990s, Pahlmeyer has been acquiring vineyards, too: in Atlas Peak and on the ridges above the Sonoma Coast. The reds are distinctly better than the hazy, unfiltered Chardonnay, which can be too overpowering. Pahlmeyer's commitment to the highest quality is beyond dispute, whatever one thinks of his wines stylistically, and his acquisition of outstanding vineyard sites bodes well for the future.

Paradigm ☆☆☆☆

PO Box 323, Oakville, CA 94562.
Tel: 944 1683. Fax: 944 9328. paradigmwinery.com
50 acres. 5,000 cases. No visits.

Owned by Ren and Marilyn Harris, this small producer, with vineyards close to Far Niente, has focused on Cabernet and Merlot, along with tiny quantities of Cabernet Franc and Zinfandel. Winemaker Heidi Peterson Barrett has ensured that quality is very high.

Robert Pecota ☆☆→☆☆☆

3299 Bennett Lane, Calistoga, CA 94515.
Tel: 942 6625. Fax: 942 6671. robertpecotawinery.com
40 acres. 20,000 cases. No visits.

Pecota's vineyards in northern Napa Valley are planted with Cabernet, Merlot, and Sauvignon Blanc, although some fruit, such as Chenin and Syrah from Monterey, is also purchased. One of Pecota's specialities is Muscat Canelli, once quite common in Napa, now rare.

WHO OWNS THE VINEYARDS?

In most of Europe, a wine estate produces wines exclusively or mostly from its own vineyards. In California, there are many comparable estates, but there are also many wineries with no vineyards, or with limited acreage, which obliges them to buy large quantities of fruit each year, either from contracted growers or on the spot market.

There are many large grape-farming companies such as Beckstoffer Vineyards or Kautz or Delicato, enterprises that sell the majority of their production. Fortunately, there also remains a plethora of smallholdings: vineyards ranging from five to one hundred acres, sometimes planted with old vines. These are an invaluable resource to winemakers trying to make wines of character and individuality, but unfortunately, some of these precious old vines are being uprooted and replaced with more profitable varieties such as Pinot Noir or Merlot.

Peju Province ☆→☆☆☆

8466 St Helena Highway, Rutherford, CA 94573.
Tel: 963 3600. Fax: 963 8680. peju.com
150 acres. 15,000 cases. Tasting room.

Tony Peju produces a wide range of wines with crowd appeal, such as his Carnival, a fairly sweet French Colombard. There are also more serious offerings such as Estate Chardonnay and Merlot, and a high-priced Reserve Cabernet. Production expanded in 2000, when newly planted vineyards in Pope Valley came on stream.

Pepi ☆☆☆

See Kendall-Jackson.
Access to Kendall-Jackson vineyards. 25,000 cases. No visits.

Robert Pepi was one of the first Napa producers to focus on Sangiovese and other Italian varieties, a trend continued by Kendall-Jackson, which bought the property in 1995. Today, it is the headquarters not only for the Pepi range, but for other Kendall-Jackson wines such as Lokoya and Cardinale. Kendall-Jackson innovations include a Central Coast Pinot Grigio and a fresh, almondy Arneis. One of the best wines is Due Baci, which is a blend of Cabernet Sauvignon from Mount Veeder and estate-grown Sangiovese.

Perelli-Minetti ☆

1443 Silverado Trail, St Helena, CA 94573. Tel: 963 8762.
8 acres. 5,000 cases. No visits.

This small business began as a hobby winery, until 1988, when a winery was built. The only wines are Chardonnay and Cabernet Sauvignon.

Joseph Phelps ☆☆→☆☆☆☆☆

200 Taplin Rd, St Helena, CA 94574.
Tel: 963 2745. Fax: 963 4831. jpwines.com
350 acres. 100,000 cases. No visits.

Under initial winemaker Walter Schug (*qv*), Phelps focused on varieties such as Riesling and Scheurebe, but since 1983, winemaker Craig Williams has shifted the emphasis to Rhône varieties. In fact, Phelps produced one of the first Syrahs in California from 1974 onwards; its Syrah is still excellent, and the Viognier is one of California's best. Le Mistral is a juicy Rhône blend, and Grenache is used to make a delicious rosé.

The standard varietals are not that exciting, and Phelps has suffered from the loss of its outstanding source of Cabernet, Eisele Vineyard, which is now the Araujo (*qv*) property. Phelps's greatest wine is Insignia, a majestic and very long-lived Bordeaux blend. The style of Insignia has changed subtly over the years, with a higher proportion of new oak being employed in the 1990s, and a greater dominance of Cabernet Sauvignon at the expense of Cabernet Franc.

Pine Ridge ☆→☆☆☆☆☆

5901 Silverado Trail, Napa, CA 94558.
Tel: 253 7500. Fax: 253 1493. pineridgewinery.com
228 acres. 80,000 cases. Tasting room.

Gary Andrus founded this impressive winery in 1978, but the business has had a chequered financial history. Nonetheless, the wines, especially the various Cabernets from different subregions of Napa, have been distinguished, as is the Bordeaux blend made from Rutherford fruit and called Andrus Reserve.

Other wines are less impressive, and although Pine Ridge is one of the few Napa wineries to specialize in Chenin, its current Chenin/Viognier blend is too sweet and soupy.

Plumpjack ☆☆☆☆

620 Oakville Crossroad, Napa, CA 94558.
Tel: 945 1220. Fax: 944 0744. plumpjack.com
53 acres. 10,000 cases. Tasting room.

The Getty family is the major investor in this winery, which was founded in 1996. Nils Venge is the winemaker. Chardonnay and Sangiovese are made from purchased fruit, as the main emphasis at Plumpjack is on estate-grown Cabernet. The Reserve Cabernet is aged in new oak for over three years.

The winery caused a stir by releasing the 1997 Reserve sealed with screw-caps as well as corks, requiring customers to buy both! It certainly attracted attention, which is exactly what the ambitious owners were hoping for.

Pride Mountain Vineyards ☆☆☆☆→☆☆☆☆☆

4026 Spring Mountain Rd, St Helena, CA 94574.
Tel: 963 4949. Fax: 963 4848. pridewines.com
80 acres. 12,000 cases. Tasting room.

Founded in 1990 by the Pride family, this estate sits high on Spring Mountain on undulating terrain. The elevation means the growing season is long, and the flavours intense. The range consists of Cabernet, Merlot, Chardonnay, and Viognier, and Syrah will be added once the vines are mature.

The reds are exceptional, with a concentration of flavour that stems from mature mountain fruit. The top wine is the Reserve Claret, but it is made in very small quantities.

Quintessa ☆☆☆☆

1040 Main St, Napa, CA 94559.
Tel: 252 1280. Fax: 252 1024. quintessa.com
170 acres. 5,000 cases. No visits.

Originally owned by Franciscan (*qv*), this ambitious estate has remained Agustin Huneeus's personal property. The winemaker is Philippe Melka, and the only wine produced is a luxurious Bordeaux blend. The vineyards are quite varied in soil and elevation, so Melka has many lots from which to compose his blend. Unsatisfactory lots are sold off.

Kent Rasmussen ☆☆☆

1001 Silverado Trail, St Helena, CA 94574. Tel: 963 5667. Fax: 963 5664.
14 acres. 24,000 cases. Tasting room.

Kent Rasmussen concentrates his efforts on Chardonnay and Pinot Noir from the Carneros region; the oaky Chardonnay has proved more consistent. He also buys in Sangiovese, Syrah, and Dolcetto, which is usually released under his second label of Ramsay.

Raymond ☆→☆☆☆☆

849 Zinfandel Lane, St Helena, CA 94574.
Tel: 963 3141. Fax: 963 8498. raymondwine.com
550 acres. 300,000 cases. Tasting room.

Roy Raymond, Sr, was in charge of the Beringer winery until 1970, and his sons, Roy and Walter, started producing their own wines in 1974. Although it remains under family ownership, the winery has had numerous makeovers in recent years. The basic wines, under a California appellation, are bottled under the Amberhill label; much of the fruit comes from the Raymonds' Monterey vineyards. The next range up in quality, Raymond Estates, is not necessarily produced from estate-grown fruit. The next tiers are Raymond Reserve and Raymond Generations. Despite this confusing hierarchy, the Raymond wines can be excellent, especially the best Cabernets.

Reverie ☆☆☆

1520 Diamond Mountain Rd, Calistoga, CA 94515. Tel: 942 6800. Fax: 942 6803.
30 acres. 2,500 cases. No visits.

This small property on Diamond Mountain, owned by Norman Kiken,
started releasing wines in the late 1990s. The steep vineyards are planted
with Bordeaux varieties, plus some Tempranillo, Roussanne, Grenache,
and Barbera. Initial releases, such as the 1998 Cabernet Franc and various
Bordeaux blends, were promising.

Ristow Estate *NR*

5040 Silverado Trail, Napa, CA 94558.
Tel: 252 4275. Fax: 415 931 5405. ristowestate.com
17 acres. 2,000 cases. No visits.

Founded in 1989 by Brazilian plastic surgeon Brunno Ristow, this property
produces only Cabernet Sauvignon. The first vintage was 1995 and the
winemaker is Pam Starr.

Ritchie Creek *NR*

4024 Spring Mountain Rd, St Helena, CA 94574. Tel and fax: 963 4661. ritchiecreek.com
8 acres. 1,200 cases. No visits.

Dentist Peter Minor founded this property as a vineyard in 1967 and started
making wine in 1974. Chardonnay dominates production, and some
Cabernet is also produced from a north-facing site that gives higher
acidities than usual in Napa Valley.

Rocking Horse ☆☆☆

PO Box 5868, Napa, CA 94581. Tel: 226 5555. Fax: 255 1506.
rockinghorsewinery.com
No vineyards. 8,000 cases. No visits.

This *négociant* winery buys in Zinfandel from Howell Mountain, and
Cabernet and Merlot from various parts of Napa Valley. The wines are
made by Jim Moore, formerly of Mondavi, and quality has been high.

Rombauer ☆☆

3522 Silverado Trail, St Helena, CA 94574. Tel: 963 5170.
No vineyards. 25,000 cases. Tasting room.

Rombauer does own vineyards but sells all its fruit, mostly Zinfandel, to
other wineries, so it is obliged to purchase fruit for its own range of wines.
These are classical varietals – Cabernet, Merlot, and Chardonnay – and a
proprietary red blend called Le Meilleur du Chai.

Round Hill *NR*

1680 Silverado Trail, St Helena, CA 94574.
Tel: 963 9503. Fax: 963 0834. roundhillwines.com
37 acres. 400,000 cases. Tasting room.

This is essentially a *négociant* winery, the majority of its wines bearing the
California appellation, although the top wines – the Napa Reserves and the

Rutherford Ranch range – are from Napa fruit. Developed by the Van Asperen family, the business was sold in 2000 to Marko Zaninovitch, a vineyard owner from Monterey, so Round Hill's future is unclear.

Rudd ☆☆☆☆

500 Oakville Crossroad, Oakville, CA 94562.
Tel: 944 8577. Fax: 944 2823. ruddwines.com
45 acres. 10,800 cases. No visits.

Leslie Rudd, the owner of the Dean & Deluca delicatessen chain, bought the former Girard winery (although not the rights to the Girard name, which were sold separately) in 1996 and has been investing a fortune in the property. He shrewdly hired David Ramey, one of California's most respected winemakers, to oversee the winery. Around the winery is a remarkable rocky vineyard, currently being replanted with Bordeaux varieties, but with the potential to make extraordinary red wine. In the meantime, Rudd produces a Bordeaux blend from the Jericho Canyon Vineyard near Calistoga, and intense, elegant Chardonnays from Carneros and Russian River. These are early days, but initial tastings show enormous promise.

Rutherford Hill ☆

200 Rutherford Hill Rd, St Helena, CA 94573.
Tel: 963 1871. Fax: 963 1878. rutherfordhill.com
190 acres. 100,000 cases. Tasting room.

Originally founded by the partners in Freemark Abbey (*qv*) as a kind of extension winery, Rutherford Hill enjoyed a fine reputation in the 1970s and early 1980s. Then quality slipped, and in 1996, the property was acquired by the Terlato Wine Group of Chicago. Quality has been mundane, but new investment may well bring improvements.

Saddleback Cellars ☆☆☆

7802 Money Rd, Oakville, CA 94562. Tel: 944 1305. Fax: 944 1325.
17 acres. 4,000 cases. No visits.

Nils Venge, winemaker for Plumpjack and other estates, has his own small winery specializing in Cabernet Sauvignon, Zinfandel, and Pinot Blanc.

St Clement ☆☆→☆☆☆

2867 St Helena Highway, St Helena, CA 94574.
Tel: 967 3033. Fax: 963 9174. stclement.com
21 acres. 25,000 cases. Tasting room.

Dennis Johns was the winemaker here for twenty years, establishing a fine reputation. In 1999, Beringer bought the property and David Schlottman was appointed as winemaker in 2000. The winery offers a range of standard varietals, mostly from bought-in Napa fruit. The Reserve Chardonnay comes from the estate's Abbots Vineyard in Carneros. The whites are somewhat characterless, but the reds, such as the Merlot and the Bordeaux blend called Oroppas, are sleek and elegant.

St Supéry ☆☆

8440 St Helena Highway, Rutherford, CA 94573.
Tel: 963 4507. Fax: 963 4526. stsupery.com
645 acres. 120,000 cases. Tasting room.

This nineteenth-century property was bought and revived by the Skalli family, whose members are major players in southern France. Most of the grapes come from their large Dollarhide Ranch in Pope Valley, where the cool nights help produce relatively light-bodied wines. The range of standard varieties and Bordeaux blends is cleanly made and sensibly priced. St Supéry has one of the valley's best visitors' centres.

V Sattui ☆

1111 White Lane, St Helena, CA 94574. Tel: 963 7774. Fax: 963 4324. vsattui.com
150 acres. 40,000 cases. Tasting room.

Daryl Sattui had the good fortune to build a tasting room and picnic grounds on the main highway through Napa. This has proved enormously popular with day-trippers, and almost all wines are sold at the cellar door. The range is populist, with blush wines and off-dry Riesling on offer, but there are also more serious wines from Cabernet and Zinfandel.

Schramsberg ☆☆☆

1400 Schramsberg Rd, Calistoga, CA 94515.
Tel: 942 6668. Fax: 942 5943. schramsberg.com
60 acres. 45,000 cases. Tasting room.

This estate was founded by Jacob Schram in 1862, and revived by Jack and Jamie Davies in the late 1960s as a sparkling-wine estate. Production is strictly *méthode champenoise*, and the wines are given prolonged ageing on the yeast. These are serious wines, but can be a touch heavy. The prestige *cuvée* is "J Schram", made only from Chardonnay and Pinot Noir and aged five years to give a rich, toasty wine. After the death of Jack Davies in 1998, Duckhorn (*qv*) took a minority share in the winery.

Screaming Eagle *NR*

PO Box 134, Oakville, CA 94562. Tel: 944 0749. Fax: 944 9271. screamingeagle.com
2 acres. 550 cases. No visits.

A finely located vineyard in Oakville yields California's most costly Cabernet, which routinely sells for silly prices at auction. The winemaker is Heidi Peterson Barrett.

Seavey *NR*

1310 Conn Valley Rd, St Helena, CA 94574.
Tel: 963 8339. Fax: 963 0232. seaveyvineyard.com
37 acres. 1,200 cases. No visits.

Bill Seavey sold his Chardonnay and Cabernet grapes to other wineries until 1990, when he started bottling his own wines, which were initially made by Gary Galleron and now by Philippe Melka. The Cabernet is greatly admired.

Selene ☆☆☆→☆☆☆☆

PO Box 313, Napa, CA 94458. Tel: 258 8119. Fax: 258 8132. selenewines.com
No vineyards. 4,000 cases. No visits.

The label of consultant winemaker Mia Klein, who specializes in outstanding
Sauvignon Blanc and an oaky Merlot from Carneros.

Sequoia Grove ☆☆☆

8338 St Helena Highway, Napa, CA 94558.
Tel: 944 2945. Fax: 983 9411. sequoiagrove.com
110 acres. 20,000 cases. Tasting room.

The Allen family bought vineyards here in 1978 and replanted them in 1995.
The Chardonnays, despite no malolactic fermentation, can be a touch drab,
but the Cabernet is excellent, especially the Reserve. There is a second label,
Allen Family Wines, sold only at the winery.

Shafer ☆☆→☆☆☆☆☆

6154 Silverado Trail, Napa, CA 94558.
Tel: 944 2877. Fax: 944 9454. shafervineyards.com
200 acres. 32,000 cases. No visits.

John Shafer came to California from Illinois in 1972, seeking a change of
career as a grape farmer. In 1978, he began producing his own wines, which
today are made by his son Doug and by Elias Fernandez. Almost all the
wines are from estate-grown fruit. The Red Shoulder Ranch Carneros
Chardonnay is much admired, but only by those who like a rich, heavy style.
The reds, however, are superb, especially the new-oaked Hillside Select
Cabernet, which has a wonderfully velvety texture. Overall, the wines are a
model of consistency, yet Shafer has not refrained from moving in new
directions, introducing a Syrah in 1999 and making a fine port-style wine,
which, because of its very limited production, is sold only at the winery.

Showket *NR*

PO Box 4350 Oakville, CA 94562.
Tel: 877 746 9538. Fax: 707 944 0131. showketvineyards.com
27 acres. 1,500 cases. No visits.

The Showkets have planted vineyards near Dalla Valle, but their first releases
were made from vineyards in Spring Mountain. They have secured the services
of Heidi Peterson Barrett as winemaker, which may explain the very high prices
demanded for the initial releases of Cabernet Sauvignon and Sangiovese.

Signorello ☆☆☆→☆☆☆☆

4500 Silverado Trail, Napa, CA 94558.
Tel: 255 5990. Fax: 255 5999. signorellovineyards.com
100 acres. 6,500 cases. Tasting room.

The Signorello family has been growing grapes in Oak Knoll since 1977 and
started producing wine in 1985. The style is luxurious, with whole-cluster
pressing for white grapes, and a high proportion of new French oak, often

heavily toasted; the wines are unfined and unfiltered. There is a sumptuous Semillon and rich Chardonnay, and exceptional Estate Cabernet. Pinot Noir is bought in from vineyards in Carneros and Russian River. Prices are high.

Silver Oak ☆☆☆

915 Oakville Crossroad, Oakville, CA 94562.
Tel: 944 8808. Fax: 944 2817. silveroak.com
338 acres. 50,000 cases. Tasting room.

Founded in 1972, Silver Oak is a Cabernet-only winery, producing bottlings from Alexander and Napa valleys. All wines are pure Cabernet, and are aged only in American oak. These are sleek, elegant, oaky wines, drinkable upon release, which partly accounts for their popularity. Co-founder Justin Meyer was the winemaker until 2000, when he sold his share to his partner, Ray Duncan. The wines are extremely well-made, but the extent to which you admire them depends greatly on your tolerance for American oak.

Silverado Vineyards ☆☆☆

6121 Silverado Trail, Napa, CA 94558.
Tel: 257 1770. Fax: 257 1538. silveradovineyards.com
300 acres. 95,000 cases. Tasting room.

Founded in 1981 by Walt Disney's widow, Lilian (who died in 1998), Silverado focuses on sensibly priced varietals, with both Cabernet and Sauvignon Blanc being the leading offerings. The wines are made in a supple, elegant, approachable style. Jack Stuart has been the winemaker from the outset.

Sinskey ☆☆☆→☆☆☆☆

6320 Silverado Trail, Napa, CA 94558. Tel: 944 9090. Fax: 944 9092.
160 acres. 20,000 cases. Tasting room.

Eye surgeon Robert Sinskey started planting vineyards in 1982, and the first vintage was 1986. The current vineyards are in Carneros and Stags Leap District, and are tended with great care for the environment. The best wines are the reds, notably the Pinot Noir and Merlot, and the occasional Cabernet Franc.

Smith-Madrone ☆☆

4022 Spring Mountain Rd, St Helena, CA 94574. Tel: 963 2283.
32 acres. 8,000 cases. No visits.

The mountain vineyards yield a lean, long-lived Cabernet Sauvignon, and one of Napa's best Rieslings.

Spottswoode ☆☆☆→☆☆☆☆☆

1902 Madrona Ave, St Helena, CA 94574.
Tel: 963 0134. Fax: 963 2886. spottswoode.com
37 acres. 8,500 cases. No visits.

Dr Jack Novak founded the property in 1972, but after his early death, his widow Mary and daughter Beth have run the estate, which has been organic since 1985. All the wines are estate-grown. Winemaker Tony Soter established the style: supremely elegant Cabernet and a stylish Sauvignon Blanc. Current winemaker Rosemary Cakebread has continued this approach since 1997. One peculiarity about the Sauvignon Blanc is that a proportion of the wine is aged in small steel drums, which allows the wine to benefit from lees contact without acquiring oaky flavours.

Spring Mountain ☆☆☆

2805 Spring Mountain Rd, St Helena, CA 94574.
Tel: 967 4188. Fax: 963 2753. springmtn.com
226 acres. 30,000 cases. No visits.

The original Spring Mountain winery declared bankruptcy in 1990, and was bought in 1992 by a consortium led by former Franciscan president Tom Ferrell. Their first task was to replant the vineyards. The first releases of a Bordeaux blend were very promising, in a dense, oaky style.

Staglin ☆☆☆☆

PO Box 680, Rutherford, CA 94573.
Tel: 944 1710. Fax: 963 8784. staglinfamily.com
50 acres. 10,000 cases. No visits.

The Staglins have replanted their vineyard on the Rutherford Bench, a site with enormous potential. The Cabernet is superb, and the Sangiovese is very fine too. Prices are high.

Stag's Leap Wine Cellars ☆☆☆→☆☆☆☆

5766 Silverado Trail, Napa, CA 94558. Tel: 944 2020. Fax: 257 7501. cask23.com
120 acres. 60,000 cases. Tasting room.

Although Warren Winiarski's acclaimed winery produces Merlot, Chardonnay, Sauvignon Blanc (the Rancho Chimiles bottling is excellent), and Riesling, it is deservedly best known for its Cabernets. There are a number of different bottlings: a Napa appellation from bought-in grapes; a SLV from the estate vineyard; Fay Vineyard, from a Stags Leap vineyard bought in 1986; and the often sublime Reserve called Cask 23. These Cabernets represent the essence of Stags Leap District: rich but elegant, sleek in texture, balanced and age-worthy. Quality has been remarkably consistent for three decades. Prices are predictably high, but Winiarski offers a range of well-made, inexpensive wines under the Hawk Crest label.

Stags' Leap Winery ☆☆

6150 Silverado Trail. Napa, CA 94558.
Tel: 944 1303. Fax: 944 9433. stagsleapwinery.com
170 acres. 130,000 cases. No visits.

Sometimes confused with its more illustrious neighbour, Stag's Leap Wine Cellars, this winery acquired a fine reputation for its sleek, glossy Petite Sirah. It also produces Chardonnay and Merlot, all made in a rather soft, luxuriant style. In 1997, the estate was bought by the group now known as Beringer Blass.

Steltzner ☆

5998 Silverado Trail, Napa, CA 94558.

Tel: 252 7272. Fax: 252 2079. steltzner.com

10 acres. 15,000 cases. Tasting room.

Dick Steltzner owns excellent vineyards in Oakville and Stags Leap, yet the wines lack finesse and concentration.

Sterling ☆→☆☆☆

1111 Dunaweal Lane, Calistoga, CA 94515.

Tel: 942 3345. Fax: 942 3466. sterlingvineyards.com

1,200 acres. 300,000 cases. Tasting room.

This flagship of the Seagram group, with its crag-top winery reached by cable car, was sold, along with the rest of the group, to Diageo in 2000, so the future evolution of the winery is uncertain.

By the late 1990s, Sterling was producing a range of sensibly priced varietal wines that lacked distinction, along with special bottlings from top vineyards in Carneros (Winery Lake Pinot Noir), Calistoga (Three Palms Merlot), and Diamond Mountain (Cabernet) that were of much better quality. Redwood Trail is a label developed for the British market: characteristic varietal wines at a low price.

Stonegate ☆

1183 Dunaweal Lane, Calistoga, CA 94515.

Tel: 942 6500. Fax: 942 9721.

215 acres. 15,000 cases. Tasting room.

In the 1980s, Stonegate developed a fine reputation for Merlot, but a change in ownership in 1996 seems to have led to slipping standards in recent years. The whites (Chardonnay, Sauvignon Blanc) are rather heavy and oily; the reds soft and flat, with jammy overtones. It remains to be seen whether the company can return to its former glory.

EATING OUT

Not surprisingly, its location among vineyards and its proximity to San Francisco has made Napa Valley a gastronomic Mecca. The French Laundry in Yountville is arguably the best restaurant in America, and it's certainly the most inventive – but you must book a month in advance. Chef Thomas Keller dazzles diners with a seemingly endless succession of tiny, exquisitely prepared and presented dishes. Other outstanding and enjoyable restaurants include Catahoula (Calistoga), Celadon and Bistro Don Giovanni (Napa), Bouchon (Yountville), and in St Helena, Tra Vigne, Terra, Mustards Grill, and Pinot Blanc. Their wine lists often feature bottles from cult wineries that are otherwise impossible to find.

Stonehedge ☆

PO Box 5182 Huntington Park, CA 90255.

Tel: 323 780 5929. Fax: 323 780 3126. stonehedgewinery.com

5 acres. 200,000 cases. No visits.

The Shahabi brothers are the owners of this winery, which draws on Napa vineyards for its major red wines, and buys in from all over California for its less expensive range. The reds can be astringent, but the Zinfandel, aged in French and American oak, is good.

Stony Hill ☆☆

Bale Grist Mill State Park Rd, St Helena, CA 94574.

Tel: 963 2636. Fax: 963 1831. stonyhillvineyard.com

40 acres. 4,000 cases. No visits.

Fred McCrae bought his mountainside estate as a weekend retreat in 1943, and only began producing wines ten years later. He concentrated on Chardonnay, for which he acquired an enviable reputation (admittedly, there was little competition in those days). They were lean wines, made from very low yields, eschewing malolactic fermentation, and seeing virtually no new oak – in short, not the Napa stereotype. They certainly aged very well.

After McCrae's death in 1977, the estate was run by his widow Eleanor, and after her death in 1991, by their son Peter. Little has changed, except that the vineyards had to be replanted in the early 1990s, after Pierce's disease wrecked them. The Chardonnay style remains discreet, but no longer finds favour with a public grown used to lavishly oaked wines.

Storybook Mountain ☆☆☆→☆☆☆☆

3835 Highway 128, Calistoga, CA 94515.

Tel: 942 5310. Fax: 942 5334. storybookwines.com

42 acres. 8,000 cases. No visits.

Since 1980, Jerry Seps has been producing nothing but Zinfandel from the most northerly estate in the valley. He makes at least three wines from his vineyards, which are planted at elevations from 600 to 1,200 feet. The wines age well.

Summers ☆☆→☆☆☆

1171 Tubbs Lane, Calistoga, CA 94515.

Tel: 942 5508. Fax: 942 4039. sumwines.com

28 acres. 7,500 cases. Tasting room.

In 1996, the genial Jim Summers, a grape farmer from Knights Valley, bought the run-down San Pietro Vara winery and fixed it up. Initial releases included fine Merlot, lush Charbono, and very drinkable Zinfandel. The second label, for wines from bought-in fruit, is Villa Andriana. A Cabernet Sauvignon will be added to the range in 2001.

Sutter Home ☆→☆☆

277 St Helena Highway, St Helena, CA 94574.
Tel: 963 3104. Fax: 963 7217. sutterhome.com
6,000 acres. 10 million cases. Tasting room.

The Trinchero family bought an abandoned Napa winery in 1947 and produced an astonishing range of wines, many of them fortified. It was Bob Trinchero who hit upon the idea of making an off-dry pink wine from Zinfandel, and so White Zinfandel was born. It has proved a phenomenal success, and the Trincheros have acquired vast acreage in distant parts of California to fuel the demand. This is now the fourth largest winery in the state. The Trincheros have also bought the Montevina winery (*qv*) in the Sierra Foothills. In 1995 they launched the more upmarket M.Trinchero label for their best Cabernet and Chardonnay.

Swanson ☆☆☆☆

1271 Manley Lane, Rutherford, CA 94573.
Tel: 944 0905. Fax: 944 0955. swansonwine.com
140 acres. 25,000 cases. No visits.

Businessman Clarke Swanson has invested a fortune in his winery and vineyards, but fortunately it shows in the wines. The vineyards are in choice corners of Oakville and Carneros, and their quality shines through. Swanson produces creamy Chardonnay, delicious Cabernet and Merlot, vigorous Sangiovese, splendid Syrah, and a fine proprietary red called Alexis. All the wines are estate-grown.

T-Vine ☆☆☆→☆☆☆☆

3120 Old Lawley Toll Rd, Calistoga, CA 94515.
Tel: 942 8685.
No vineyards. 4,000 cases. No visits.

Owner/winemaker Greg Brown produces small lots of wine from Napa vineyards: Chardonnay, Petite Sirah, Zinfandel, and a Bordeaux blend called "T". The Grenache is one of California's finest, and the Syrah is extremely concentrated. Only the rather obvious, oaky Chardonnay disappoints.

Philip Togni ☆☆☆☆→☆☆☆☆☆

3780 Spring Mountain Rd, St Helena, CA 94574.
Tel: 963 3731. Fax: 963 9186.
10 acres. 2,500 cases. No visits.

The British-born Togni is a true California veteran, having been winemaker at Mayacamas and Chalone in the 1950s. He planted his own vineyards high on Spring Mountain in 1981. The mainstay is a noble Cabernet: some 1980s vintages were over-tannic, but since the 1990s, the wines have been magnificent. His other wine is an enchanting sweet red from Black Hamburg called Ca' Togni, but Pierce's disease has more or less eliminated commercial production.

Trefethen ☆☆

1160 Oak Knoll Ave, Napa, CA 94558.
Tel: 255 7700. Fax: 255 0793. trefethenwine.com
650 acres. 100,000 cases. Tasting room.

This large southern Napa property has been owned by the Trefethen family since 1968, and Swiss-born Peter Luthi has been the winemaker since 1985. The relatively cool climate means that Trefethen usually does better with Chardonnay and Riesling than with Cabernet, although in good years, such as 1997, very good Cabernet Sauvignon and Cabernet Franc were made. The wines are well-made but play safe and lack excitement. In 1997, an exceedingly expensive Reserve Cabernet called Halo was also produced.

Tudal ☆

1015 Big Tree Rd, St Helena, CA 94574.
Tel: 963 3947. Fax: 963 9288. tudalwinery.com
7 acres. 2,000 cases. No visits.

Since 1979, Arnold Tudal has been making Cabernet from his dry-farmed, low-yielding vineyards. Quality is uneven.

Turley Wine Cellars ☆☆☆

3358 St Helena Highway, St Helena, CA 94574. Tel: 963 0940. Fax: 963 8683.
15 acres. 12,000 cases. No visits.

After Larry Turley and John Williams (*see* Frog's Leap) went their separate ways in 1994, Turley remained at the original frog farm to pursue his goal of making forceful, extracted wines from a dozen or more old-vine Zinfandel and Petite Sirah vineyards. The wines are controversial. Their powerful, high-alcohol style has attracted fulsome praise from the American wine press. Others, such as myself, find some of the wines simply undrinkable, although a handful are better balanced and undoubtedly impressive. You pays your money – a lot of money – and you makes your choice. Ehren Jordan, not Larry Turley's famous sister, Helen, makes the wines.

Turnbull ☆☆☆→☆☆☆☆

8210 St Helena Highway, St Helena, CA 94562.
Tel: 963 5839. Fax: 963 4407. turnbullwines.com
187 acres. 10,000 cases. Tasting room.

Founded in 1979, this estate was bought by Patrick O'Dell in 1993. Since then, quality has been impressive, and there are delicious, supple wines from Merlot, Sangiovese, Syrah, and Cabernet Sauvignon. There's a juicy Rhône blend called Old Bull Red, and a pricy Bordeaux blend called Oakville.

Viader ☆☆☆☆

1120 Deer Park Rd, Deer Park, CA 94576. Tel: 963 3816. Fax: 963 3817. viader.com
23 acres. 4,000 cases. No visits.

Argentine-born Delia Viader only does one thing, but she does it supremely well. Her eponymous wine is a blend of Cabernet Franc and Cabernet

Sauvignon, from grapes grown organically on rocky Howell Mountain soils. Tony Soter was the initial winemaker from 1989, replaced in 1999 by Charles Hendricks. The wine is rich and succulent, and benefits from ageing.

Villa Mt Eden ☆☆☆

8711 Silverado Trail, St Helena, CA 94574. Tel: 963 9100. Fax: 963 7840.
600 acres. 200,000 cases. Tasting room.

Of nineteenth-century origin, the winery has passed through many hands until its purchase in 1986 by the Stimson-Lane group, who own Chateau Ste Michelle in Washington State. They have retained Mike McGrath as winemaker, who has been here since 1982. The property leases vineyards in Yountville, and also in Monterey and Paso Robles. Parcels of grapes are also bought in from excellent vineyards throughout the state.

The standard range of wines is not exceptional, but there are very good blends under the Grand Reserve label, and the finest lots emerge as Signature Series wines. In general, the reds, notably Zinfandel, Syrah, and Cabernet, are better than the whites. In 2000 the winery launched a new and inexpensive Coastal range.

Vine Cliff ☆☆☆☆

7400 Silverado Trail, Napa, CA 94558.
Tel: 944 1364. Fax: 944 1252. vinecliff.com
40 acres. 12,000 cases. No visits.

Napa's largest winery was located here in the 1880s, but phylloxera finished it off. The estate was bought in 1984 by hotelier Charles Sweeney, who has invested heavily in terraced organic vineyards and a winery; the first vintage of the reborn Vine Cliff was 1993. The wines (Chardonnay, Cabernet, Merlot, and a Bordeaux blend) are opulent in style and show great promise.

Vineyard 29 *NR*

2929 St Helena Highway, St Helena, CA.
Tel: 963 2449. Fax: 963 5271. vineyard29.com
6 acres. 1,000 cases. No visits.

Named after its address, this micro-winery follows the usual formula, producing only Cabernet aged in new oak. In 2000, the original owners sold it to Silicon Valley tycoon Chuck McMinn, who hired Philippe Melka as the winemaker, so the style established by Heidi Peterson Barrett may change. This cult winery is highly regarded by those who have tasted the wine.

Von Strasser ☆☆☆☆

1510 Diamond Mountain Rd, Calistoga, CA 94515.
Tel: 942 0930. Fax: 942 0454. vonstrasser.com
15 acres. 3,500 cases. No visits.

Originally planted in the early 1970s, this vineyard neighbouring Diamond Creek was bought by Rudy von Strasser in 1990. He doubled the vineyard density and began producing very intense Cabernet with considerable

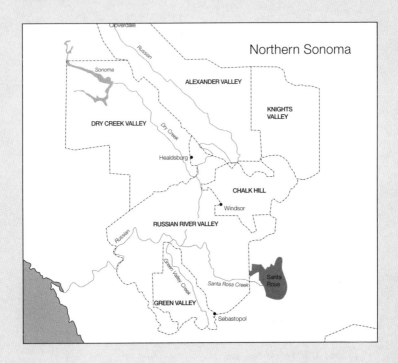

Northern Sonoma

Cloverdale

Russian

Sonoma

ALEXANDER VALLEY

KNIGHTS VALLEY

DRY CREEK VALLEY

Dry Creek

Healdsburg

CHALK HILL

Windsor

RUSSIAN RIVER VALLEY

Russian

Green Valley Creek

Santa Rosa Creek

Santa Rosa

GREEN VALLEY

Sebastopol

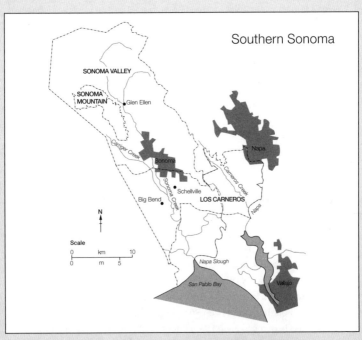

Southern Sonoma

SONOMA VALLEY

SONOMA MOUNTAIN

Glen Ellen

Carriger Creek

Napa

Sonoma

Sonoma Creek

Schellville

LOS CARNEROS

Carneros Creek

Big Bend

Napa

N

Scale

0   km   10
0   m   5

Napa Slough

San Pablo Bay

Vallejo

finesse and a very limited Reserve (a Bordeaux blend), as well as oaky Chardonnay from purchased fruit. Strasser also makes 8,000 cases from purchased Napa grapes under the Freestone label.

Whitehall Lane ☆☆

1563 St Helena Highway, St Helena, CA 94574.

Tel: 963 9454. Fax: 963 7035. whitehalllane.com

110 acres. 32,000 cases. Tasting room.

Founded by the Finkelstein brothers (*see* Judd's Hill) in 1979, this successful winery was sold to Tom Leonardini in 1993. Its star turn has always been Merlot, much of which is bought in from Knights Valley, although some vintages have been somewhat jammy and obvious. There is also a fresh Carneros Chardonnay and a delicate Cabernet.

ZD ☆☆☆

8383 Silverado Trail, Napa, CA 94558. Tel: 963 5188. Fax: 963 2640. zdwines.com

40 acres. 25,000 cases. Tasting room.

Founded in 1969 by the two aircraft engineers whose initials form the winery name, ZD has concentrated on Chardonnay, much of which is released under the California appellation. The Pinot Noir, Merlot, and Cabernet can be very attractive, and overall, this family-operated winery is underrated.

Sonoma County

Note: as in Napa, the area code is 707 except where otherwise indicated.

Adler Fels ☆→☆☆

5325 Corrick Lane, Santa Rosa, CA 95409.

Tel: 539 3123. Fax: 539 3128. adlerfelswinery.com

No vineyards. 15,000 cases. No visits.

Adler Fels has developed a reputation for its white wines, varying from dry Sauvignon Blanc to off-dry Gewurztraminer and, more recently, Sangiovese. The wines are made by owner David Coleman. They lack consistency.

Alderbrook ☆☆

2306 Magnolia Dr, Healdsburg, CA 95448.

Tel: 433 5987. Fax: 433 1862. alderbrook.com

65 acres. 50,000 cases. Tasting room.

Founded twenty years ago, Alderbrook has experienced numerous changes of ownership, the latest being in 2001, when the property was bought by the Terlato Wine Group, which also owns Rutherford Hill. This makes it difficult to assess its performance. Alderbrook produces a full range of varietal wines, mostly from Dry Creek and Russian River Valley. They are cleanly made, with pronounced varietal character and a well-judged oak influence.

Alexander Valley Vineyards ☆☆

8644 Highway 128, Healdsburg, CA 95448.
Tel: 433 7209. Fax: 433 9408.
150 acres. 80,000 cases. Tasting room.

This well-established estate was founded in 1962 by aircraft executive Harry Wetzel, whose son Hank is the current winemaker. The winery offers a full range of varietal wines, including plump, fleshy Cabernet Sauvignon and Merlot, and delightful Cabernet Franc. Prices are reasonable.

Arrowood ☆☆☆☆→☆☆☆☆☆

14347 Highway 12, Glen Ellen, CA 95442.
Tel: 938 5170. Fax: 938 1543. arrowoodvineyards.com
30 acres. 30,000 cases. Tasting room.

Richard Arrowood was the winemaker at Chateau St Jean (*qv*) from 1974 to 1990, where he made a sensational range of single-vineyard white wines as well as some of the best late harvest Rieslings to have emerged from California. In the 1980s, he began his own winery, relying mostly on purchased fruit from top Sonoma vineyards. In 2000, the property was bought by Robert Mondavi, but Richard Arrowood stays on as a kind of lessee for the time being.

The wines are of the very highest quality. Sometimes the regular bottlings are preferable to the richer, more overbearing Reserves; it is not perverse, for example, to prefer the regular Chardonnay to the very oaky, voluptuous Reserve. There is attractive Pinot Blanc, and delicious Viognier, wisely kept out of new oak. Arrowood made very few red wines at St Jean, but is clearly as gifted with Cabernet and Merlot as with Chardonnay and Sauvignon. He is one of the few producers to bottle a varietal Malbec, and the toasty Syrah shows great promise.

The range is topped off with gorgeous late harvest wines from Riesling and Viognier. Grand Archer is the second label, and can offer exceptional value; Mondavi plans to increase production of Grand Archer to around 20,000 cases.

Belvedere ☆☆

4035 Westside Rd, Healdsburg, CA 95448.
Tel: 433 8236. Fax: 431 0826. belvederewinery.com
500 acres. 75,000 cases.
Tasting room at 250 Center St, Healdsburg, CA 95448. Tel: 431 4430.

This winery has been through changes of ownership and strategy, but seems to be on a more even keel now that financier William Hambrecht, who owns 500 acres of vineyards in Sonoma, is in charge. Bob Bertheau is the current winemaker, and wines are produced from a range of sites throughout Sonoma. The leading varieties at present are Chardonnay and Merlot.

Benziger ☆→☆☆☆

1883 London Ranch Rd, Glen Ellen, CA 95442.

Tel: 935 4064. Fax: 935 3018.

85 acres. 180,000 cases. Tasting room.

Founded in 1980 by Bruno Benziger, this became one of Sonoma's great success stories after the Benziger family established brands such as Glen Ellen and MG Vallejo, which were sold to Heublein in 1993. Thereafter, Joe Benziger and Terry Nolan were more free to concentrate on producing smaller lots of wines with character. Some of the basic wines are dilute and lack interest, but there are usually more exciting bottles on offer, too, such as the Sonoma Mountain Bordeaux blend called Tribute. Many of the more individual wines were released under the Imagery Series label, which has now been developed as an independent brand (*qv*).

Buena Vista ☆

18000 Old Winery Rd, Sonoma, CA 95476.

Tel: 252 7117. Fax: 252 0392. buenavistawinery.com

1360 acres. 420,000 cases. Tasting room.

This historic estate was once the property of Agoston Haraszthy, who imported countless cuttings from Europe to Sonoma in the mid-nineteenth century. Abandoned after phylloxera, it was identified and restored in the 1960s. In 1979, the German Racke corporation bought Buena Vista; in 2001, it sold the company to Allied Domecq. With almost all the vineyards being located in Carneros, many of the wines are made from Carneros fruit, though there are also varietal wines from purchased fruit under the California appellation. Chardonnay dominates. The top wines bear the Grand Reserve label. Despite access to well-located organically farmed vineyards, quality has been uninspired. Prices are modest.

Davis Bynum ☆→☆☆☆

8075 Westside Rd, Healdsburg, CA 95448.

Tel: 433 5852. Fax: 433 4309.

25 acres. 18,000 cases. Tasting room.

Davis Bynum began his professional life as a San Francisco newspaperman. As a hobby winemaker, he developed a brand call Barefoot Bynum, which proved very successful; he sold the brand in 1979 in order to concentrate on the vineyards he had bought in the Russian River Valley. Their grapes were supplemented with outstanding Pinot Noir from neighbouring properties such as Rochioli and Allen vineyards. Gary Farrell (*qv*) was the winemaker for many years, but the current occupant of that post is David Georges.

The white wines are sound, but Bynum's strength lies with Pinot Noir: the basic bottling is the Russian River Valley, then there is a Limited Edition, and in top vintages, Le Pinot from Allen or Rochioli fruit only. There is also a Bordeaux blend called Eclipse.

TOP RED MERITAGE WINES FROM SONOMA

Cinq Cépages (Chateau St Jean), Legacy (Stonestreet), Les Pavots
(Peter Michael), Marlstone (Clos du Bois), Reserve Alexandre (Geyser Peak),
Trésor (Ferrari-Carano).

Canyon Road ☆

19550 Geyserville Ave, Geyserville, CA 95441.
Tel: 857 3417. Fax: 857 3545. canyonroadwinery.com
122 acres. 200,000 cases. Tasting room.

Daryl Groom, winemaker at Geyser Peak (*qv*), also makes wines from
vineyards owned by the Trione family of Geyser Peak. They are cheap,
simple wines with minimal oak-ageing that bear the California appellation.
Half the production is of Chardonnay. There is an allied range called
Venezia, which includes a Sangiovese and a white Bordeaux blend from
Alexander Valley.

Carmenet ☆☆→☆☆☆

1700 Moon Mountain Dr, Sonoma, CA 95476.
Tel: 996 5870. Fax: 996 5302. carmenetwinery.com
97 acres. 50,000 cases. No visits.

Founded in 1982, Carmenet was acquired in 1984 by the Chalone group.
The winery built a good reputation for Sauvignon Blanc, although none of
the grapes were estate-grown. (In 1996, two-thirds of the vineyards were
destroyed by a bush fire.) The vineyards are situated high on volcanic soils
and are better suited to red Bordeaux varieties, which have become the
main focus of the winery in the 1990s.

The basic reds are the Dynamite Cabernet and Merlot, and there is a
Bordeaux blend called Moon Mountain Reserve, an old-vine Zinfandel, and
a few bottlings from single vineyards.

Chalk Hill ☆☆

10300 Chalk Hill Rd, Healdsburg, CA 95448.
Tel: 838 4306. Fax: 838 9687. chalkhill.com
300 acres. 75,000 cases. No visits.

San Francisco lawyer Fred Furth bought an estate here in 1972, and after
some false starts in the vineyard, focused on Chardonnay, Sauvignon Blanc,
Cabernet, and Merlot. About half the production is Chardonnay. Chalk Hill
enjoyed brief renown when David Ramey was the winemaker here in the
early 1990s, but overall, the estate's wines have been lacklustre. A little Pinot
Gris is also produced, and the occasional late harvest Semillon, which can
be delicious.

Chateau St Jean ☆☆→☆☆☆☆

8555 Highway 12, Kenwood, CA 94542.
Tel: 833 4134. Fax: 833 4200. chateaustjean.com
250 acres. 175,000 cases. Tasting room.

A group of grape farmers from the Central Valley founded this estate
in 1973 and built a winery three years later. Their initial winemaker, Richard
Arrowood (*qv*), dazzled the wine world by fashioning numerous single-
vineyard Sauvignons and Chardonnays, and also produced some of
California's finest sweet wines from Riesling, Sauvignon, and Semillon. He
left in 1990 to focus on his own winery, and the present winemaker is Steve
Reeder. In 1996 the winery was sold to Beringer, and in 2000, became
incorporated into its Australian purchaser Mildara-Blass.

The single-vineyard wines are mostly a thing of the past, as they were not
always easy to sell. However, there is still a Petite Etoile Sauvignon, and
Chardonnays from Robert Young and Belle Terre, the latter usually being the
fatter wine. Chardonnay is by far the most important wine for Chateau St Jean,
although Reeder plans to increase red-wine production. But great strides have
been made with red wines: the splendid Cabernet-dominated Cinq Cépages,
and the lovely Merlots. Sadly, very little sweet wine is still being made here.

These are hedonistic wines, richly fruity, high in alochol, and probably
best enjoyed fairly young. It is hard to think of white wines more typically
Californian in style and structure.

Chateau Souverain ☆☆→☆☆☆☆

400 Souverain Rd, Geyserville, CA 95441.
Tel: 433 8281. Fax: 433 5174. chateausouverain.com
325 acres. 145,000 cases. Tasting room.

After a complex and chequered history, Souverain was bought by Beringer in
1996, and in 2000 was absorbed into Beringer's new owners, Mildara-Blass. As
yet there has been no change in winemaking or strategy. Mostly red grapes are
grown in the winery's Alexander Valley vineyards, so all Chardonnay is bought
in. The best Chardonnay is usually from Russian River Valley. With the
exception of the delicious Syrah, the reds are aged in a blend of French and
American oak. Since 1996, Ed Killian has been the winemaker and has raised
standards to an impressive level. The whites are a touch plump and buttery, but
the reds are concentrated and opulent, and the reserve bottlings are first-rate.
Given the quality, the wines represent good value for money, too.

Christopher Creek ☆☆

641 Limerick Lane, Healdsburg, CA 95448.
Tel: 433 2001. Fax: 431 0183. christophercreek.com
10 acres. 4,000 cases. Tasting room.

This small vineyard and winery was bought in 1997 by Fred Wasserman
from the Central Valley. He and winemaker Chris Russi have expanded

the range of wines. To the Chardonnay, Petite Sirah, and Syrah they have
added Viognier and Zinfandel. Quality is average.

Cline ☆☆☆→☆☆☆☆

24737 Highway 121, Sonoma, CA 95476.
Tel: 963 4310. Fax: 935 4319. clinecellars.com
150 acres. 90,000 cases. Tasting room.

The Cline brothers' winery originated in Oakley in Contra Costa County,
where they own a splendid old vineyard planted by their grandfather
with traditional varieties, notably Mourvedre, Zinfandel, and Carignane.
In 1991, they relocated to southern Sonoma, where they planted Rhône
varieties. These varieties reflect the strength of the winery, which turns out
a range of delicious Zinfandels, Mourvedre, Syrah, and Viognier, as well as
Carignane and Marsanne for the adventurous. Some of the wines are a
touch weird, but overall, this is a treasure-trove for those seeking wines
of genuine individuality.

Clos du Bois ☆☆→☆☆☆

19410 Geyserville Ave, Geyserville, CA 95441.
Tel: 857 1651. Fax: 857 1667. closdubois.com
900 acres. 1,000,000 cases. Tasting room.

The brainchild of Frank Woods, who created the winery and began planting
the vineyards, Clos du Bois has grown to be one of the largest producers of
Alexander Valley wines. The basic range is from Sonoma County, then there
are Appellation Reserves from Alexander Valley, and then the wines that
have made the winery's reputation: the Vineyard Designates from the
estate's best parcels, such as Briarcrest Chardonnay and the Bordeaux blend
called Marlstone. But now that competition has grown within Alexander
Valley, Clos du Bois no longer stands out as a pace-setter.

David Coffaro ☆☆☆

7485 Dry Creek Rd, Geyserville, CA 95441. Tel: 433 9715. Fax: 433 6008. coffaro.com
20 acres. 3,000 cases. No visits.

A grape grower since the 1970s, Coffaro has developed an extensive list of
small-volume wines, some of which are proprietary blends, using both his
own grapes and those purchased from his neighbours. The emphasis is on
Zinfandel, Mourvedre, Carignane, and Syrah. Quality is a bit erratic, but the
wines can be exciting. Most of them are sold as futures to a loyal following.

BR Cohn ☆☆

15140 Highway 12, Glen Ellen, CA 95442.
Tel: 938 4064. Fax: 938 4585. brcohn.com
65 acres. 20,000 cases. Tasting room.

Bruce Cohn used to be a rock-group manager and bought this property in
1974; the first vintage was 1984, with Helen Turley as the winemaker until
1987. There are two main ranges: Silver Label for wines from purchased

fruit, and Gold Label for estate-grown wines. The Carneros Chardonnay is light and crisp, and Cohn is better known for reds, notably Merlot and Cabernet. They are stylish but fairly light, as well as being expensive for the quality.

H Cotturi *NR*

6725 Enterprise Rd, Glen Ellen, CA 95442.
Tel: 525 9126. Fax: 542 8039. cotturiwinery.com
7 acres. 6,000 cases. No visits.

The Cotturi family's property deserves mention as one of California's best-known organic estates, although their strict observance means sulphur dioxide is not used during the winemaking, with often detrimental effects on wine quality and stability. Zinfandel is the major variety.

La Crema ☆☆☆→☆☆☆☆

18700 Geyserville Ave, Geyserville, CA 95441.
Tel: 433 4474. Fax: 857 3813. lacrema.com
250 acres. 110,000 cases. No visits.

The original La Crema winery went bankrupt, and was revived by Kendall-Jackson (*qv*), which bought the property in 1993. It specializes in Burgundian varieties from the Sonoma Coast. The best white is the Russian River Chardonnay, and there is also a Reserve Zinfandel from Dry Creek and Russian River fruit. The most widely available Pinot Noir is the Sonoma Coast bottling, but all the Pinots are made in a very traditional manner in large, open-top fermenters, and aged for ten months in twenty per cent new barriques.

Dashe *NR*

2900 Main St, Alameda, CA 95401.
Tel: 510 865 0267. Fax: 510 865 0266. dashecellars.com
No vineyards. 7,000 cases. No visits.

Michael and Anne Dashe have specialized in producing small quantities of mostly Dry Creek Valley Zinfandel and Sangiovese. At first, they made their wines at Cline Cellars, but since 1998, they have operated their own small winery in Alameda. Their approach is to be as non-interventionist as possible.

Dehlinger ☆☆☆☆

6300 Guerneville Road, Sebastopol, CA 95472. Tel: 823 2378. Fax: 823 0918.
45 acres. 10,000 cases. No visits.

Tom Dehlinger is one of California's most committed producers of Pinot Noir. He has mapped his vineyards very precisely, so as to identify the specific characteristics of each parcel. This often results in multiple bottlings from any vintage. The wines are often aged in oak puncheons, which can hold from 72 to 120 gallons, rather than barriques, and consequently the wines spend longer in wood; the style usually favours rich fruitiness over delicacy and finesse. Dehlinger also produces small quantities of Cabernet, Chardonnay, Syrah, and other varieties.

DeLoach ☆☆→☆☆☆☆

1791 Olivet Rd, Santa Rosa, CA 94501.
Tel: 526 9111. Fax: 526 4151. deloachvineyards.com
970 acres. 180,000 cases. Tasting room.

Former fireman Cecil DeLoach built up his now substantial estate by buying up vineyards from old-timers who felt there was no future in the wine business. He established his reputation as a Zinfandel producer, and still releases a number of single-vineyard bottlings from each vintage. The Chardonnay, Cabernet, and Pinot Noir can be very enjoyable, too. When conditions permit, a fine, late harvest Gewurztraminer is also made.

Basic wines are bottled under the California appellation, and the best wines, essentially the reserves, carry the designation "OFS". These are given special treatment, such as longer oak-ageing, but are very expensive.

De Lorimier ☆☆

2001 Highway 128, Geyserville, CA 95441.
Tel: 546 7718. Fax: 857 3263. delorimierwinery.com
100 acres. 12,000 cases. Tasting room.

This low-key Alexander Valley winery specializes in Bordeaux blends. The two main ones are the white Spectrum and the red Mosaic, but there are also two Chardonnays and occasional late harvest wines from either Sauvignon or Semillon.

Dry Creek Vineyards ☆☆☆

3770 Lambert Bridge Rd, Healdsburg, CA 95448.
Tel: 433 1000. Fax: 433 5329. drycreekvineyard.com
200 acres. 130,000 cases. Tasting room.

Boston businessman David Stare acquired this property in 1972 and has a pursued a steady course ever since, concentrating on well-balanced, understated varietal wines at a sensible price. This is not the place for fat, blowsy wines. The house specialty is probably Sauvignon Blanc, as well as a delicious unoaked Chenin Blanc. The reds are sleek and elegant, a touch herbaceous in cooler vintages. Both Zinfandel and Petite Sirah can be excellent. There was a change of winemaker in 2000, when the veteran Larry Levin was replaced by Jeff McBride.

Duxoup ☆☆

9611 West Dry Creek Rd, Healdsburg, CA 95448. Tel: 433 5195.
2,000 cases. No visits.

A quirky operation run by Andrew Cutter, who buys in fruit from Dry Creek Valley vineyards and processes it in a low-tech winery. The most interesting wines have been the Syrah and Charbono, made in vibrantly fruity style. The unusual name of the winery apparently derives from Andrew Cutter's habit of intoning, "It's as easy as duck soup."

Everett Ridge ☆☆☆→☆☆☆☆

435 West Dry Creek Rd, Healdsburg, CA 95448.
Tel: 433 1637. Fax: 433 7024. everettridge.com
110 acres. 7,000 cases. Tasting room

Formerly known as Bellerose, this property was bought in 1996 by the Air family. The vineyards are located principally in Dry Creek Valley, but also in Sonoma Valley and Mendocino, which is the source of a lively Sauvignon Blanc. This is one of the few California vineyards that is cultivated biodynamically. The wines show great promise: a tight, peppery Estate Cabernet, a crisp Chardonnay, and a spicy, concentrated, old-vine Zinfandel.

Gary Farrell ☆☆☆☆

10701 Westside Rd, Healdsburg, CA 95448.
Tel: 433 6616. Fax: 433 9060. garyfarrell.com
45 acres. 12,000 cases. No visits.

Although one of California's most respected winemakers, the almost reclusive Farrell had no winery of his own until 2000, when he moved into a well-equipped new facility in the Russian River Valley. Until then, he had used the facilities at Davis Bynum (*qv*), where he used to be the winemaker. He founded his label in 1982 and has always specialized in Pinot Noir from the valley's top vineyards, including Rochioli; when young, these wines can seem tight and restrained in style, but they can age very well. The Pinots are made in a Burgundian style, with a cold soak before fermentation and punching down the cap by hand.

Bynum also produces small lots of Merlot, Zinfandel, and some Chardonnay; and there are occasional bottlings from Bien Nacido Vineyard in Santa Barbara.

Ferrari-Carano ☆☆☆→☆☆☆☆

8761 Dry Creek Rd, Healdsburg, CA 95448.
Tel: 433 6700. Fax: 431 1742. ferrari-carano.com
650 acres. 120,000 cases. Tasting room.

The Caranos are hoteliers from Reno, and there is no lack of showmanship at the estate they have created with great flair in Dry Creek Valley. Visitors relish the beautiful gardens and the Italianate villa, which serves as a hospitality centre. All this pizzazz should not lead one to suppose the wines are meretricious. Under the guiding hand of winemaker George Bursick since 1985, they are of excellent quality. Bursick can draw on vineyards that stretch from Alexander Valley down to Carneros to fashion elegant, oaky whites from Chardonnay and Sauvignon.

The reds are going from strength to strength, the Merlot and Cabernet being supplemented with a Cabernet/Sangiovese blend called Siena and a Bordeaux blend called "Trésor". The style is richly fruity and seductive.

Field Stone ☆

10075 Highway 128, Healdsburg, CA 95448.
Tel: 433 7266. Fax: 433 2231. fieldstonewinery.com
130 acres. 15,000 cases. Tasting room.

A former cattle ranch in Alexander Valley, Field Stone has been producing wines since the late 1970s. Cabernet Sauvignon is the major wine, and there is also sound Chardonnay and Sauvignon Blanc.

Fisher ☆☆☆

6200 St Helena Rd, Santa Rosa, CA 95404. Tel: 539 7511. Fax: 539 3601.
75 acres. 8,500 cases. No visits.

Founded in 1974, Fred Fisher owns vineyards in Napa as well as Sonoma. His top Chardonnay and Cabernet are bottled under the Coach Insignia label, this being a reference to the source of the Fishers' wealth: Body by Fisher carriagework on Detroit motorcars. There are also occasional single-vineyard releases, notably the very expensive Wedding Vineyard Cabernet from a mountain site. The style of all the wines is rich and bold.

Flowers ☆☆☆☆

28500 Seaview Rd, Cazadero, CA 95421.
Tel: 847 3361. Fax: 847 3740. flowerswinery.com
66 acres. 10,000 cases. No visits.

Walt Flowers is a nurseryman from Pennsylvania who purchased land here in the early 1990s. His Camp Meeting Ridge Vineyard soon became celebrated for supplying exquisite Chardonnay and Pinot Noir to wineries such as Kistler. Since 1994, Walt and Joan Flowers have been producing their own wines. The basic wines carry the Sonoma Coast appellation; then there are wines from Camp Meeting Ridge. At the top of the range comes Moon Select. The wines are aged in a good deal of new oak, but they do not come across as overly oaky because of the intensity of the fruit. The glory of these vineyards is that, despite the cool temperatures, there is constant sunlight and excellent ventilation. Prices are high, but quality is exceptional and improving from year to year.

Foppiano ☆→☆☆

12707 Old Redwood Highway, Healdsburg, CA 95448.
Tel: 433 7272. Fax: 433 0565. foppiano.com
200 acres. 185,000 cases. Tasting room.

Louis Foppiano is the latest member of the family to run this estate, one of the properties originally established by Italian immigrants in the nineteenth century. The wines are slightly old-fashioned, fruity and accessible but also quite tannic and assertive. The Foppiano style favours robust reds such as Zinfandel and Petite Sirah. The second label is Riverside Farms. There is also a reserve range of Cabernet and Chardonnay bottled under the Fox Mountain label. All the wines are good value, but they are unlikely to excite the discerning palate.

Fritz ☆☆→☆☆☆

24691 Dutcher Creek Rd, Cloverdale, CA 95425.

Tel: 894 3389. Fax: 894 4781. fritzwinery.com

90 acres. 20,000 cases. Tasting room.

Founded in 1980 by Arthur Fritz, the winery is located in northern Sonoma. Half the production is of Chardonnay, which is sourced from a number of well-known Sonoma vineyards. They can be blowsy. The Rockpile Vineyard Cabernet is inconsistent, but there is a peppery Rogers' Reserve Dry Creek Zinfandel from very old vines. One house specialty is Melon, the Loire grape often mistakenly planted (and labeled) in California as Pinot Blanc.

Gallo Sonoma ☆☆→☆☆☆

3387 Dry Creek Rd, Healdsburg, CA 95448. Tel: 431 5500. Fax: 431 5515.

3,000 acres. 500,000 cases. No visits.

In the mid-1980s, the all-powerful Gallo family, conscious of their image as low-quality producers, began buying up vineyards and land in Sonoma, much to the annoyance of neighbouring vineyard owners, even though the Gallos pledged that their farming would be close to organic and would respect the environment. Their county-wide holdings now include the Frei, Barrelli Creek, Chiotti, and Stefani vineyards, as well as the Two Rock Ranch, Laguna Ranch, and Twin Valley Ranch. These disparate and very large vineyards allow them to bottle a wide range of wines, which are produced at the sprawling winery at the Frei estate. When the first wines were released in 1991, even the fiercest critic of the imperial Gallos had to admit that they were of good quality, especially the reds. As well as the single-vineyard wines, the Gallos released 4,000 cases each of varietals known, rather confusingly, as the Estate Range; these were high-priced, but not significantly better than the regular bottlings.

Gan Eden ☆☆

4950 Ross Rd, Sebastopol, CA 95472. Tel: 829 5686. Fax: 829 0993. ganeden.com

No vineyards. 15,000 cases. No visits.

Since 1985, Craig Winchell has produced a range of kosher varietals, mostly from Alexander Valley fruit. The Cabernet is burly and rich, but the Pinot Noir can be light and the Chardonnay rather sweet.

ITALIAN HERITAGE

Many of Sonoma's vineyards and wineries were founded at the end of the nineteenth century by Italian immigrants. Many of these businesses are still in operation, and remain family businesses now being run by third- or fourth-generation descendants. Italian-origin wineries include Foppiano, Martini & Prati, Pedroncelli, Rafanelli, Sebastiani, and Seghesio.

Geyser Peak ☆☆☆

2281 Chianti Rd, Geyserville, CA 95441.
Tel: 857 9463. Fax: 857 3545. peakwinesinternational.com
1,200 acres. 600,000 cases. Tasting room.

Australia comes to Sonoma County! Indeed, Penfolds at one time owned half of this property, although ownership subsequently reverted to the original owners, the Trione family, and in 1997 to Fortune Brands. The Australian influence lives on, however, in the form of Daryl Groom, the former winemaker for Grange at Penfolds, and his assistant, Mick Schroeter, another Penfolds alumnus. They moved swiftly to eliminate the cheaper ranges that had dogged the winery's reputation.

The style of Geyser Peak is very much one favouring forward fruit. This is typified by Australian-style blends such as Semchard, which blends Livermore Valley Semillon with Sonoma Chardonnay. There is also a wide range of standard varietals, all cleanly made and enjoyable. In addition, there are (again, Australian-style) limited-production wines released under Bin numbers, such as the Bin 2 Cabernet. Probably the best wine is Reserve Alexandre, a Bordeaux blend made only in exceptional years. And, inevitably, there is a Shiraz aged in American oak. Groom is a very gifted winemaker who has shown it is possible to produce good-quality wines in large volumes.

Gundlach-Bundschu ☆☆→☆☆☆

2000 Denmark St, Sonoma, CA 95476. Tel: 938 5277. Fax: 938 9460.
375 acres. 40,000 cases. Tasting room.

The fact that no one can pronounce the Bavarian name doesn't prevent the winery from receiving a stream of visitors to its charmingly located Sonoma headquarters. The vineyards were established in the 1850s, but Prohibition forced the operation to close; however, a descendant, Jim Bundschu, replanted the vineyards in 1967 and re-established the winery. The company is known for its Chardonnay and Riesling, but the red wines can be excellent and surprisingly long-lived. Prices are reasonable.

Hafner ☆☆☆

4280 Pine Flat Rd, Healdsburg, CA 95448. Tel: 433 4606.
100 acres. 10,000 cases. No visits.

The Hafners are primarily grape farmers in Alexander Valley who sell most of their crop to other wineries. But since 1982, they have released wines under their own name; most of their production is of Chardonnay.

Hamel ☆☆☆☆

PO Box 1355, Healdsburg, CA 95448. Tel/fax: 433 9055.
No vineyards. 1,500 cases. No visits.

Kevin Hamel was the winemaker at Preston until 2001. Since 1994, he has also been developing his own label, focusing on impressive Syrah.

Hanna ☆☆

5345 Occidental Rd, Santa Rosa, CA 95401. Tel: 575 3330. hannawinery.com
OR: 9280 Highway 128, Healdsburg, CA 95448. Tel: 431 4310. Fax: 431 4314.
500 acres. 30,000 cases. Tasting room.

Founded by surgeon Elias Hanna, the winery's first vintage was 1985.
Winemaker Stephen Sullivan, who was replaced in 2000 by Jeff Hinchcliffe,
established a reputation for good Cabernet, Sauvignon Blanc, and
Chardonnay. The Merlot is supple but disappointing.

Hanzell ☆☆☆

18596 Lomita Ave, Sonoma, CA 95476. Tel: 996 3860. Fax: 996 3962.
33 acres. 3,000 cases. No visits.

Paper tycoon James Zellerbach was a Burgundy enthusiast who decided to
create his own estate on Burgundian principles in 1957. He was one of the
first to plant French clones of Pinot Noir and Chardonnay. After his death in
1963, Hanzell became moribund until its revival by new owners; the current
proprietors are the de Brye family, of Australian origin. Bob Sessions has
been making the wines since 1973, and the style has only evolved slightly:
the Chardonnay is twenty per cent barrel-fermented, and only twenty–five
per cent of the wine goes through malolactic fermentation; nonetheless they
come across as rich, ripe wines. The Pinot is made in a slightly funky, meaty
style which has both admirers and detractors.

Hartford Court ☆☆☆→☆☆☆☆

8075 Martinelli Rd, Forestville, CA 95436.
Tel: 887 1532. Fax: 887 7158. hartfordcourt.com
45 acres. 2,500 cases. No visits.

This winery has been owned by Jackson Family Estates since 1993; previously,
it was called Domaine Laurier and belonged to the VinTech group. The
property is managed by Don Hartford, who is married to Jess Jackson's
daughter, Jennifer; the winemaker is Mike Sullivan. The winery specializes in
Pinot Noir, Chardonnay, and Zinfandel from single vineyards in the Russian
River Valley. There are also blends under the Sonoma Coast appellation.
Some of the wines are marked by excessive acidity, but others are impeccable.
There are also boldly flavoured and long-lived Zinfandels from dry-farmed
vineyards, vinified, like the Pinot Noir, in open-top fermenters and with
punching down the cap. The wines are expensive but made with great care.

Hop Kiln ☆☆

6050 Westside Rd, Healdsburg, CA 95448. Tel: 433 6491. Fax: 433 8162.
128 acres. 10,000 cases. Tasting room

The winery was created in 1975 by psychiatrist Martin Griffin. The range
was eclectic, including a Gewurztraminer/Riesling blend, a Valdiguié, a
Zinfandel called Primitivo, and a Big Red blend of just about everything.
In 2001, the winery was offered for sale.

Imagery Estates ☆☆→☆☆☆

14335 Highway 12, Glen Ellen, CA 95442. Tel: 935 4515. imagerywinery.com
20 acres. Approx 3,000 cases. Tasting room.

The winery, tasting room, and art gallery are all offshoots of the Benziger winery; indeed, Joe Benziger makes these wines, which used to form part of his family's range. Since 2000, they've had their own home. What's on offer is the Artist Collection range of relatively uncommon Burgundian, Italian, and Rhône varieties; and the Vineyard Collection of pricy, single-vineyard Cabernets. The quality is variable – excellent Barbera, mediocre Sangiovese – and prices seem set too high.

Iron Horse ☆☆→☆☆☆☆

9786 Ross Station Rd, Sebastopol, CA 95472. Tel: 887 1507. Fax: 887 1337.
250 acres. 40,000 cases. Tasting room.

The Sterlings bought and expanded these Green Valley vineyards in 1976. They also have access to Alexander Valley fruit, allowing them to produce Cabernet and Sauvignon Blanc as well as Burgundian varieties. The wines are made by Barry Sterling's son-in-law Forrest Tancer and David Munksgard. The Chardonnay is lean and Chablis-like, the Pinot Noir surprisingly full and forward. But the reputation of Iron Horse rests on its splendid sparkling wines, which are aged for at least four years on the yeast. There are numerous *cuvées*: the basic one is Classic Brut; there is also a Blanc de Noirs called Wedding Cuvée, and a sweetish sparkler known as Russian Cuvée.

J Wine Company ☆☆☆

1147 Old Redwood Highway, Healdsburg, CA 95448.
Tel: 431 5400. Fax: 431 5410. jwine.com
200 acres. 30,000 cases. Tasting room.

This offshoot of Jordan was established by Tom Jordan's daughter with the primary goal of producing sparkling wine called "J". It is a roughly equal blend of Pinot Noir and Chardonnay, is aged for three years on the yeasts, and is well-balanced and elegant. An increasing amount of still Pinot is also made.

Jordan ☆☆☆

1474 Alexander Valley Rd, Healdsburg, CA 95448.
Tel: 431 5250. Fax: 431 5259. jordanwinery.com
275 acres. 75,000 cases. Tasting room.

Oilman Tom Jordan founded this large estate in 1972, but in recent years Mendocino fruit has been blended into both the Cabernet and Chardonnay. The formula is simple: still wines from Cabernet and Chardonnay, and a sparkling wine. The wines were met initially with acclaim, but although supple and well-crafted, they are essentially bland.
(*See also* "J", *above.*)

Kendall-Jackson

Wine Country Store

337 Healdsburg Ave, Healdsburg, CA 95448. Tel: 433 7102. kjwines.com

None of the Kendall-Jackson and Jackson Family wineries – La Crema, Hartford Court, Stonestreet – are open for visits and tastings, but their wines can be tasted here.

Kenwood ✩✩→✩✩✩✩

9592 Highway 12, Kenwood, CA 95452. Tel: 833 5891. Fax: 833 1146.

350 acres. 300,000 cases. Tasting room.

Founded by the Lee family in 1970, Kenwood was taken over by their partner, Gary Heck, the owner of Korbel, in 1998, although some Lees are still actively involved. The range of wines is broad, but Kenwood has always had a deservedly high reputation for its Sauvignon Blanc, produced from Carneros and Russian River fruit. The basic range, known as White Label, is a reliable collection of Sonoma County wines. There are also single-vineyard wines from the Jack London Ranch (leased by Kenwood) and from various old-vine Zinfandel sites. The Artists' Series Cabernet Sauvignon, aged in new barriques, can be first-rate.

Kistler ✩✩✩✩→✩✩✩✩✩

4707 Vine Hill Rd, Sebastopol, CA 95472. Tel: 823 5603. Fax: 823 6709.

120 acres. 23,000 cases. No visits.

In the 1970s, Steve Kistler and Mark Bixler bought a remote property in the Mayacamas Mountains, which they planted mostly with Chardonnay. Before long, the wines had acquired a cult reputation. Kistler takes an almost scientific approach to winemaking, which is essentially Burgundian. He was one of the first Californian winemakers to ferment Chardonnay in small barrels and to encourage malolactic fermentation; racking is minimal and the wines are usually bottled without fining or filtration. With his track record, he has no difficulty obtaining wonderful grapes from Sonoma's top vineyards, and there have been about ten different vineyard-designated wines. Pinot Noir is made in smaller quantities, but can be equally fine. Cabernet production was abandoned in 1993.

At their best, Kistler Chardonnays have an intensity and a mineral complexity unmatched by other California Chardonnays. Unfortunately, a couple of recent wines have shown a toasty, forward, blowsy style that one can only hope is an aberration and not a new direction.

Korbel ✩

13250 River Rd, Guerneville, CA 95446.

Tel: 887 2294. Fax: 869 2981.

1,000 acres. 2 million cases. Tasting room.

Founded in the nineteenth century, Korbel has been owned by the Heck family since 1954. This is California's largest producer of *méthode champenoise* sparkling wine. There are numerous *cuvées*, of which the flagship is the Le Premier Reserve, which is barrel-fermented. The more regular *cuvées* are of modest quality.

Kunde ☆☆→☆☆☆☆

10155 Highway 12, Kenwood, CA 95452. Tel: 833 5501. Fax: 833 2204. kunde.com
800 acres. 130,000 cases. Tasting room.

The Kunde family has been growing grapes in Sonoma Valley for a century, and still sells 26 grape varieties to other wineries. There used to be a Kunde winery, but it closed in 1944. Fortunately, the family reopened it in 1990 and now produces a wide range of well-crafted wines. The Estate Series includes Zinfandel from very old vines and different *cuvées* of Chardonnay; the Reserve Series focuses on Cabernet and Chardonnay, and there is a Rhône series for Viognier and Syrah. The wines are very accessible, extremely well-made, and quite good value. The large tasting room is one of the most hospitable in the Sonoma Valley.

Lake Sonoma ☆

9990 West Dry Creek Rd, Geyserville, CA 95441. Tel: 431 1550. Fax: 431 8356.
20 acres. 10,000 cases. Tasting room.

Owned by Korbel (*qv*) since 1996, Lake Sonoma is best known for straightforward Sauvignon Blanc, Zinfandel, Merlot, and Chardonnay.

Lambert Bridge ☆☆☆

4085 West Dry Creek Rd, Healdsburg, CA 95448. Tel: 431 9600. Fax: 433 3215.
5 acres. 20,000 cases. Tasting room.

After a complex history, this winery closed down in 1992 but was revived the following year by the Chambers family. Most of the fruit is bought in from various Sonoma regions. These are attractive wines: a sleek Sauvignon, good Chardonnay, oaky Merlot, and a Bordeaux blend called Crane Creek Cuvée.

Landmark ☆☆☆→☆☆☆☆

101 Adobe Canyon Rd at Highway 12, Kenwood, CA 95452.
Tel: 833 1144. Fax: 833 1164.
20 acres. 20,000 cases. Tasting room.

Damaris Deere Ethridge's estate has benefitted from advice from Helen Turley to become one of Sonoma's top Chardonnay producers. The basic "Overlook" blend, sourced from various Sonoma County vineyards, is of very good quality and consistency. There are also special bottlings, such as the Damaris Reserve and Two Williams Vineyard. The Pinot Noir is also worth looking out for.

Laurel Glen ☆☆☆☆

6611 Sonoma Mountain Rd, Glen Ellen, CA 95442. Tel: 526 3914. Fax: 526 9801.
25 acres. 65,000 cases. No visits.

Patrick Campbell has an unusual background for a Sonoma winemaker. A philosophy graduate from Harvard, he became the farming manager for a

SONOMA WINE IN ONE HOUR

Rohnert Park is a sprawling suburb of Santa Rosa. One of its few claims to fame is the Sonoma County Wine Center, where you can taste and buy a wide range of wines, and pick up information about wineries, restaurants, and tourist attractions. There is also a demonstration vineyard, where you can learn about grape varieties and viticulture. The address is 5000 Roberts Lake Rd, Rohnert Park, CA 94928. Tel: 586 3795. It's open daily from 9am to 5pm.

Zen monastery before planting his own vines. At first, he sold grapes, but in 1981, he began producing Laurel Glen. These Cabernet vineyards lie above the fog line, but the grapes struggle to ripen, and yields are very low. In some years, Laurel Glen can have punishing tannins, but in good vintages it is a highly concentrated and noble Cabernet. Any wine not up to scratch is declassified into Counterpoint, a second label that can offer good value. To rustle up cash flow, Campbell also makes Terra Rosa and Reds, cheap-and-cheerful blends from purchased fruit; these account for the overwhelming majority of the cases made.

Ledson ☆

7335 Highway 12, Santa Rosa, CA 95409. Tel: 833 2330. Fax: 996 6996. ledson.com
38 acres. 5,000 cases. Tasting room.

Built as a private home, this grotesque Addams Family residence on Highway 12 became a winery in 1993. The range of wines is very wide, and includes many produced from non-Sonoma grapes. Most of the wines are crowd-pleasers, sold alongside many other products in the large and popular tasting room.

Limerick Lane ☆☆☆

1023 Limerick Lane, Healdsburg, CA 95448. Tel: 433 9211. Fax: 433 1652.
33 acres. 3,500 cases. Tasting room.

This small winery has a well-deserved reputation for the Zinfandel produced from its Collins Vineyard, but Hungarian immigrant Ted Markoczy has not been able to resist the lure of his native Furmint variety. He has discontinued his dry Furmint, as Californians couldn't learn to love its acidic structure, but his Tokaj-style, late harvest wine is impressive if overpriced. There is also a good Syrah.

Marcassin ☆☆☆

PO Box 332, Calistoga, CA 94515. Tel: 258 3608. Fax: 942 5633.
19 acres. 2,500 cases. No visits.

This is the private label of celebrity winemaker Helen Turley and her husband John Wetlaufer. It is also the name of their Sonoma Coast vineyard, where they grow Pinot Noir and Chardonnay. They also buy in fruit from cool-climate Sonoma vineyards, which are bottled as small-volume, single-vineyard wines. They epitomize the Turley style: ultra-ripe fruit, minimal intervention, high alcohol. Prices are high and the wines have a cult following.

Martinelli ☆→☆☆☆☆

3360 River Rd, Windsor, CA 95492. Tel: 525 0570. Fax: 525 8463.
200 acres. 7,000 cases. Tasting room.

The Martinellis have been growing grapes and apples since the 1860s, and have been producing their own wines since 1987. They have two claims to fame: the hefty Zinfandels made from their Jackass Vineyard, and the advice of Helen Turley, whose photograph adorns the tasting room. Other than Zinfandel and some Chardonnay bottlings, the wines are dull.

Martini & Prati ☆

2191 Laguna Rd, Santa Rosa, CA 95401. Tel: 823 2404. Fax: 829 6151.
No vineyards. 100,000 cases. Tasting room.

Owned by the Martini family since 1902, this large winery is now allied to a company called ConeTech. It produces a wide range of mostly Italian varieties, and is launching a premium range of conventional varieties under the Tower Hill name. You can still buy jug wines here, and they are surprisingly quaffable.

Matanzas Creek *NR*

6097 Bennett Valley Rd, Santa Rosa, CA 95404.Tel: 528 6464. Fax: 571 0156.
310 acres. 45,000 cases. Tasting room.

In the 1980s, Sandra and Bill McIver developed this luxurious estate into one of California's leading producers of Sauvignon Blanc, Chardonnay, and Merlot. They made history of a sort by releasing the ultra-premium Journey Chardonnay and Merlot in 1992 for unprecedently high prices, which were not justified by the quality.

In 2000, the estate was bought by Jess Jackson, and the long-term winemakers, Bill Parker and Susan Reed, left in 2001. The original owners established a fine reputation for Chardonnay, Sauvignon Blanc, and Merlot, and it will be interesting to see what changes the new proprietors will make.

Mazzocco Vineyards ☆☆

1400 Lytton Springs Rd, Healdsburg, CA 95448.
Tel: 431 8159. Fax: 431 2369. mazzocco.com
50 acres. 17,000 cases. Tasting room.

The winery's first releases were in 1985, but eye surgeon Thomas Mazzocco's property was sold five years later. The winemaker since 1993 has been Phyllis Zouzounis, and most of the wines are from Alexander Valley or Dry Creek. Quality has lacked consistency, although I have encountered peppery Zinfandel and good Cabernet and a Bordeaux blend called Matrix.

Peter Michael ☆☆☆☆→☆☆☆☆☆

12400 Ida Clayton Rd, Calistoga, CA 94515. Tel: 942 4459. Fax: 942 0209.
130 acres. 15,000 cases. No visits.

Sir Peter Michael, an electronics tycoon from England, bought a large ranch
in Knights Valley in 1981, and produced his first wines in 1987. Enormous
resources have been invested in the vineyards, with spectacular results,
despite many changes of winemaker (the present incumbent is Luc Morlet).
For the Chardonnays, the winemaking is Burgundian, but it's the vineyards
that differentiate the wines: Mon Plaisir comes from Alexander Valley,
Clos du Ciel from Howell Mountain, and the stunning La Carrière from the
Michael estate. In addition, there is a fine Sauvignon Blanc called Après
Midi, and a fine Bordeaux blend called Les Pavots. Not surprisingly, the
wines are expensive.

   The secret of the winery's very high quality seems to be the close alliance
between the vineyard management and the winery procedures. Vinification
and barrel-ageing techniques seem closely matched to the special quality of
fruit derived from the estate's varied vineyards. The result is wines of great
concentration and complexity, and a respect for *terroir* unusual in California.

Michel-Schlumberger *NR*

4155 Wine Creek Rd, Healdsburg, CA 95448. Tel: 433 7427. Fax: 433 0444.
65 acres. 25,000 cases. Tasting twice daily.

This costly winery was built in 1984, but sold in 1993 to Jacques
Schlumberger. It is best known for Cabernet, though Chardonnay, Pinot
Blanc, Syrah, and Merlot are also produced.

Mietz *NR*

1345 West Dry Creek Rd, Healdsburg, CA 95448.
Tel: 433 7103. Fax: 433 8578. mietzcellars.com
5 acres. 3,000 cases. No visits.

Mietz produces red wines from the Russian River and Dry Creek valleys,
Merlot being a specialty. Its reputation has been rising steadily in recent years.

Mill Creek ☆

1401 Westside Rd, Healdsburg, CA 85448.
Tel: 433 5098. Fax: 431 1714. mcvonline.com
75 acres. 15,000 cases. Tasting room.

The winery offers a wide range of fairly lacklustre wines, although the Estate
Merlot and Cabernet are a notch better.

Murphy-Goode ☆☆☆

4001 Highway 128, Geyserville, CA 95441. Tel: 431 7644. Fax: 431 8640.
350 acres. 90,000 cases. Tasting room.

This Alexander Valley winery was founded in 1988 by two grape growers
who were having difficulties selling all their production to other wineries.
They specialize in Sauvignon Blanc and produce three different *cuvées*.

The regular Fumé is fermented in steel tanks and aged only briefly in oak; the Reserve Fumé is barrel-fermented and goes through partial malolactic fermentation. "The Deuce" is fermented and aged in new barriques and goes through full malolactic fermentation, resulting in a richer style. Wines other than Sauvignon – Pinot Blanc, Chardonnay, Merlot, and Cabernet Sauvignon – can be very good, too, if not exceptionally concentrated: .

Nalle ☆☆☆☆

2383 Dry Creek Rd, Healdsburg, CA 95448. Tel: 433 1040. Fax: 433 6062.
No vineyards. 2,500 cases. No visits.

Doug Nalle buys Zinfandel from four growers of old-vine Zinfandel, and fashions a beautifully balanced wine that is far more pleasurable than some of the over-extracted, monster Zins currently in fashion. The wine is ripe, elegant, and hedonistic. Nalle also produces a little Cabernet Sauvignon.

Pedroncelli ☆→☆☆

1220 Canyon Rd, Geyserville, CA 95441.
Tel: 857 3531. Fax: 857 3812. pedroncelli.com
105 acres. 80,000 cases. Tasting room.

The Pedroncellis are another of the old Italian families who settled here a century ago. Most of the wines are made from fruit purchased in various parts of northern Sonoma. The style is frankly commercial, without great fruit concentration, depth, or consistency. The wines have the merit of being inexpensive. In 1995, a range of Single and Special Vineyard Selections pushed quality up a further notch.

Pezzi King ☆☆☆→☆☆☆☆

3805 Lambert Bridge Rd, Healdsburg, CA 95448.
Tel: 431 9388. Fax: 431 9389. pezziking.com
60 acres. 35,000 cases. Tasting room.

Jim Rowe founded this Dry Creek Valley winery in 1994, and Cecile Lemerle makes the wines. The best bear the Hillside Estate label; there is also an excellent Small Lot Reserve Zinfandel. These reds show outstanding promise.

Porter Creek ☆☆

8735 Westside Rd, Healdsburg, CA 95448. Tel: 433 6321. Fax: 433 4245.
21 acres. 3,000 cases. Tasting room.

Since 1987, this winery has specialized in Pinot Noir and Chardonnay vinified with indigenous yeasts. For good measure, there are small lots of other wines, such as a surprisingly charming Carignane and Syrah.

Preston ☆☆☆→☆☆☆☆

9282 West Dry Creek Rd, Healdsburg, CA 95448. Tel: 433 3372. Fax: 433 5307.
100 acres. 7,000 cases. Tasting room.

Since 1975, Lou Preston and his winemakers, notably Kevin Hamel, have turned out a delightful collection of balanced and characterful wines from grapes that are mostly organically farmed. The whites were always good here:

fine Sauvignon, delicious Viognier and Marsanne; reds included lively Barbera, old-vine Zinfandel, juicy Syrah. Lou Preston is now contemplating retirement and production is diminishing. His leisure is our loss.

Quivira ☆☆☆

4900 West Dry Creek Rd, Healdsburg, CA 95448.
Tel: 431 8333. Fax: 431 1664. quivirawine.com
75 acres. 25,000 cases. Tasting room.

The winemaker here, Grady Wann, has maintained consistency, releasing a series of splendid, fruity Zinfandels and blends: the Dry Creek Cuvée from Rhône varieties, and the Cabernet Cuvée. These are among the best and most typical red wines of Dry Creek Valley, offering rich fruit and great reliability, all at sensible prices.

Rabbit Ridge ☆☆

3921 Westside Rd, Healdsburg, CA 95448. Tel: 431 7128. Fax: 431 8018.
40 acres (plus 200 in Paso Robles). 360,000 cases. Tasting room.

Owner/winemaker Erich Russell has expanded his winery with remarkable speed, offering a vast range of varietals and bizarre blends. Unfortunately, the expansion was too fast for the local authorities, who have threatened legal action for alleged coding violations. Russell has retaliated by decamping to Paso Robles, where he is now constructing a new winery. In the meantime, he retains his tasting room in Healdsburg. Quality has always been hit-and-miss, but prices are low.

Rafanelli ☆☆☆☆

4685 West Dry Creek Rd, Healdsburg, CA 95448. Tel: 433 1385. Fax: 433 3836.
50 acres. 10,000 cases. Tasting room.

The Rafanellis still think of themselves as grape growers, but David Rafanelli and his daughter Rashell happen to make absolutely delicious Zinfandel and Cabernet: fruity, concentrated, balanced, with no trace of portiness. They are aged in French oak and bottled without fining or filtration. Exemplary.

Ravenswood ☆☆→☆☆☆☆

18701 Gehricke Rd, Sonoma, CA 95476. Tel: 938 1960. Fax: 938 9459.
13 acres. 600,000 cases. Tasting room.

In the late 1970s and early '80s, Zinfandel-obsessed Joel Peterson began producing splendid red wines from a cramped garage near Sonoma. In 1991, he moved to the former Haywood winery, and serious expansion got under way. His inexpensive Vintners Blends account for most of the production, and Ravenswood still turns out magnificent and varied Zinfandels, as well as some exceptional Cabernet and Merlot, and small lots of Cabernet Franc, Petite Sirah, and Gewurztraminer. The basic winemaking principles have remained unaltered, fortunately: indigenous yeasts and no filtration. In 2001, Ravenswood was bought by the Constellation corporation, but there seems no immediate threat to the Ravenswood style.

The tasting room offers an excellent opportunity to compare the different styles of Zinfandel produced by all the major regions of California. There are succulent wines from Sonoma old vines, Lodi, Amador, and Mendocino, as well as celebrated single-vineyard bottlings from Old Hill, Monte Rosso, Teldeschi, Big River, Wood Road, Dickerson, Belloni, and other prized vineyards, all of whose owners know that their grapes are in skilled and experienced hands at Ravenswood.

J Rochioli ☆☆☆→☆☆☆☆

6192 Westside Rd, Healdsburg, CA 95448. Tel: 433 2305. Fax: 433 2358.
161 acres. 10,000 cases. Tasting room.

The Rochiolis are essentially grape growers, and most of the best Pinot Noir producers in Sonoma queue up to get their hands on their fruit. Tom Rochioli also leases the Allen Vineyard and makes small quantities of wines from specific parcels within both vineyards. The Pinot Noir is the best, vinified and aged in a Burgundian fashion, but the Sauvignon Blanc and Chardonnay are good, too. Unfortunately, the best wines are almost never seen in the tasting room, as they are produced in minute quantities and are snapped up on release by restaurants and collectors.

Rutz Cellars ☆☆→☆☆☆

3637 Frei Rd, Sebastopol, CA 95472. Tel: 823 0373. Fax: 823 4564. rutzcellars.com
No vineyards. 3,000 cases. No visits.

Fred Williams buys in grapes from top Sonoma vineyards. Rutz is best known for Pinot Noir, which can be over-extracted, and also makes a powerful, toasty Chardonnay that can sometimes be a tad clumsy.

St Francis ☆☆→☆☆☆☆

8450 Highway 12, Kenwood, CA 95452.
Tel: 833 4666. Fax: 833 6534. stfranciswine.com
400 acres. 380,000 cases. Tasting room.

Tom Mackey has been making the wines here since 1983 and has developed a fine reputation for Merlot in particular. The reds are significantly better than the whites, and are mostly aged in American oak. In addition to the

EATING OUT

Sonoma County restaurants are less grand and costly than their Napa counterparts, but you can eat extremely well here. A few wineries, such as Topolos and Chateau Souverain, have their own restaurants, but the wine list can be restricted. In Healdsburg, try the tiny Ravenous or Bistro Ralph, where the food is usually based on what the chef can find at the local farmer's market; in Santa Rosa there is Café Lolo, and in Graton the rustic but laid-back Willow Wood Café.

standard bottlings, which are of dependable quality, there are numerous reserve and single-vineyard bottlings of Merlot, Zinfandel, Cabernet Sauvignon, and Cabernet Franc. These are powerful, earthy, and intense, but can lack finesse. Nonetheless the overall quality here is very high and consistent.

Sausal ☆→☆☆☆

7370 Highway 128, Healdsburg, CA 95448.
Tel: 433 2285. Fax: 433 5136. sausalwinery.com
130 acres. 10,000 cases. Tasting room.

The Demostene family are rightly proud of their Zinfandel vineyard, which was planted in 1877, the oldest in Alexander Valley. This is the source of their Century Zinfandel; there are two other Zinfandel bottlings from marginally less ancient vines. Their other wines are less interesting. All are estate-grown.

Scherrer ☆☆☆→☆☆☆☆

4940 Ross Rd, Sebastopol, CA 95472. Tel: 824 1933. Fax: 823 8980.
28 acres. 4,000 cases. No visits.

Fred Scherrer is a grape grower who has sold most of his fruit to other producers, notably Greenwood Ridge, but he has also been producing small quantities of impressive Zinfandel under his own name. His oldest Zinfandel vineyard dates from 1912. The winery also buys in Pinot Noir and Chardonnay from the Russian River Valley.

Sebastiani *NR*

389 Fourth St. East, Sonoma, CA 95476.
Tel: 938 5532. Fax: 933 3370. sebastiani.com
400 acres. 180,000 cases. Tasting room.

This venerable winery has suffered from family feuds over the years, and in 2000 most of the brands were sold off. This has resulted in a huge drop in production, which had peaked at eight million cases. Nonetheless, there is a conscientious attempt to offer a wide range of wines providing good value for money. In ascending order of seriousness and price, the ranges are Sonoma County (formerly known as Cask Series), Appellation Selection, Vineyard Selection, and Proprietary Series. In addition, there are the more anonymous brands such as Nathanson Creek. Because of the wide and constantly fluctuating ranges of wines offered, it is very difficult to assess the overall quality of the winery.

Seghesio ☆☆☆→☆☆☆☆

14730 Grove St, Healdsburg, CA 95448. Tel: 433 3579. Fax: 433 0545. seghesio.com
350 acres. 80,000 cases. Tasting room.

Edoardo Seghesio's descendants still run the winery a century after he founded it. For many years they sold bulk wines to producers such as Gallo, but created their own label in 1983. Eighty-five per cent of the wines are estate-grown from vineyards in northern Sonoma. Seghesio is famous for having the oldest Sangiovese vines in Sonoma, from which it produces a small quantity of wine; and cuttings were used to plant new vineyards from the best clones. There is a strange Italian/Bordeaux blend called Omaggio, and a splendid collection of Zinfandels, of which the San Lorenzo is probably the best by a whisker.

Simi ☆☆☆→☆☆☆☆

16275 Healdsburg Ave, Healdsburg, CA 95448.
Tel: 433 6981. Fax: 433 6253. simiwinery.com
600 acres. 170,000 cases. Tasting room.

This nineteenth-century estate remained in the hands of the family until the 1950s. Thereafter there were repeated changes of ownership, and since 1999 it has been part of the Constellation group. In the 1980s, its celebrated winemaker was Zelma Long, and the current incumbent is New Zealander Nick Goldschmidt. The Cabernet and Chardonnay have always been reliable, and there is also good Sauvignon Blanc and an unusual red blend called Altaire from Pinot Noir, Pinot Meunier, and Cabernet Franc. More recently, a range of Carneros wines has been added.

Sonoma-Cutrer ☆☆☆

4401 Slusser Rd, Windsor, CA 95492. Tel: 528 1181. Fax: 528 1561. sonomacutrer.com
1,100 acres. 130,000 cases. No visits.

In 1973, Brice Cutrer Jones began to grow Pinot Noir and Chardonnay for sale to other wineries, but then founded his own all-Chardonnay winery in 1981. At first, his three wines – Russian River Ranches, Cutrer Vineyard (now known as The Cutrer), and Les Pierres – met with acclaim, but in the 1990s the winery's achievement was superseded by other Sonoma producers. Now owned by Brown-Forman it remains a major player in the Chardonnay stakes, and also produces a limited number of double magnums as Founders Reserve.

Stonestreet ☆☆☆→☆☆☆☆

4611 Thomas Rd, Healdsburg, CA 95448. Tel: 433 9463. Fax: 433 9469.
1,500 acres. 60,000 cases. No visits.

Acquired by Jess Jackson in 1989, Stonestreet's strength is its access to fruit from the former Gauer Ranch in Alexander Valley, a large vineyard also bought by Jess Jackson. The Chardonnay is rich, and accounts for about half the production. There is a Bordeaux blend called Legacy, aged in new oak, and a very impressive Christopher's Vineyard Cabernet, grown at 2,400 feet and aged in mostly new oak.

Rodney Strong ☆☆

11455 Old Redwood Highway, Healdsburg, CA 95448.
Tel: 431 1533. Fax: 433 0921. rodneystrong.com
900 acres. 490,000 cases. Tasting room.

Rodney Strong, a former dancer, has a long history as a grape grower and wine producer in Sonoma, although he is no longer associated with the winery that bears his name; it is now owned by Klein Foods. Continuity has been maintained by the long-term winemaker Rick Sayre. The estate's vineyards are scattered across the county, and at the top end there are some impressive bottles such as the Alexander's Crown Cabernet. But overall, the wines, especially those under the Sonoma County appellation, are light and frankly dull.

Joseph Swan ☆→☆☆☆

2916 Laguna Rd, Forestville, CA 95436.

Tel: 573 3747. Fax: 575 1605. swanwinery.com

13 acres. 4,500 cases. Tasting room (weekends only).

Swan was a pioneer of Dry Creek Zinfandel, and subsequently of fine Pinot Noir. After his death in 1988, son-in-law Rod Berglund took over the property. Little has changed, and Swan still focuses on small lots of mostly red wine. Quality is very mixed: there are some splendid Zinfandels, alongside rather funky or porty wines, and there is a similar disparity among the Pinots.

F Teldeschi ☆→☆☆

3555 Dry Creek Rd, Healdsburg, CA 95448. Tel: 433 6626. Fax: 433 3077.

80 acres. 2,000 cases. Tasting room.

The Teldeschis are grape farmers of long standing, and began bottling their own wines in 1985, with Dan Teldeschi as winemaker. The Zinfandels are well thought of, but in my experience they are too burly and lacking in fruit intensity.

Topolos at Russian River ☆☆

5700 Gravelstein Highway, Forestville, CA 95436.

Tel: 887 1562. Fax: 887 1399. topolos.com

26 acres. 18,000 cases. Tasting room.

Michael Topolos runs a determinedly old-fashioned winery, using organic, and in some cases, biodynamically grown fruit from his vineyards. He also buys in grapes from other vineyards in Sonoma County. The overall style of the wines is hefty and extracted; they are not for the timorous. But his Zinfandel, Alicante, and Carignane have a hearty authenticity, and the Zinfandel port is delicious.

Marimar Torres ☆☆☆→☆☆☆☆

11400 Graton Rd, Sebastopol, CA 95472.

Tel: 823 4365. Fax: 823 4496.

81 acres. 15,000 cases. No visits.

In 1982, with some advice from her celebrated brother Miguel, Marimar Torres bought this Green Valley property. She has focused on Chardonnay and Pinot Noir, paying scrupulous attention to viticulture and clonal selection. In 2000, she acquired acreage in Sonoma Coast, which will add twenty acres of Pinot Noir. With her cool-climate vineyards, the emphasis is on finesse and length of flavour rather than power.

Trentadue *NR*

19170 Geyserville Ave, Geyserville, CA 95441. Tel: 433 3104. Fax: 433 5825.
250 acres. 20,000 cases. Tasting room.

One of the sources for Ridge's celebrated "Geyserville" blend, the Trentadue vineyards also supply a wide range of wines to the Trentadue's own winery. As well as typical Geyserville varieties such as Zinfandel and Petite Sirah, there is an interesting field blend called Old Patch Red.

Unti ☆☆

4202 Dry Creek Rd, Healdsburg, CA 95448.
Tel: 433 5590. Fax: 433 5591. untivineyards.com
21 acres. 4200 cases. No visits.

A new player in Dry Creek, producing supple Zinfandel and a little Syrah and Sangiovese.

Valley of the Moon ☆

777 Madrone Rd, Glen Ellen, CA 95442.
Tel: 996 6941. Fax: 996 5809. valleyofthemoonwinery.com
60 acres. 30,000 cases. Tasting room.

A successful nineteenth-century producer, Valley of the Moon was revived by Kenwood (*qv*) in 1996, and was absorbed by Kenwood's new owner Korbel (*qv*). It produces a very wide range of wines, mostly under the Sonoma County appellation. The top wines are the Syrah and the polyglot Bordeaux blend called Cuvée de la Luna. Initial releases have proved simple and thin.

Viansa ☆☆→☆☆☆

25200 Highway 121, Sonoma, CA 95476.
Tel: 935 4700. Fax: 996 4632. viansa.com
90 acres. 25,000 cases. Tasting room.

Sam Sebastiani left the family winery in 1986 and set off in a new direction, creating a Californian version of an Italian food-and-wine market on a hilltop in southern Sonoma. The wines are both varietal and blends bearing fantasy names such as Stellante and Prindelo. Not everything succeeds, but there are delicious, cleanly made wines on offer, such as the Pinot Grigio and Arneis, the Lambrusco-style Stellante, and some of the higher-priced Premier Wine Selections.

Wellington ☆☆→☆☆☆

11600 Dunbar Rd, Glen Ellen, CA 95462.
Tel: 939 0708. Fax: 939 0378. wellingtonvineyards.com
22 acres. 6,000 cases. Tasting room.

Peter Wellington and his Australian co-winemaker Chris Loxton make a wide range of wines from estate and purchased fruit. Quality is variable, but the best wines include the Mohrhardt Ridge Cabernet, the Sauvignon Blanc, the Bordeaux blend called Victory Reserve, and the Russian River Zinfandel.

Mark West *NR*

9060 Graton Rd, Graton, CA 95444.

Tel: 824 2401. Fax: 824 5287. markwestwinery.com

No vineyards. 25,000 cases. Tasting room.

This winery, founded in 1974 by Bob Ellis, has been through numerous changes of ownership. In 2000, it was bought by brothers Derek and Courtney Benham of the Codera Wine Group; they also owned the Blackstone Winery (*qv*) until its sale in 2001. I have not tasted the current range of wines.

Wild Hog Vineyards ☆

PO Box 189, Cazadero, CA 95421. Tel: 847 3687.

5 acres. 2,000 cases. No visits.

At this small organic estate in the hills of the Sonoma Coast, Daniel Schoenfeld produces Pinot Noir as well as wines such as Nebbiolo and Dolcetto from purchased grapes.

Williams-Selyem ☆☆☆☆-☆☆☆☆☆

6575 Westside Rd, Healdsburg, CA 95448. Tel: 433 6425. Fax: 433 6546.

No vineyards. 7,000 cases. No visits.

Burt Williams and Ed Selyem built a formidable reputation in the 1980s for Pinot Noirs made in a careful, instinctive, artisanal fashion from grapes purchased from exceptional vineyards, initially in Russian River Valley, and later supplemented by Sonoma Coast fruit. These delicious, velvety wines soon attracted a cult following. Sadly, back problems persuaded Ed Selyem to retire in 1998, and the winery was sold to grape farmer John Dyson, who has installed Bob Cabral as winemaker alongside Burt Williams. To the relief of the winery's many fans, quality has been maintained.

Yoakim Bridge ☆☆☆

7209 Dry Creek Rd, Healdsburg, CA 95448. Tel: 431 1236. Fax: 433 8511.

5 acres. 2,500 cases. Tasting room.

The first vintage here was 1997, and first releases of the Zinfandel were promising, with delicious fruit and a firm structure.

Carneros

All area codes are 707 except where otherwise indicated.

Acacia ☆☆→☆☆☆

2750 Las Amigas Rd, Napa, CA 94559. Tel: 226 9991. Fax: 226 1685. acaciawinery.com

90 acres. 60,000 cases. Tasting room.

Founded in 1979, Acacia began as a Pinot Noir and Chardonnay specialist, focusing on single-vineyard wines. In 1986, the property was bought by the Chalone Group, although the founding winemaker, Mike Richmond, is still

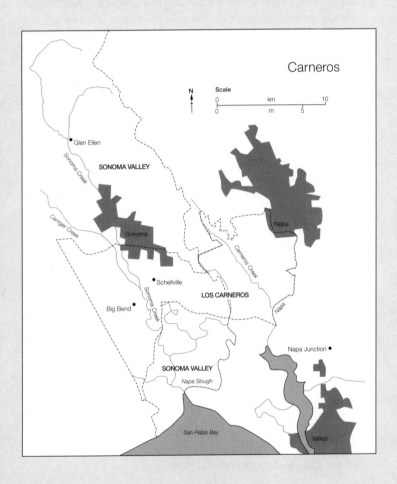

involved. The return of phylloxera forced a change of policy on Acacia, and in 1993 it ceased to make single-vineyard bottlings; instead it produced regular and reserve bottlings. Then, in 1999, Acacia reverted to single-vineyard wines once again.

The winemaking is generally non-interventionist and the wines have considerable purity of flavour. After a prolonged dull patch, Acacia returned to form with its fie 1999 Pinots.

Adastra NR

2545 Las Amigas Rd, Napa, CA 94559. Tel/fax: 255 4818. adastravw.com
20 acres. 2,000 cases. No visits.

The Thorpe family developed a vineyard in the early 1990s. Most of the fruit is sold to other wineries, but since 1995, small quantities of Chardonnay and Merlot have been produced, with Pinot Noir added in 2002. Pam Starr is the consultant winemaker, and only French oak is used.

Arietta NR

4050 Spring Mountain Rd, St Helena, CA 94574.
650 cases. No visits.

John Kongsgaard and Fritz Hatton lease a parcel within Hudson Vineyard in Carneros to make a high-priced single wine, a Cheval-Blanc-style blend of Cabernet Franc and Merlot.

Artesa ☆☆☆

1345 Henry Rd, Napa, CA 94558. Tel: 224 1668. Fax: 224 1672. artesawinery.com
175 acres. 50,000 cases. Tasting room.

Founded in 1979 by the Cordoniu winery in Spain, the Carneros branch was designed as an ultra-modern, sparkling-wine facility. The first releases were in 1991. Although the quality of the wines was high, they were not commercially viable, and in the late 1990s the operation was revamped. Don Van Staaveren and Todd Graff were brought in as winemakers, and the name was changed to Artesa. The production of sparkling wines was diminished, and that of still wines from Chardonnay, Pinot Noir, and Merlot increased; more acreage will be planted in Alexander Valley. All the sparkling wines spend at least three years on the yeast.

Bouchaine ☆☆

1075 Buchli Station Rd, Napa, CA 94559.
Tel: 252 9065. Fax: 252 0401. bouchaine.com
104 acres. 15,000 cases. No visits.

Founded in 1981 by wealthy investors from Delaware, Bouchaine has been through numerous changes of direction. The current winemaker, appointed in 1999, is David Stevens, and the initial emphasis on Pinot Noir has been switched to Chardonnay. Over the years, Bouchaine has been active in vineyard research, experimenting with various Pinot clones. Quality is variable.

Carneros Creek ☆☆→☆☆☆

1285 Dealy Lane, Napa, CA 94558.
Tel: 253 9463. Fax: 253 9465. carneros-creek.com
175 acres. 40,000 cases. Tasting room.

Francis Mahoney started out as a producer of Zinfandel and Cabernet from purchased fruit, but soon caught the Pinot bug, and launched clonal selection trials in collaboration with the University of California. Eventually he chose the five clones he considered best. There are three styles of Pinot: the light, early drinking Fleur de Carneros; the regular Blue Label; and the excellent Signature Reserve. Quality, rather surprisingly, is patchy.

Codorniu

See Artesa.

Domaine Carneros ☆☆→☆☆☆

1240 Duhig Rd, Napa, CA 94558. Tel: 257 0101. Fax: 257 3020. domaine.com
200 acres. 45,000 cases. Tasting room.

A large, ungainly château, modelled on the eighteenth-century Château de la Marquetterie, looms over the Carneros hills, signalling the presence here of the Taittinger family from Reims. Fortunately, the wines are crafted with more taste than the winery, and for many years Eileen Crane was the skilled and thoughtful winemaker, always aiming to produce fizz with delicacy and elegance. In some *cuvées*, the *dosage* can be a touch intrusive. The smoky, oaky Famous Gate Pinot Noir is worth looking out for too.

Gloria Ferrer ☆☆→☆☆☆☆

23555 Highway 121, Sonoma, CA 95476.
Tel: 996 7256. Fax: 996 0720. gloriaferrer.com
450 acres. 100,000 cases. Tasting room.

Owned by the Ferrer family from the Penedès in Spain, where they own the Freixenet cava house, this modern sparkling-wine facility was constructed in the late 1980s. It offers a wide range of styles. The basic wine is the unexciting Sonoma Brut, an over-fruity *blanc de noirs*, and the elegant, crisp Royal Cuvée, which is aged for six years on the yeasts. Those looking for a more concentrated, toasty style should try the superb Carneros Cuvée (aged seven years). The commercial difficulties of selling sparkling wines profitably has led to an increasing emphasis on still wines, which now account for half the production. The Pinot Noir is charming but light; they also offer Chardonnay, Merlot, and Syrah.

MacRostie *NR*

17246 Woodland Ave, Sonoma, CA 95476. Tel: 996 4480. Fax: 996 3726.
22 acres. 12,000 cases. No visits.

Steve MacRostie makes the wine at Roche, and under his own name makes mostly Chardonnay, Pinot Noir, and some Merlot from well-known Carneros vineyards.

Mont St John ☆

5400 Old Sonoma Rd, Napa, CA 94559. Tel: 255 8864. Fax: 257 2778.
160 acres. 22,000 cases. Tasting room.

Louis Bartolucci originally established Mont St John as an organic vineyard in 1976. Much of the fruit was sold to other wineries, but since 1978, the property has produced a wide range of wines. Pinot Noir and Chardonnay, from which one would expect good things, are disappointing. Other wines such as Riesling and Gewurztraminer are made in an off-dry style.

Roche ☆

28700 Arnold Dr, Sonoma, CA 95476. Tel: 935 7115. Fax: 935 7846.
38 acres. 20,000 cases.

Doctors Joe and Genevieve Roche developed vineyards here in the 1980s and opened a winery in 1990. The winery focuses on Chardonnay and Pinot Noir, but to date, quality has been modest and irregular.

Saintsbury ☆☆☆→☆☆☆☆

1500 Los Carneros Ave, Napa, CA 94559.
Tel: 252 0592. Fax: 252 0595. saintsbury.com
54 acres. 55,000 cases. No visits.

David Graves and Richard Ward founded this winery in 1983, after honing their skills at other wineries. In 1986, they began planting vineyards which now account for thirty per cent of their requirements. In 1990, they bought the Brown Ranch near the winery; this primarily provides fruit for reserve bottlings. The only wines are Chardonnay and Pinot Noir. The Reserve Chardonnay is usually of much greater interest than the regular bottling. Pinot comes in three versions: Garnet, a charming, delicate style for early drinking, the regular bottling, and the beautifully balanced, fruity Reserve. From the mid-1990s, there has also been a Brown Ranch Pinot Noir of great intensity. The style is toasty, but this seems to match the fruit quality well.

Schug ☆☆☆

602 Bonneau Rd, Sonoma, CA 95476.
Tel: 939 9363. Fax: 939 9364. schugwinery.com
42 acres. 20,000 cases. Tasting room.

Walter Schug was born and was trained in winemaking in the Rheingau, but emigrated to California in 1959. He made his name as the winemaker for Phelps, producing succulent late harvest wines from Riesling and Scheurebe. In 1990, he established his own winery, with a shift in emphasis to Burgundian varieties. His own vineyards adjoin the Sangiacomo Vineyard, from which he buys fruit. His top wines are the Heritage Reserves, and the Carneros appellation bottlings can also be very fine. Merlot and Cabernet Sauvignon are made from fruit purchased in various parts of the North Coast. The wines have improved greatly in recent years: they may lack weight but they are elegant and not over-extracted, and show freshness and vitality.

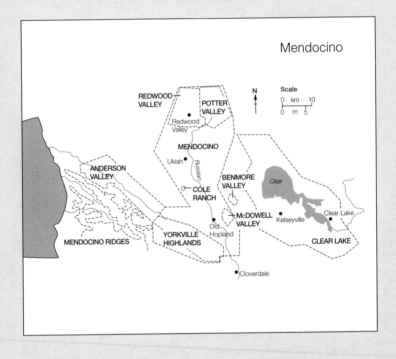

Truchard ☆☆☆→☆☆☆☆

3234 Old Sonoma Rd, Napa, CA 94559.
Tel: 253 7153. Fax: 253 7234. Truchardvineyard.com
167 acres. 10,000 cases. No visits.

Tony Truchard is a doctor-turned-grape farmer. He still supplies grapes to other wineries but has been bottling his own wines since 1989. Unlike most Carneros producers, who focus on Burgundian varieties, Truchard has had surprising success with Merlot and Syrah. Even the Cabernet Sauvignon from here is sleek and elegant. In 2000, Roussanne and Tempranillo were added to the range. He has a light touch with new French oak, and the wines are stylish rather than powerful.

Mendocino County

Area codes are the same as for Napa and Sonoma – namely 707 – unless otherwise indicated.

Brutocao ☆→☆☆

13500 Highway 101, Hopland, CA 95449.
Tel/fax: 744 1066. brutocaocellars.com
475 acres. 15,000 cases. Tasting room.

Leonard and Albert Brutocao were grape growers in the 1940s, selling to other wineries. Steven Brutocao has, since 1991, been producing a range of wines under the family label. They can be uneven and some vintages have been over-oaked.

Claudia Springs ☆☆→☆☆☆

2160 Guntly Rd, Philo, CA 95466. Tel: 895 3926. claudiasprings.com
25 acres. 3,000 cases. Tasting room in Boonville (see end of chapter).

Since 1989 Bob Klindt has been producing a range of single-vineyard Zinfandels, as well as Pinot Noir, Chardonnay, and delicious Viognier.

Edmeades ☆☆☆→☆☆☆☆

5500 Highway 128, Philo, CA 95466. Tel: 895 3232. Fax: 895 3237.
63 acres. 10,000 cases. No visits.

In 1962, Dr Donald Edmeades planted vineyards in Anderson Valley, and a winery was built ten years later. Despite acclaim for some of the early wines, which were made by Jed Steele, the business fared badly and closed in the late 1980s. In 1992, it was bought by Kendall-Jackson and is now part of Jackson Family Farms. The winemaker, Van Williamson, has turned out some impressive single-vineyard Zinfandels and Petite Sirah, and there is some good Chardonnay and Pinot Noir, too. More Pinot Noir is being planted in northern Anderson Valley.

Enotria

See Monte Volpe.

Fetzer ☆☆→☆☆☆☆

12625 East Side Rd, Hopland, CA 95449.
Tel: 744 7600. Fax: 744 7605. fetzer.com
2,000 acres. 3 million cases. Tasting room.

Barney Fetzer starting planting vineyards in Mendocino in 1958, and a decade later his sons started producing wine. Thanks to sound quality and reasonable prices, the winery prospered. So much so that the property was bought by the Brown-Forman company, which also owns Villa Mount Eden in Napa (*qv*), in 1992. The Fetzer family still sells grapes to the winery that bears their name, as the winery vineyards supply only fifteen per cent of its requirements. A substantial and growing proportion of the vineyards are organic, and Fetzer is one of the few American wineries with its own cooperage.

There are numerous ranges of wines. The inexpensive Bel Arbor range includes Sundial Chardonnay (the biggest seller at 850,000 cases), Valley Oaks Cabernet, and Eagle Peak Merlot, all of which are highly successful and inexpensive. The Barrel Select is rather higher in quality. The Reserve range features single-vineyard wines from all parts of California. In 2000, a range called Mariah was introduced; its wines are from grapes grown high up in the new Mendocino Ridge AVA. Finally, Bonterra, which was spun off as a separate brand and company in 1995, but maintains links with the parent company, and produces a range of ten wines (notably Chardonnay and Viognier) from organically grown grapes.

The Fetzer winemakers (Dennis Martin and Phil Hurst) as well as Bob Blue of Bonterra do not aim for heavy extraction. Indeed, some of the white wines are deceptively lean and crisp, but they are very well-made and finely balanced. The cheaper wines and the Bonterra range offer outstanding value for money. The Fetzer wines may not be the most thrilling in the North Coast, but they never disappoint.

Fife ☆☆☆→☆☆☆☆

3620 Road B, Redwood Valley, CA 95470.
Tel: 485 0323. Fax: 485 0832. fifevineyards.com
37 acres (24 in Napa, 13 in Mendocino). 20,000 cases. No visits.

Dennis Fife was an executive at Inglenook and became aware of the quality of Mendocino fruit – so in 1991 he founded his own label. He has acquired vineyards in Redwood Valley and also in Napa Valley, so his wines come from both. Winemaker John Buechsenstein produces a wide range of excellent and dense red wines, both single varietals and blends such as Max Cuvée, which is composed primarily of Syrah and Petite Sirah. The wines are rich and oaky and just the right side of overpowering.

Frey ☆

14000 Tomki Rd, Redwood Valley, CA 95470.
Tel: 485 5177. Fax: 485 7875. freywine.com
60 acres. 37,000 cases. No visits.

Dr Paul Frey planted organic vineyards in the 1960s and a winery followed in 1980. After his death, some of his twelve children took over. Frey offer a wide range of wines, including some made from biodynamically cultivated grapes, but the adherence to organic principles (no sulphites) can result in some very unsatisfactory bottles. They are best drunk young.

Gabrielli ☆☆→'☆☆☆

10950 West Rd, Redwood Valley, CA 95470.
Tel: 485 1221. Fax: 485 1225. gabrielliwinery.com
13 acres. 8,000 cases. Tasting room.

This innovative winery is located in the northern part of Redwood Valley. Gabrielli often works with Mendocino oak barrels, which can give very good results, although barriques are also used.

The range is expanded by single-vineyard wines from Pinot Noir, and there is a bizarre but characterful white blend called Ascenza. Quality can be hit-and-miss, but the best wines (notably Syrah and Sangiovese) are at times excellent.

Goldeneye *NR*

9200 Highway 128, Philio, CA 95466.
Tel: 895 3814. goldeneyewinery.com
50 acres. 1,000 cases. No visits.

The former Gemello estate in Anderson Valley was bought by the Duckhorns (*qv*) of Napa Valley in 1996. The long-term plan is to produce outstanding Pinot Noir, aged in new French oak.

TO FILTER OR NOT TO FILTER

It has become common in recent years for Californian winemakers who are opposed to routine filtration to blazon the word "unfiltered" on the label. In part, this is because certain American wine writers, notably Robert Parker, have championed the cause of unfiltered wines. It is true that certain filtration techniques can strip a wine of aroma, colour, and flavour. On the other hand, the routine avoidance of filtration opens up the risk of bacterial infection and spoilage. Wines aged for at least eighteen months in barrel are probably clear enough to be bottled without filtration; younger wines and most white wines will still be hazy. Limpidity may be largely cosmetic, but cloudiness in a wine is not, as some seem to believe, an intrinsic sign of quality.

Greenwood Ridge ☆☆☆

5501 Highway 128, Philo, CA 95466.
Tel: 895 2002. Fax: 895 2001. greenwoodridge.com
16 acres. 7,000 cases. Tasting room.

In 1973, the Green family bought an existing vineyard 1,200 feet up in Anderson Valley. Allan Green's first vintage was 1980. It has now been recognized that these ridge-top vineyards are capable of producing outstanding fruit, and this winery's Riesling, Cabernet, and Merlot can be first-rate.

Green also sources from other Mendocino vineyards for Chardonnay and Sauvignon Blanc, and his Zinfandel is bought from Scherrer (*qv*) in Sonoma. Late harvest Rieslings can be exceptional.

Handley ☆→☆☆☆

3151 Highway 128, Philo, CA 95466.
Tel: 895 3876. Fax: 895 263. handleycellars.com
49 acres. 15,000 cases. Tasting room.

Milla Handley makes a full range of wines, but is best known for her sparkling wines, which can be very good. The most serious of them is the *blanc de blancs*, aged for five years on the yeasts. She may also be the only California producer to market a dry Pinot Meunier. In addition to the twenty-nine acres she owns in Anderson Valley, Handley owns twenty in Dry Creek, from which she produces Chardonnay and Sauvignon.

Hidden Cellars *NR*

PO Box 448, Talmage, CA 95481.
Tel: 462 0301. Fax: 462 8144. hiddencellars.com
No vineyards. 30,000 cases. No visits.

In the 1980s, founding winemaker Dennis Patton focused on Chardonnay and other white wines, but by the 1990s he was concentrating on old-vine reds from long-established Mendocino vineyards. By 1997, he was bottling ten different Zinfandels and four Petite Sirahs, and overall quality was very high.

In 1999, Parducci (*qv*) bought the business. Parducci's own difficulties mean that Hidden Cellars is also up for sale.

Husch ☆☆

4400 Highway 128, Philo, CA 95466.
Tel: 895 3216. Fax: 895 2068. huschvineyards.com
240 acres. 30,000 cases. Tasting room.

The Oswald family own vineyards here in Anderson Valley and an equally large property in Ukiah Valley. German-born Fritz Meier makes a wide range of wines, of which the best are usually the Pinot Noir and the Chardonnay. Gewurztraminer is a specialty, and is sometimes made in a late harvest style.

Jepson ☆☆

19400 Highway 101, Ukiah, CA 95482.

Tel: 468 9036. Fax: 468 0362. jepsonwine.com

110 acres. 22,000 cases. Tasting by appointment.

The former Baccala estate was bought by Robert Jepson in 1986, and he soon inaugurated the production of sparkling wine of good quality. In 2000, he brought in a new winemaker, Alison Schneider. By the late 1990s, the wines were more serious: sound Chardonnay and Pinot Noir, and some Viognier. The Sauvignon Blanc can be too sweet and confected.

Lazy Creek *NR*

4610 Highway 128, Philo, CA 95466. Tel: 895 3623.

20 acres. 3,000 cases. No visits.

Founded by Swiss chef Hans Kobler, the estate and winery were sold to landscape architect Josh Chandler in 1999. Kobler, who remains at Lazy Creek as consultant winemaker, has developed a fine reputation for Gewurztraminer.

Lolonis ☆☆→☆☆☆

1905 Road D, Redwood Valley. CA 95470.

Tel: 925 938 8066. Fax: 925 938 8069. lolonis.com

300 acres. 30,000 cases. No visits.

The Lolonis family, of Greek origin, have been growing grapes in Redwood Valley since the 1920s. Much of the fruit, which today is organically farmed, is still sold to other wineries, but since the 1980s, the family has also been producing its own wines. The Zinfandel can be particularly persuasive, and there is also worthwhile Chardonnay and Cabernet, and a proprietary red called Petros. Quality has been improving through the 1990s.

Lonetree ☆☆☆

PO Box 401, Philo, CA 95466. Tel: 463 0635. Fax: 468 0848. lonetreewine.com

75 acres. 2,000 cases. Tasting room in Boonville (see end of chapter).

John Scharffenberger is the owner of the lofty Eaglepoint Ranch in Ukiah Valley. Its Zinfandel grapes are much sought after by other wineries, but since 1994 Scharffenberger has produced some impressive Zinfandel and Sangiovese and powerful Syrah from his vineyards.

See also Pacific Echo.

McDowell Valley Vineyards ☆☆→☆☆☆☆

3811 Highway 175, Hopland, CA 95449.

Tel: 744 1053. Fax: 744 1826. mcdowellsyrah.com

330 acres. 20,000 cases. Tasting room.

McDowell is celebrated for nurturing what must be the oldest Syrah in California: vines from 1948 and 1959. So enamoured is McDowell of Rhône varieties that, since 1996, it has been making nothing else. The Mendocino Syrah comes from younger vines, but is nonetheless delicious, but the old-vine Reserve is magnificent and long-lived. The Viognier is splendid, and more complex than the very enjoyable Marsanne and the dry, refreshing Grenache Rosé.

McNab Ridge *NR*

2350 McNab Ranch Rd, Ukiah, CA 95482.

Tel: 462 2423. Fax: 462 9263. mcnabridge.com

65 acres. 6,000 cases. No visits.

Octogenarian John Parducci bought this property, previously known as Zellerbach Vineyard, in 1999. Its range consists of Chardonnay, Cabernet, and Merlot.

Mendocino Hill ☆☆→☆☆☆

PO Box 749, Hopland, CA 95449.

Tel: 744 1302. Fax: 744 2034. mendocinohill.com

20 acres. 2,000 cases. Tasting room.

Founded in 1991, Mendocino Hill produced rather tannic wines initially, but by the late 1990s the wines had improved. There is delicious Syrah and a sweetish, oaky Sangiovese/Cabernet blend called Villa Mendo.

Monte Volpe ☆☆☆

1170 Bel Arbres Rd, Redwood Valley, CA 95470.

Tel: 485 9463. Fax: 485 9742.

70 acres. 15,000 cases.

Tasting room at 13251 Highway 101, Hopland, CA 95449.

Greg Graziano, one of Mendocino's most dynamic winemakers, founded this label in 1991, and as the name suggests, it specializes in Italian varietals and blends. Not everything succeeds, but in general quality is high, and there aren't many places in California where you can sample Tocai Friulano.

Graziano, somewhat confusingly, has two other labels. Domaine Saint Gregory specializes in the Pinot family, and makes, among other wines, some invigorating Pinot Bianco. Enotria is in effect a subsidiary of Monte Volpe, since it, too, focuses on Italian varieties, but only those native to Piedmont, such as Arneis, Dolcetto, Nebbiolo, and Barbera.

Navarro ☆☆→☆☆☆☆

5601 Highway 128, Philo, CA 95466.

Tel: 895 3686. Fax: 895 3647. navarrowine.com

85 acres. 30,000 cases. Tasting room.

Ted Bennett and Deborah Cahn bought this ranch in Anderson Valley in 1973 and soon realized the conditions were best suited to cool-climate grape varieties. Their Riesling, both in its off-dry and botrytized versions, can be exquisite, refreshed by a keen acidity. The wines are made in an Alsatian style, so that varieties such as Pinot Gris and Gewurztraminer are aged in large oval casks. The Pinot Noir, on the other hand, is aged in French oak and can be impressive.

Pacific Echo ☆→☆☆

8501 Highway 128, Philo, CA 95466.

Tel: 895 2311. Fax: 895 2758. pacific-echo.com

97 acres. 40,000 cases. Tasting room.

John Scharffenberger, who owns Lonetree (*qv*), developed this Anderson Valley property in order to produce sparkling wine. At first, the wines were released under his own unwieldy name, until the present name was adopted by new French owners in 1998. The wines are made from traditional Champagne varieties, and include a *crémant* and a vintage *blanc de blancs*. They are robust and can be earthy.

Parducci *NR*

501 Parducci Rd, Ukiah, CA 95482.

Tel: 463 5350. Fax: 462 7260.

250 acres. 350,000 cases. Tasting room.

The oldest winery in Mendocino, founded in 1932, has been through numerous changes of ownership. A relaunch in the late 1990s clearly did not succeed, and by 2001, many of the vineyards had been sold off and the winery was on the market.

Pepperwood Springs *NR*

1200 Holmes Ranch Rd, Philo, CA 95466.

Tel/fax: 895 2920.

4 acres. 2,000 cases. No visits.

Founded in 1981 in Anderson Valley, the winery was sold to Eric Stirling in 2001 and is unlikely to continue in its present form.

Roederer Estate ☆☆☆☆

7000 Highway 128, Philo, CA 95466.

Tel: 895 2288. Fax: 895 2120.

350 acres. 55,000 cases. Tasting room.

Jean-Claude Rouzaud, the head of Roederer, searched long and hard for a base for a California winery. He shrewdly settled on Anderson Valley, where the growing season resembles that of Champagne, and installed Dr Michel Salgues as his winemaker in 1985.

The wines are made with the same care as those in France, employing up to twenty per cent reserve wines in the Estate Brut. The top *cuvée* is the vintage L'Ermitage, but often the Estate Brut rivals it in quality. Unlike so many California sparkling wines, those from Roederer have finesse and a lovely citric freshness. The rosé is excellent, too.

Domaine Saint Gregory

See Monte Volpe.

Other Tasting Centres

In 2001, three wineries – Claudia Springs, Lonetree, and Raye's Hill – set up a cooperative tasting room at 17810 Farrer Lane, Boonville, CA 95415. Tel: 895 3993.

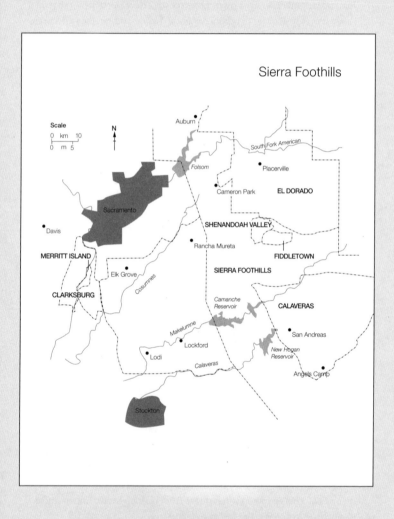

Sierra Foothills

Amador Foothill Winery ☆

12500 Steiner Rd, Plymouth, CA 95669.
Tel: 209 245 6307. Fax: 245 3580. amadorfoothill.com
11 acres. 7,000 cases. Tasting room.

Ben Zeitman and Katie Quinn came to Plymouth in the 1980s and
supplement their own grapes with purchases of old-vine Zinfandel
from leading local vineyards.

Despite their commitment and experience, the wines are disappointing.
The Sauvignon Blanc and Semillon can be tart and thin; the reds, including
the Zinfandels, can be earthy and tannic. On the other hand, the 1999
Carignane and Sangiovese had much more vibrant fruit.

Boeger ☆☆→☆☆☆

1709 Carson Rd, Placerville, CA 95667.
Tel: 530 622 8094. Fax: 622 8112. boegerwinery.com
82 acres. 22,000 cases. Tasting room.

Greg Boeger farms at heights of up to 3,000 feet, growing no fewer than
thirty varieties. Consequently, he can offer a wide range of wines, and they
can be rather hit-and-miss. Usually reliable are the Zinfandels (especially the
Walker bottling), Viognier, Barbera, and some of the weird blends such as
Migliore, which mixes together varieties from Italy, southern France, and
Zinfandel. It's best to make good use of the tasting room, which is located in
a nineteenth century winery.

Chatom *NR*

1969 Highway 4, Douglas Flat, CA 95229.
Tel: 209 736 6500. Fax: 736 6507. chatomvineyards.com
65 acres. 25,000 cases. Tasting room.

The wines produced here in the mid-1990s were of a poor standard,
but a new winemaker, Scott Klann, has been appointed, so quality
may be improving.

Deaver ☆→☆☆

12455 Steiner Rd, Plymouth, CA 95669.
Tel: 209 245 4099. deavervineyard.com
400 acres. 4,000 cases. Tasting room.

The Deaver Ranch is one of Amador's most celebrated vineyards,
with Zinfandel surviving from 1881. There was a vineyard dating from
1855 planted with the Mission grape, but it expired of uneconomic
old age in 1997.

Deaver still sells most of its fruit to other wineries. Its own wines are
inconsistent: lime-scented Chardonnay, delicate Mourvedre, sleek Barbera,
and peppery but rather fruitless Zinfandel.

WOMEN WINEMAKERS

In California, women are not consigned to the role of tasting-room hostesses.
For many years, some of the state's top winemakers have been women.

- Helen Turley (Marcassin and consultant)
- Heidi Peterson Barrett (consultant)
- Cathy Corison (Corison)
- Lane Tanner (Lane Tanner)
- Mia Klein (Selene and consultant)
- Zelma Long (consultant)
- Sandi Belcher (Long)
- Gina Gallo (Gallo Sonoma)
- Alison Schneider (Jepson)
- Rosemary Cakebread (Spottswoode)
- Sara Steiner (Calera)

Dobra Zemlya ☆

12505 Steiner Rd, Plymouth, CA 95669. Tel: 209 245 3183. Fax: 209 245 5022.
15 acres. 1,500 cases. Tasting room.

The Croatian Milan Matulich and his American wife Victoria have farmed
here for many years, but only began producing their own wines in 1997, all
from estate-grown grapes. The Sangiovese and Syrah, both aged in mostly
American oak, were mediocre, but a cask sample of 2000 Viognier was quite
promising. The neighbours speak well of this new winery, but quality at
present seems dim.

Easton

See Terre Rouge.

Ironstone ☆☆→☆☆☆

1894 Six Mile Rd, Murphys, CA 95247.
Tel: 209 728 1251. Fax: 209 728 1275. ironstonevineyards.com
4,400 acres. 500,000 cases. Tasting room.

When visiting the vast visitors' centre the Kautz family have constructed at
their Ironstone winery, it is easy to overlook the wine, since so much else is
on offer. But the Kautzes are growers with vast acreage in Lodi and the
Central Valley, and some 70 acres in the Foothills. All their wines are labelled
under the California appellation to give them maximum flexibility, except for
the Reserve wines, which come from Foothills fruit. Steve Millier has been
making the wines here since 1988 and has done a fine job of combining
large-volume production with decent quality and sensible prices. The
winery releases most standard varietals and a juicy Cabernet Franc. Rather

than Syrah, they produce Shiraz, as they like the peppery Australian style. Another Kautz specialty is Symphony, a weird cross between Muscat of Alexandria and Grenache Gris. Usually made in an off-dry style, it is heavily scented and very much a minority taste. The "port" is good. Other labels for simpler wines include Cinnamon Grove.

Karly ☆→☆☆☆

11076 Bell Rd, Plymouth, CA 95669.
Tel: 209 245 3922. Fax: 209 245 4874. karlywines.com
20 acres. 11,000 cases. Tasting room.

Buck and Karly Cobb planted their vineyard in mineral-rich soil with good drainage; the cultivation is essentially organic. They also buy in some grapes from other growers. They are best known for their Zinfandels, but some of them can be too jammy and porty, a frequent problem with Amador Zinfandel. The Mourvedre is imposing, if a touch too alcoholic, but the Orange Muscat is often sensational.

Latcham *NR*

2860 Omo Ranch Rd, Mt Aukum, CA 95656. Tel: 530 620 6834. Fax: 530 620 5578.
Tasting room.

This Eldorado winery has a fine reputation for Cabernet Sauvignon, Cabernet Franc, and Zinfandel.

Lava Cap ☆☆→☆☆☆

2221 Fruitridge Rd, Placerville, CA 95667.
Tel: 530 621 0175. Fax: 621 4399. lavacap.com
60 acres. 15,000 cases. Tasting room.

These remarkable vineyards are planted at a height of between 2,400 and 2,800 feet, and both Cabernet and Chardonnay manage to ripen here. Thomas Jones makes the wines and singles out for attention the "Stromberg" range from very low-yielding vines grown at 3,200 feet.

Madrona ☆☆☆→☆☆☆☆

High Hill Rd, Camino, CA 95709. Tel: 530 644 5948. Fax: 644 7517. madrona-wines.com
35 acres. 10,000 cases. Tasting room.

If Eldorado County is mostly known for amiable rusticity, Madrona shows what can be done in this high-elevation region from vineyards some 3,000 feet up. Dick Bush planted them in 1973, and finds that he can successfully grow varieties associated with Bordeaux, the Rhône varieties, and the Douro Valley. In some years there is a struggle to avoid vegetal flavours and excessive tannins, but for the most part, the wines are polished and successful. The whites are invigorating: fine Chardonnay, Gewurztraminer, and Riesling. Zinfandel, Merlot, and Cabernet are all impressive, as is the Bordeaux blend called Quintet. In some vintages, it is even possible to make intense, late harvest wines from Riesling and/or Chardonnay. Recently, winemaker Hugh Chappelle departed for Flowers (*qv*), so changes may lie ahead.

Milliaire *NR*

276 Main St, Murphys, CA 95247.

Tel: 209 728 1658. Fax: 209 728 8774. milliarewinery.com

No vineyards. 2,500 cases. Tasting room (Friday to Monday).

Steve Millier's day job is winemaker for Ironstone (*qv*) but for almost twenty years he has produced small amounts of wine under his own label.

Montevina ☆→☆☆

20680 Shenandoah School Rd, Plymouth, CA 95669.

Tel: 209 245 6942. Fax: 209 245 6617. montevina.com

400 acres. 100,000 cases. Tasting room.

It was the Trinchero family of Sutter Home in Napa Valley who first put the Foothills on the map when they realized how superb its old-vine Zinfandel could be. When the Montevina estate (the first winery to be built here since Prohibition) came on the market in 1988, they bought it. They continued to produce standard varietals, but at the same time they planted many other varieties, mostly Italian. It was a matter of trial and error, and unsuitable clones or varieties were eliminated. As well as varietal wines from Barbera, Sangiovese, and Pinot Grigio, there are various blends such as Montanaro (Barbera and Zinfandel) and Matrimonio (Nebbiolo, Barbera, Sangiovese, Refosco, Zinfandel). The best wines are bottled under the Terra d'Oro label. There is no doubting Montevina's commitment to Italian varieties, but performance has been disappointing: all too often the wines lack fruit and body.

Nevada City Winery *NR*

321 Spring St, Nevada City, CA 95959.

Tel: 916 265 9463. Fax: 916 265 6860. ncwinery.com

No vineyards. 8,000 cases. Tasting room.

Founded in 1980, this winery is located in the northern Foothills. A wide range of wines is on offer, from commercial blush wines to more serious bottlings from Foothills fruit and from North Coast grapes. When climate permits, small quantities of late harvest Riesling and Sauvignon Blanc are made.

Nine Gables ☆

10778 Shenandoah Rd, Plymouth, CA 95669. Tel: 209 245 3949. Fax: 209 245 3693.

5 acres. 1,750 cases. Tasting room (Thursday to Sunday).

The Notestine family began producing wines in 2000, mostly from purchased fruit. Unfortunately, the first vintage was marred by oxidative and faulty whites, and tannic, earthy Barbera and Syrah.

Renaissance ☆☆→☆☆☆

12585 Rice's Crossing Rd, Renaissance, CA 95962.

Tel: 530 692 2222. Fax: 530 692 2497.

365 acres. 25,000 cases. No visits.

A quasi-religious organization called the Fellowship of Friends, based in San Francisco, acquired this remote site in 1971 and spent a fortune developing its terraced vineyards and in creating a winery and art museum. The elevation is high – between 1,700 and 2,300 feet – and the soil is rocky, so yields are low. Under first Karl Werner and subsequently Gideon Beinstock, Renaissance has acquired a reputation for Sauvignon Blanc and for late harvest wines, but it also produces a range of red wines from Syrah, Pinot Noir, Cabernet, and Zinfandel, as well as a "Claret Prestige" blend. The reds are rich and long-lived, but can sometimes be too tannic and dry.

Renwood ☆☆☆☆

12225 Steiner Rd, Plymouth, CA 95669.
Tel: 530 245 6979. Fax: 530 245 3732. renwood.com
700 acres. 30,000 cases. Tasting room.

Renwood began life as the Santino winery in 1979 (the Santino name is now used as Renwood's second label) but displayed a new surge of energy after it was acquired by banker Robert Smerling in 1992. Smerling has invested enormously in the vineyards, launching a major project to preserve and perpetuate the existing "heritage" vines of Zinfandel from the Foothills.

At the same time, Renwood buys in grapes to produce around seven bottlings of mostly old-vine Zinfandels that successfully combine fruit, power, oakiness, and intensity. They rarely show the porty character that can mar Amador Zinfandel. The Barberas are equally successful, and even the Nebbiolo shows promise. Renwood's "port" is made from Portuguese varieties, and there is a bizarre Ice Zin made with cryo-extraction and tasting better than it sounds.

Shenandoah Vineyards ☆☆→☆☆☆

12300 Steiner Rd, Plymouth, CA 95669. Tel: 209 245 4455. Fax: 209 245 5156.
45 acres. 15,000 cases. Tasting room.

Under the same ownership as Sobon (*qv*), Shenandoah offers a cheaper range of wines on the whole, but there are also some serious bottlings under the Special Reserve or Vintner's Selection labels. One of the specialties is Zingiovese, a juicy blend of Zinfandel and Sangiovese, and the company releases Italian varieties as well as Cabernet. Finally, there are port-style wines and Muscats. The wines offer very good value for money, and quality overlaps with the more upmarket Sobon wines.

Sierra Vista ☆☆☆→☆☆☆☆

4560 Cabernet Way, Placerville, CA 95667.
Tel: 530 622 7221. Fax: 530 622 2413. sierravistawinery.com
42 acres. 10,000 cases. Tasting room.

John MacCready taught engineering in Sacramento and bought this lovely property in 1972, intending to grow grapes. But soon he was trying his hand at winemaking.

He planted Syrah in 1979 and this has become his most important wine, with an outstanding bottling, Red Rock Ridge, from the original block. The

Cabernet is on the chunky side, and there are some robust Zinfandels. The Viognier can be delicious, and there is a Tavel-style rosé called Belle Rose. Quality has remained very consistent over the years.

Sobon Estate ☆→☆☆☆☆

14430 Shenandoah Rd, Plymouth, CA 95669.

Tel: 209 245 6554. sobonwine.com

84 acres. 10,000 cases. Tasting room.

Scientist Leon Sobon bought this ranch in 1977, and in 1989 acquired the former D'Agostini winery, the oldest in the Foothills. Leon's son, Paul, is now the winemaker, and all the wines are estate-grown from dry-farmed organic vineyards. Sobon has an enviable reputation for its excellent Zinfandels, the top bottlings being the Fiddletown and Rocky Top. These are very ripe, powerful Zinfandels, with the occasional jamminess of Amador fruit. Sobon also does well with Rhône varieties such as Syrah, Roussanne, and Viognier. Recently, they have introduced a Signature Select Program for small lots of exceptional wines.

Stevenot ☆☆

2690 San Domingo Rd, Murphys, CA 95247.

Tel: 209 728 3436. Fax: 209 728 3710. stevenotwinery.com

50 acres. 30,000 cases. Tasting room.

Stevenot was the first winery to open in Calaveras County. It was originally a cattle ranch, but owner Barden Stevenot began planting vines in 1974. As well as standard varietals, there is a little Tempranillo, a rarity in the Foothills. Most of the wines are aged in American oak, including the Chardonnay.

Story ☆☆

10525 Bell Rd, Plymouth, CA 95669. Tel: 209 245 6208. Fax: 209 245 6619.

43 acres. 3,500 cases. Tasting room.

The peculiarity of Story is that it is one of the last wineries in California to produce wines from the Mission grape that was originally brought here by Spanish missionaries two centuries ago. The vines are eighty years old, and the wines work best when made in an off-dry style or as sweet wine. Story also produces good Zinfandel and a little Gewurztraminer.

Domaine de la Terre Rouge ☆☆☆→☆☆☆☆

10801 Dickson Rd, Fiddletown, CA 95629. Tel: 209 245 3117. Fax: 209 245 5415.

70 acres. 15,000 cases. Tasting room.

William Easton founded his winery in 1987. Rather confusingly, there are two labels: Terre Rouge focuses on Rhône-style wines, the Easton label on everything else. The winemaking here is unusually sophisticated for the Foothills and shows that Amador fruit can attain remarkable finesse. The Viognier and Roussanne are both aromatic and spicily oaky, and there is a fine, white, Rhône-style blend called Enigma. The Mourvedre is somewhat tarry and dry, and the Syrahs are more successful. Of the three Syrah bottlings, the best is the elegant Sierra Foothills; the Sentinel Oak Vineyard is rated more highly by Easton but can be over-extracted.

Under the Easton label there is delicious Barbera, stylish and persistent. There's a range of Zinfandels. The Estate Zinfandel tastes overripe, but the Shenandoah and Fiddletown bottlings are excellent. A white wine called Notoma is a white Bordeaux blend, but the oak overwhelms the fruit.

TKC Vineyards ☆

11001 Valley Dr, Plymouth, CA 95669. Tel: 209 245 6428. Fax: 209 245 4006.
6 acres. 1,500 cases. Tasting room (weekends).

TKC produces small lots of Zinfandel, Mourvedre, and Cabernet Sauvignon, but the wines are dry and fruitless.

Villa Toscano ☆☆☆

10600 Shenandoah Rd, Plymouth, CA 95669.
Tel: 209 245 3800. Fax: 209 245 3332. villatoscano.com
105 acres. 45,000 cases. Tasting room.

Amid the rustic architecture of Amador County, this gleaming "Tuscan" villa, with its pretty gardens and ponds, adds a glitzy note more usually associated with Napa than the Foothills. The estate was created by Jerry Wright, who hired Gordon Binz, formerly of Renwood, as winemaker. Initial releases have been very promising: a lush Syrah and a ripe, spicy Zinfandel.

Vino Noceto ☆☆☆

11011 Shenandoah Rd, Plymouth, CA 95669.
Tel: 209 245 6556. Fax: 209 245 3446. noceto.com
12 acres. 5,000 cases. No visits.

It took courage for Suzy and Jim Gullett to specialize exclusively in Sangiovese, but they did their research, planted the best Tuscan clones, and since 1990 have made some very convincing wines, including a reserve. To complicate their life further, they also produce a little sparkling Muscat called Frivolo.

San Francisco Bay

Ahlgren ☆☆☆

20320 Highway 9, Boulder Creek, CA 95006.
Tel: 831 338 6071. Fax: 831 338 9111. ahlgrenvineyard.com
26 acres. 2,500 cases. Tasting room (Saturday only).

Dexter Ahlgren buys in some impressive Santa Cruz Mountain Cabernet, but goes further afield for some of his other wines: to Monterey for Chardonnay, to Livermore for Zinfandel, and to Paso Robles for Nebbiolo. Quantities of each wine are tiny.

Bargetto ☆→☆☆☆

3535 North Main St, Soquel, CA 95073.

Tel: 831 475 2258. Fax: 831 475 2664. bargetto.com

20 acres. 35,000 cases. Tasting room on Cannery Row, Monterey.

Founded in 1933 and now run by the third generation, this winery shows vigour and enterprise. Some of its best wines come from Santa Cruz Mountains fruit (Chardonnay, Merlot, and Cabernet), but it is also enthusiastic about Italian varieties such as Pinot Grigio and Dolcetto, which are purchased from the Central Coast. The best Italianate wine is "La Vita", a pricy, Piedmontese-style blend, with fine acidity and a slight but welcome tartness. In general, quality is variable.

Bonny Doon ☆☆→☆☆☆☆

10 Pine Flat Rd, Bonny Doon, CA 95060. Tel: 408 425 3625. Fax: 408 425 3856.

140 acres. 200,000 cases. Tasting room.

Randall Grahm, a wildly clever philosophy student, drifted into winemaking in the early 1980s, eventually founding Bonny Doon in 1983. He began conventionally enough, producing Chardonnay and Pinot Noir. But he grew bored with Chardonnay, his Pinot vines proved too vigorous, and quality was not exceptional. Profoundly convinced that California's climate is far better suited to Mediterranean varieties than Burgundian ones, he turned his inventive attention to Rhône and Italian varieties. Soon he was mimicking, with remarkable success, the great wines of Châteauneuf-du-Pape and Bandol.

If it's unfashionable, Grahm will try his hand at it. He offers Riesling, occasional Charbono, and some brilliant Nebbiolo and Syrah. Le Sophiste is a remarkable white Rhône blend. Then, too, there are the cheaper wines such as Ca' del Solo Big House Red. There are wines that come and go, reflecting Grahm's restlessness.

He is viewed with some suspicion in California: his often caustic wit does not go down well with worshippers of cult wines from Napa. Grahm is a hedonist, a populist, and a brilliant marketing man. He casts an envious glance back at the Old World, whose wines he so much admires (whether tannic Madiran or racy Riesling), and then acknowledges that in California even the shrewdest grape farmer or winemaker is still in the dark about the mysteries of *terroir*.

Although some of his wines are remarkably good, Randall Grahm's major contribution has been to make people reconsider assumptions long taken for granted. As one of the original "Rhône Rangers", he made the strongest possible case, both intellectually and in the bottle, for regarding balmy California as a Mediterranean rather than an Atlantic climate. When the rest of the industry was becoming increasingly monolithic, Grahm gloried in diversity. When Napa moved in the direction of cult wines at preposterous

prices, Bonny Doon began producing mass-market, food-oriented blends of good quality. Randall Grahm has succeeded in being an intellectual and a populist simultaneously.

David Bruce ☆→☆☆☆☆

21439 Bear Creek Rd, Los Gatos, CA 95030.
Tel: 408 354 4214. Fax: 408 395 5478. davidbrucewinery.com
15 acres. 60,000 cases. Tasting room.

A bottle of Richebourg gave dermatologist David Bruce his conversion experience. In the 1960s, he acquired vineyards 2,200 feet up in the Santa Cruz Mountains, and began producing exciting Pinot Noir and Chardonnay. He was beset with problems: Pierce's disease, bacterial problems, and poor corks reduced his production and damaged his reputation, but he has bounced back. Quality has always been irregular, since in addition to his small volume of estate wines, he also produces wines from purchased grapes from various parts of Santa Cruz, Paso Robles, and Monterey. But now and again he makes a great Pinot Noir or Petite Sirah or Zinfandel, wines that are powerful, complex, and memorable.

Byington ☆☆

21850 Bear Creek Rd, Los Gatos, CA 95030. Tel: 408 354 1111. Fax: 408 354 2782.
9 acres. 20,000 cases. Tasting room.

Founded in 1987 by steel manufacturer Bill Byington, this winery has had a chequered past. There has been some fine Santa Cruz Mountains Cabernet, but also an eclectic range including Napa Merlot and Mendocino Gewurztraminer that have often failed to impress. In 1999, a new winemaker was hired, the eccentric Don Blackburn, who made fine wines at Bernardus in Monterey.

Cinnabar ☆☆☆

23000 Congress Springs Rd, Saratoga, CA 95070.
Tel: 408 741 5858. Fax: 408 741 5860. cinnabarwine.com
32 acres. 15,000 cases. No visits.

Founded in 1983 by Tom Mudd, this small winery specializes in estate-grown Chardonnay, Pinot Noir, and Cabernet Sauvignon from mountain vineyards. Chardonnay and Merlot are also bought in from Central Coast sites, and there is a Bordeaux blend called "Mercury Rising". Consultant winemaker George Troquato ensures that quality is steady.

Clos La Chance ☆☆☆

21511 Saratoga Heights Dr, Saratoga, CA 95070.
Tel: 408 741 1796. Fax: 408 741 1198. closlachance.com
5 acres. 15,000 cases. No visits.

The name oozes pretension, but Bill Murphy's Santa Clara winery makes some fine Santa Cruz Mountains Chardonnay, a fresh, clean Napa Chardonnay, graceful Cabernet Sauvignon and Cabernet Franc, as well as Merlot from Central Coast fruit. Jeff Ritchey is the winemaker.

DRY-FARMED VINEYARDS

This term often appears on wine labels. The great majority of California vineyards are irrigated, for the simple reason that if they were not, the vines could die after a hot, dry summer. On the other hand, some varieties are robust enough to be cultivated without irrigation – dry-farmed – and the fact that the vine is not over-nourished contributes to the concentration of the resulting wine. Thus, many dry-farmed vineyards, often planted with Zinfandel or Petite Sirah, are revered for the quality of their fruit. But it should not be assumed that dry-farmed is always the same as well-farmed.

Concannon ☆☆→☆☆☆

4590 Tesla Rd, Livermore, CA 94550.
Tel: 925 456 2505. Fax: 925 456 2511. concannonvineyard.com
200 acres. 75,000 cases. Tasting room.

Founded by Irish immigrant James Concannon in 1883, the winery weathered Prohibition by selling altar wines. In the 1980s, it was bought and sold a few times, until in 1992 it was acquired by its neighbour, Wente (*qv*). Today, it produces a wide range of wines, some from the San Francisco Bay appellation and thus utilizing local grapes; but most wines are sold under the Central Coast or California appellations. Its more successful wines include a lightly herbaceous Cabernet Sauvignon, and a burly, peppery Petite Sirah. There are also red and white Bordeaux blends called Assemblage.

Cooper-Garrod ☆☆→☆☆☆

22600 Mount Eden Rd, Saratoga, CA 95070.
Tel: 408 867 7116. Fax: 408 741 1169. cgv.com
21 acres. 3,000 cases. Tasting room.

This dry-farmed estate specializes in Chardonnay, Cabernet Sauvignon, and Cabernet Franc, as well as a Bordeaux blend called "Fine Claret".

Cronin ☆☆☆→☆☆☆☆

11 Old La Honda Rd, Woodside, CA 94062.
Tel: 650 851 1452. Fax: 851 5696.
3 acres. 2,000 cases. No visits.

In the midst of a hillside suburb, Duane Cronin descends into his basement to produce a range of exceptional Chardonnays, bought in from Santa Cruz and a wine of great personality. The winemaking is artisanal, but none the worse for that. Continuity is the problem here, as vineyard sources dry up and production of favourite wines – a Zinfandel from Gilroy, Sauvignon from Santa Cruz – has to crease. Cronin enjoys a loyal following, so his wines are greatly admired and quite hard to find.

Fellom Ranch Vineyard *NR*

17075 Montebello Rd, Cupertino, CA 95014. Tel/fax: 408 741 0307.

14 acres. 1,500 cases. No visits.

With a high vineyard adjoining the legendary Monte Bello of Ridge Vineyards (*qv*), Roy Fellom aims high to produce fine Cabernet and Merlot, as well as Zinfandel from Santa Clara fruit.

Thomas Fogarty ☆☆→☆☆☆

5937 Alpine Rd, Portola Valley, CA 94028.

Tel: 650 851 6777. Fax: 650 851 5840. fogartywinery.com

21 acres. 20,000 cases. Tasting room.

Dr Thomas Fogarty and his winemaker, Michael Martella, have expanded production by buying in additional fruit from Carneros, Monterey, and Edna Valley. Fogarty has a fine reputation for Gewurztraminer, sourced from Monterey, and for Pinot Noir, Chardonnay, and Merlot from his Santa Cruz Mountains vineyards.

Fortino ☆

4525 Hecker Pass Highway, Gilroy, CA 95020.

Tel: 408 842 3305. Fax: 408 842 8636.

52 acres. 35,000 cases. Tasting room.

This Santa Clara winery was founded in 1970. Its present range includes old-fashioned oddities such as semi-sweet sparkling wine from French Colombard and cream sherry. But there are also concessions to more international tastes, with barrel-fermented Chardonnay, Merlot, and old-vine Zinfandel. The wines are light and lack distinction.

Hallcrest *NR*

379 Felton Empire Rd, Felton, CA 95018. Tel: 408 335 4441.

5 acres. 5,000 cases. Tasting room.

The Hallcrest winery dates from the 1940s and became well-known for its Cabernet . It closed in 1969, reopened as Felton Empire, and was acquired in 1987 by John Schumacher. The specialty is Riesling, as well as standard varietals. There is also an organic range under the Organic Wine Works label.

Hecker Pass Winery ☆

4605 Hecker Pass Highway, Gilroy, CA 95020. Tel: 408 842 8755. Fax: 408 842 9799.

20 acres. 4,000 cases. Tasting room.

This third-generation winery does little to enhance the reputation of Santa Clara. The wines are tart, attenuated, and rustic.

Jory ☆→☆☆☆

3920 Hecker Pass Highway, Gilroy, CA 95020.

Tel: 805 995 2764. Fax: 805 995 2635. jorywinery.com

No vineyards. 5,000 cases. No visits.

Stillman Brown founded this Santa Clara winery in 1986, and has assembled a range of blended wines under names such as Black Hand and Zeppelin which contain a healthy dose of southern French varieties. There is also more serious, and very expensive, Chardonnay and Syrah.

Kathryn Kennedy ☆☆☆→☆☆☆☆

13180 Pierce Rd, Saratoga, CA 95070. Tel: 408 867 4170. kathrynkennedywinery.com
7 acres. 3,000 cases. No visits.

Kathryn Kennedy set out in 1979 to do one thing and to do it well. She and her winemaking son, Marty Mathis, produce small quantities (800 cases) of rich, oaky Cabernet. Recently, the range has been expanded by the introduction of Santa Cruz Mountains Syrah and a Merlot-dominated blend called Lateral.

Lucas ☆☆☆

18196 North Davis Rd, Lodi, CA 95240. Tel: 209 368 2006. lucaswinery.com
20 acres. 1,000 cases. No visits.

David Lucas specializes in Zinfandel from his own eighty-year-old vines, and makes what is clearly the most elegant expression of this grape in Lodi. The wines receive prolonged maceration, are aged in twenty-five per cent new oak, mostly French, and are bottled unfiltered. He also makes a small amount of Chardonnay.

Mondavi Woodbridge ☆→☆☆

5950 East Woodbridge Rd, Acampo, CA 95220.
Tel: 209 369 5861. Fax: 209 365 2739. woodbridgewines.com
No vineyards. 6,500,000 cases. No visits.

This vast winery is based in Lodi, where Robert Mondavi grew up. Working closely with local growers, it produces large quantities of drinkable, if unexceptional, wines. As well as standard varietals, there is some Pinot Grigio and a port-style wine from Portuguese varieties known as Portacinco. Quality seems to have slipped somewhat in recent years.

Mount Eden ☆☆☆→☆☆☆☆

22020 Mount Eden Rd, Saratoga, CA 95070.
Tel: 408 867 5832. Fax: 408 867 4329. mounteden.com
40 acres. 20,000 cases. No visits.

The heart of this property is the vineyard established by Martin Ray, a pioneer of modern California winemaking in the post-war years. Ray was a quarrelsome man and lost control of his estate in the 1970s. Today, Mount Eden is owned by Jeff and Eleanor Patterson. Parts of the vineyard are very old and give tiny crops of Chardonnay, Pinot Noir, and Cabernet of intense concentration. The bulk of production is an Edna Valley Chardonnay made in a full, tropical-fruit style.

Murrieta's Well ☆☆→☆☆☆

3005 Mines Rd, Livermore, CA 94550.
Tel: 925 456 2390. Fax: 447 4837. murrietaswell.com
90 acres. 8,000 cases. Tasting room (weekends only).

This old winery was resurrected in 1990 by Philip Wente as a joint venture with Chilean winemaker Serghio Traverso. The vineyards are organically cultivated. The two main wines are blends called Vendimia. The white combines Sauvignon, Semillon, and Muscat Canelli; it is well-balanced and fresh but a touch neutral. The red consists of Cabernet, Merlot, and Zinfandel, an attractive and stylish wine. There is also a Zinfandel from eighty-year-old vines.

Pedrizetti *NR*

1645 San Pedro Ave, Morgan Hill, CA 95037.
Tel: 408 779 7389. Fax: 408 779 9083. pedrizetti.com
No vineyards. 50,000 cases. Tasting room.

This Santa Clara property, founded in 1913, was bought by the Pedrizettis in 1945. Ed Pedrizetti is the current winemaker. The wines have been rustic, but the winery is now said to be up for sale.

Peirano ☆☆→☆☆☆

21831 North Highway 99, Acampo, CA 95220. Tel: 209 369 9463. peirano.com
300 acres. Tasting room (Friday to Sunday).

Lance Randolph owns this fifth-generation family vineyard in Lodi, and first made wines in 1992. The winemaker is Michael Carr. He produces a stylish Zinfandel that is not too extracted, and has recently added some white varieties to the range: Chardonnay, Sauvignon Blanc, and Viognier. There is also a limited production of Cabernet, Merlot, and Shiraz.

Picchetti *NR*

13100 Montebello Rd, Cupertino, CA 95014.
Tel: 408 741 1310. Fax: 408 269 8565. picchetti.com
12 acres. 6,000 cases. Tasting room (weekends only).

The core of this property (known as Sunrise Winery until 1998, when it was bought by Leslie Pantling) is an ancient Zinfandel vineyard, the Picchetti Ranch. This is supplemented by Chardonnay from Santa Cruz Mountains, Syrah from Paso Robles, Merlot from Napa and Sonoma, and Cabernet from Santa Cruz Mountains and Alexander Valley.

Ridge ☆☆☆☆→☆☆☆☆☆

17100 Montebello Rd, Cupertino, CA 95015.
Tel: 408 867 3233. Fax: 408 868 1350. ridgewine.com
520 acres. 68,000 cases. Tasting room.

This nineteenth-century property was revived in the early 1960s by a band of investors, and Paul Draper was hired as winemaker. Over thirty years later he is still here. Draper's calm guidance has given Ridge consistency of both quality and style.

Ridge has become best-known for its magnificent estate Cabernet, known as Monte Bello, and for the stunning collection of Zinfandels. Ridge, a fanatic about *terroir*, sourced his Zinfandel fruit from up to thirty five vineyards, but now the range has been slimmed down. The principal bottlings are the Geyserville field blend, Lytton Springs, and Paso Robles.

The Ridge Zinfandels are all beautifully balanced: no excesses of oak or alcohol. In addition, there is fine Chardonnay and Merlot from Santa Cruz Mountains, and fine Petite Sirah from York Creek in Napa. Draper ages most of the red wines in American oak, but so skillful is the cooperage land so careful the oak-ageing process that many wine drinkers would not detect its presence.

Paul Draper has been a shining example to more than one generation of California winemakers. He is a scrupulous and thoughtful winemaker, never applying a formula, but adapting his techniques to the nature of the fruit. Balance counts for more than power, complexity for more than flashiness. In a sense he is more European than Californian in his approach, but he would no doubt bristle at the statement. His fondness for Zinfandel and his use of American oak for his top wine demonstrate his pride in the typicity of California wines, and for sheer consistency there are few winemakers in the state who can match his achievement.

Roudon-Smith ☆☆

2364 Bean Creek Rd, Santa Cruz, CA 95066.
Tel: 408 438 1244. roudonsmith.com
12 acres. 2,000 cases. Tasting room (Saturday only).

Two engineers from Los Angeles founded this property in 1972 and built a winery in 1979. They focused on Santa Cruz Mountains fruit: Chardonnay, Cabernet, and Pinot Noir. They also bought in red grapes from Paso Robles. The founders are thinking about retirement, so production has been dropping sharply in recent years, and plans about the business's future remain unclear.

St Amant ☆→☆☆☆

1 Winemaster Way, Lodi, CA 95240. Tel: 209 367 0646.
43 acres. 5,000 cases. No visits.

Tim Spencer has cultivated Portuguese varieties since the 1970s, but his vineyards had to be replanted after they were attacked by phylloxera. His Tres Cachos port is aged three years in barriques and is dense and impressive. Drawing on vineyards both in Lodi and the Sierra Foothills, he also makes old-vine Zinfandel, Cabernet Sauvignon, rich, ripe Syrah, and a tiny amount of Roussanne.

Santa Cruz Mountain Vineyard ☆☆☆

2300 Jarvis Rd, Santa Cruz, CA 95065.
Tel/fax: 408 426 6209.
14 acres. 2,500 cases. No visits.

Restaurateur Ken Burnap bought this old property in the late 1960s and developed a fine reputation for powerful Cabernet and intense Pinot Noir, all made in a deliberately low-tech way. They are robust, somewhat old-fashioned wines that are greatly admired by the winery's loyal followers.

THE JUDGMENT OF PARIS

In 1976, an English wine merchant named Steven Spurrier organized a blind tasting in Paris, pitting the new wines of California against the famous growths of France. The mostly French jury, eminent and experienced, placed a Chateau Montelena Chardonnay and a Stag's Leap Wine Cellars Cabernet Sauvignon ahead of the best from Burgundy and Bordeaux. French pride was deeply wounded, especially since the tasting became a worldwide sensation. No doubt the French wines were more closed-in and austere than their more exuberant and approachable Californian counterparts, but at the very least the tasting made the world realize that Napa Valley could producing some amazingly good wines – even from very young vines!

Sarah's Vineyard ☆☆

4005 Hecker Pass Highway, Gilroy, CA 95030.

Tel: 408 842 4278. Fax: 408 842 3252.

10 acres. 2,000 cases. Tasting room (Saturday only).

The Otteman family's property has been producing small quantities of Chardonnay, Riesling, Merlot, and Pinot Noir since 1983. Quality, initially high, has subsequently been inconsistent.

Savannah-Chanelle ☆☆→☆☆☆☆

23600 Congress Springs Rd, Saratoga, CA 95070.

Tel: 408 741 2930. Fax: 408 867 4824. savannahchanelle.com

14 acres. 12,000 cases. Tasting room.

This beautiful mountainside property has been through various owners and name changes until 1996, when it was bought by the present owner Mike Ballard. The wines are sometimes over-oaked, but there are some excellent bottles, such as the Estate Cabernet Franc and the tarry Estate Zinfandel. Pinot Noir is sleek but lacks depth.

Nonetheless, even in its first few vintages, this estate has shown itself quite capable of producing classy wines, and once it has settled into its stride, it seems destined to become one of the top properties of the region. Watch this space.

Silver Mountain Vineyards *NR*

PO Box 3636, Santa Cruz, CA 95063.

Tel: 408 353 2278. silvermountainvineyards.com

11 acres. 3,500 cases. No visits.

These vineyards are planted at 2,000 feet. Chardonnay is the major wine, and some bottlings are from organically grown grapes. There is also a Bordeaux blend from Central Coast fruit called Alloy.

Solis ☆

3920 Hecker Pass Rd, Gilroy, CA 95020.

Tel: 408 847 6306. Fax: 847 5188. soliswinery.com

12 acres. 6,000 cases. Tasting room.

David Vanni's Santa Clara winery produces a range of wine from estate-grown fruit, including Chardonnay, Riesling, Sangiovese, and Merlot. There are other wines from grapes purchased in the Central Coast. Quality is mixed.

Spenker ☆

17303 North DeVries Rd, Lodi, CA 95242. Tel: 209 367 0467. Fax: 209 368 5746.

60 acres. 2,000 cases. No visits.

The Spenker family has been growing Zinfandel for some time, but only started producing wine in 1994. Initial releases met with great acclaim, but they struck me as raw and astringent.

Storrs ☆☆☆

303 Potrero St, Santa Cruz, CA 95060. Tel: 408 458 5030. Fax: 408 458 0464.

No vineyards. 6,000 cases. Tasting room.

Storrs specialize in Santa Cruz Mountains Chardonnays from various vineyards. They are barrel-fermented and made in a rich style, with full malolactic fermentation and prolonged lees contact.

Sycamore Creek *NR*

12775 Uvas Rd, Morgan Hill, CA 95037. Tel: 408 779 4738. Fax: 408 779 5873.

14 acres. 3,500 cases. Tasting room (weekends only).

Jeff Runquist makes the wines for this estate, which was acquired by a Japanese sake producer in 1989. There are some ninety-year-old Carignane and Zinfandel vines on the property, as well as more youthful Chardonnay and Cabernet.

Ivan Tamas ☆☆→☆☆☆

5443 Tesla Rd, Livermore, CA 94550.

Tel: 925 456 2380. Fax: 925 456 2381. ivantamas.com

6 acres. 60,000 cases. Tasting room.

Founded in 1984 as a partnership between Tamas and Steve Mirassou, this winery specializes in Livermore wines (Trebbiano, Sangiovese, Zinfandel, Chardonnay) as well as wines sourced from Monterey and other parts of California.

Troquato Vineyards *NR*

247 More Ave, Los Gatos, CA 95030. Tel: 408 866 6700.

20 acres. 1,000 cases. No visits.

George Troquato is a well-known winemaker in the Santa Cruz region, working for a number of estates. This is his family property situated in Santa Clara, and specializes in small lots of Chardonnay, Merlot, Cabernet, and Zinfandel.

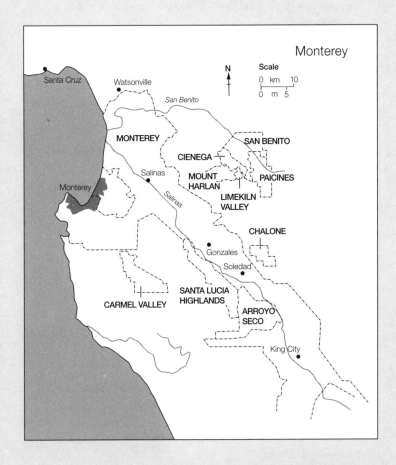

Wente Vineyards ☆☆→☆☆☆

5565 Tesla Rd, Livermore, CA 94550.

Tel: 925 456 2300. Fax: 925 456 2319. wentevineyards.com

3,000 acres. 400,000 cases. Tasting room.

Founded by Carl Wente in 1883, this winery is still owned by the same family. Its base remains firmly in Livermore, and many of its wines are sourced from the 1,400 acres here, supplemented by large vineyards in Monterey. The basic range of standard varietals is called Family Selection; Vineyard Selections are estate-grown, and there are also some reserve bottlings. Quality is sound but somewhat bland: nothing offends, but little excites. There is a small production of good sparkling wine that is aged five years on the yeasts.

Woodside Vineyards *NR*

340 Kings Mountain Rd, Woodside, CA 94062. Tel: 650 851 3144. Fax: 650 851 5037.

17 acres. 2,000 cases. Tasting room.

This long-established estate incorporates La Questa, one of the historic vineyards of the region, now reduced to a single acre of Cabernet! The range consists of small lots of standard varietals.

Monterey County

Unless otherwise indicated, the area code for the wineries listed below is 831.

Bernardus ☆☆→☆☆☆☆

5 West Carmel Valley Rd, Carmel Valley, CA 93924.

Tel: 659 1900. Fax: 659 1676. bernardus.com

50 acres. 50,000 cases. Tasting room.

This estate is owned by Bernardus Pon, a Dutch wine distributor and racing driver. For many years, the wines were made by the Francophile Don Blackburn, but since 1999 the winemaker has been Mark Chesebro, though the basic style remains the same. The principal estate wine is a Bordeaux blend called Marinus, which in recent vintages has been magnificent. Many of the other wines, including the Chardonnay, are made from purchased fruit, often from well-known vineyards in Carneros or Santa Barbara, but with these wines, quality is more patchy.

Chalone ☆☆☆→☆☆☆☆☆

Stonewall Canyon Rd and Highway 146, W. Soledad, CA 93960.

Tel: 678 1717. Fax: 678 2742. chalonevineyard.com

300 acres. 40,000 cases. Tasting room.

It's a steep drive up from the flat valley floor to the vineyards 2,000 feet up in the Gavilan Mountains. Vines – Chenin and Chardonnay – were first planted here in 1919. Philip Togni (*qv*), who made the wines here in the early 1960s, recalls how hard it was to make wines this high up when you had no water supply! In 1965, Richard Graff bought the property, which then became part of the Chalone group, and went on to acquire Acacia, Carmenet, and Edna Valley Vineyards, as well as non-Californian properties.

Michael Michaud was the winemaker from 1983 to 1998, but during that period the quality began to slip. There had been remarkable and long-lived wines from Chalone, but increasingly, musty flavours began to creep in. Dick Graff was killed in a plane crash in 1998, and later that year Michaud left. Dan Karlsen replaced him, and made some radical changes. He eliminated the Reserve bottlings, and got rid of the fungal problems in the winery that had caused the bacterial problems that led to mustiness in many of the wines. Since 1999, Chalone has seen a return to its former glory. The wines are concentrated, vibrant, and minerally. They have recovered their sense of place. The range will be expanded: there was a superb Viognier in 1999 and there will be Syrah from 2000.

Chateau Julien ☆☆

8940 Carmel Valley Rd, Carmel Valley, CA 93923.
Tel: 624 2600. Fax: 624 6138. chateaujulien.com
182 acres. 175,000 cases. Tasting room.

The pretty, English-style tasting centre in Carmel Valley disguises the fact that this is a fairly large operation owned by a company called Great American Wineries. The wines sold under the Chateau Julien label are the top of the range: Estate Vineyard wines from their Salinas vineyards, and then there are the Private Reserves. There are also much larger volumes of simpler varietal wines under the Garland Ranch and Emerald Bay Coastal labels. The wines are well-made but have never been exciting.

Durney.

See Heller.

Galante NR

18181 Cachagua Rd, Carmel Valley, CA 93924.
Tel: 1 800 GALANTE. Fax: 831 659 9525. galantevineyards.com
70 acres. 15,000 cases. No visits.

Jack Galante specializes in Cabernet Sauvignon, which come from various blocks in his vineyard. He also produces some Merlot and Sauvignon Blanc, but these are only available from the winery.

Georis NR

4 Pilot Rd, Carmel Valley, CA 93924. Tel: 659 1050. Fax: 659 1054. georiswinery.com
27 acres. 2,000 cases. Tasting room.

Walter Georis is a restaurateur from Belgium who has a low-yielding vineyard in Carmel Valley. His first vintage was 1986, and he had the foresight to focus on Merlot. There have been occasional bottlings of

RIESLING COUNTRY

Monterey County has become California's headquarters for the Riesling grape, and many of the best examples now come from here. Unfortunately, prices remain low, and how long the renaissance will continue it is hard to say. Top grower Paraiso Springs grafted over its vines in 2000. Leading producers include: Jekel, Lockwood, Lohr, Mirassou, Ventana, and Wente.

Cabernet, too, and in 1999, when frost severely damaged his crop, Georis bought in some Cabernet Franc and Sauvignon Blanc. A visit to the tasting room is not very rewarding, since it is not possible to taste the Merlot.

Hahn

See Smith & Hook.

Heller Estate ☆→☆☆☆

69 West Carmel Valley Rd, Carmel Valley, CA 93924. Tel: 659 6220. Fax: 659 6226.
120 acres. 25,000 cases. Tasting room.

This property was founded in 1968, when Bill Durney gave his name to a vineyard planted on a former cattle ranch. After his death in 1989, Durney Vineyards went through changes in ownership. Today, the property is owned by Gilbert Heller, who renamed the winery, and the wines are made by Rex Smith. The grapes, mostly Bordeaux varieties, are farmed organically. The Cabernet has been quite tannic in the past, whereas the Merlot is more fleshy and opulent; the white wines can be disappointing. The second label is Cachagua.

Jekel ☆☆→☆☆☆

40155 Walnut Ave, Greenfield, CA 93927. Tel: 674 5525. Fax: 674 3769.
327 acres. 150,000 cases. Tasting room.

Bill Jekel planted this Arroyo Seco vineyard in the 1978. He was a controversial character who believed that soil played no part in the quality of a wine. In short, *terroir* is bunk. Arguably his views were erroneous, but he made some excellent wines until he sold the estate to the Brown-Forman company in 1992. The new owners increased the proportion of red wines but the Gravelstone Chardonnay remains the most popular and reasonably priced wine. Rick Boyer is the winemaker.

Joullian ☆☆☆

2 Village Dr, Carmel Valley, CA 93924. Tel: 659 8100. Fax: 659 2802.
40 acres. 12,000 cases. Tasting room.

Ridge Watson has been making the wines here for almost two decades, keeping a watchful eye on the deep-soiled vineyards as well as the barriques. The best wine is usually the Cabernet, and the rather light

Zinfandel is the only one from Carmel Valley. The Sauvignon Blanc is usually spicy and melony, and the sleek, fresh Chardonnays are made from purchased fruit.

Lockwood ☆☆→☆☆☆

59020 Paris Valley Rd, Salinas, CA 93902.
Tel: 642 9200. Fax: 644 7829. lockwood-wine.com
1,850 acres. 80,000 cases. No visits.

This large vineyard was planted by a consortium of investors in 1981 and most of the fruit is sold to other wineries, but a winery was built in 1990. Some of the regular bottlings are rather bland, but the Sauvignon Blanc can be excellent. The best wines are marketed under the Very Special Reserve label.

J Lohr ☆☆→☆☆☆

1000 Lenzen Ave, San Jose, CA 95126.
Tel: 408 288 5057. Fax: 408 993 2276. jlohr.com
2,000 acres. 750,000 cases. Tasting room.

Jerry Lohr began planting mostly white-grape vineyards in Monterey in 1972, and planted more in 1988 in Paso Robles, even though his headquarters remains in San Jose. Jeff Meier has made the wines since 1984. This is essentially a commercial winery, focusing on sensibly priced wines that are well-crafted and offer good value.

There are special bottlings that can be of very high quality, notably the Hilltop Cabernet and the new-oaked Arroyo Vista Chardonnay. There's a pleasant, off-dry Riesling, a fresh Pinot Blanc, and Syrah in a fairly beefy style. Overall, the wines may lack complexity, but they are reliably consistent.

Meador Estate ☆☆→☆☆☆

2999 Monterey-Salinas Highway, Monterey, CA 93940.
Tel: 375 0741. Fax: 375 0797. meadorestates.com
300 acres. 1,600 cases. Tasting room.

Doug Meador is an opinionated grape farmer and the owner of Ventana Vineyard (*qv*) in Arroyo Seco, which supplies Sauvignon Blanc, Gewurztraminer, and other varieties to leading wineries. He has recently launched his own label, offering high-priced Chardonnay, Chenin Blanc, Sauvignon Blanc, and Syrah from specific blocks within his vineyards.

Mer Soleil ☆☆

See Caymus.
390 acres. 9,000 cases. No visits.

Chuck Wagner of Caymus (*qv*) in Napa started planting Chardonnay in the Santa Lucia Highlands in 1988. From these grapes he makes an opulent, exotic wine that wins high praise from those who like fruit-salad Chardonnay.

Mirassou ☆→☆☆

3000 Aborn Rd, San Jose, CA 95135.

Tel: 408 274 4000. Fax: 408 270 5881. mirassou.com

1,000 acres. 105,000 cases. Tasting room.

Founded in 1854, Mirassou is now run by the sixth generation of the family. Most of their vineyards are in Monterey, where they were pioneers of grape farming until they discovered, to their cost, that Cabernet and Zinfandel wouldn't ripen properly. These errors were corrected long ago. The top range is the Showcase Selection Chardonnay and Pinot Noir; there are also Single Vineyard Designations, Harvest Reserves, and the larger-volume Coastal Selections. There is a separate sparkling wine facility in Los Gatos. Quality is unremarkable.

Monterey Vineyard ☆→☆☆

800 S. Alta St, Gonzales, CA 93926. Tel: 408 675 2316. Fax: 408 675 4019.

1,200 acres. 750,000 cases. No visits.

Founded in 1973 as a kind of 9,600-acre cooperative, this winery has been through numerous changes. Owned since 1983 by Seagram, it became part of the Diageo group after its acquisition of Seagram. At present, the range consists of modestly priced standard varietals.

Monterra ☆☆

51955 Oasis Rd, King City, CA 93930. Tel: 386 5650. monterrawine.com

9,000 acres. No visits.

Monterra is the label used by the giant Delicato company for wines made from Monterey fruit, in effect from the vast San Bernabe vineyard near King City. Bottlings include a fresh Sangiovese, a variety not often encountered in Monterey.

Morgan ☆☆→☆☆☆

526 Brunken Ave, Salinas, CA 93901.

Tel: 751 7777. Fax: 751 7780. morganwinery.com

65 acres. 30,000 cases. No visits.

Founded in 1992 by Dan Lee, the original winemaker at Jekel (*qv*). Dean de Korth makes the wines. As well as Monterey Chardonnay and Pinot Noir, there are wines made from fruit purchased in Carneros and Alexander Valley. The wines are made in a rich, ripe style but can lack complexity.

Paraiso Springs ☆☆→☆☆☆

38060 Paraiso Springs Rd, Soledad, CA 93960. Tel: 678 0300. Fax: 678 2584.

1,800 acres. 20,000 cases. Tasting room.

Rich Smith is a grape farmer with 3,000 acres under his control. Only a small part of his best vineyards in the Santa Lucia Highlands are used for his own label. The wines are charming though somewhat lacking in concentration and structure. The Pinot Blanc is attractive, and the Riesling (last vintage 1999, alas) was a lovely wine. The Pinot Noir and Syrah show the most promise.

Pavona ☆☆→☆☆☆

88 Abrego St, Monterey, CA 93940. Tel: 646 1506. Fax: 649 8919.

No vineyards. 4,000 cases. No visits.

Richard Kanakaris and his winemaker, Ron Bunnell, specialize in buying grapes from leading vineyards in Monterey, such as Paraiso Springs, and Paso Robles, and fashioning fresh, modern-style wines.

San Saba Vineyard *NR*

1075B, South Main St, Salinas, CA 93901.

Tel: 753 7222. sansaba.com

70 acres. 5,000 cases. No visits.

Retired plastic surgeon Mark Lemmon bought this property in 1975 and produced his first vintage in 1981. With the exception of the Pinot Noir, all the wines are estate-grown, with Chardonnay the leading variety. Joel Burnstein is the winemaker.

Scheid ☆

1972 Hobson Ave, Greenfield, CA 93827.

Tel: 386 0316. Fax: 386 0127. scheidvineyards.com

6,000 acres. 5,000 cases. Tasting room.

The Scheids own or control vast acreage in Monterey, and started producing their own wines in 1991. The wines are mostly dilute.

Smith & Hook ☆→☆☆

37700 Foothill Rd, Soledad, CA 93960.

Tel: 678 2132. Fax: 678 0557. hahnestates.com

1275 acres. 40,000 cases. Tasting room.

This large estate is owned by software tycoon Nicky Hahn, and the first vintage was 1979. There is also a second label simply named "Hahn". Despite access to some fine vineyards, the wines are disappointing, with some lean, astringent, and occasionally herbaceous reds, and rather flabby whites. The top wines are bottled under the Baroness Reserve label, but seem scarcely worth the considerable extra outlay. Art Nathan is the winemaker.

Talbott ☆☆☆

53 W. Carmel Valley Rd, Carmel Valley, CA 93924.

Tel: 659 3500. Fax: 659 3515. talbottvineyards.com

550 acres. 24,000 cases (including Logan). Tasting room.

The Talbotts made their fortune from neckties, and applied some of it to the purchase of vineyards in various parts of Monterey. They sell most of their grapes, and the Chardonnay from Sleepy Hollow Vineyard is much sought after, but also produce three Chardonnays of their own: Diamond T Estate, Sleepy Hollow, and the barrel selection known as Cuvée Cynthia. There is also Pinot Noir produced from the Case Vineyard close to the winery. Logan is the estate's second label. Overall, the wines are opulent and oaky, and expensive.

Ventana Vineyard ☆☆

Winery: 2999 Monterey-Salinas Highway, Monterey, CA 93940.
Tel: 831 372 7415. Fax: 831 655 1855.
300 acres. 35,000 cases. Tasting room.

The iconoclastic grape farmer Doug Meador produces two ranges of wines:
the limited-production, high-quality Meador Estate (*qv*), and the more cheap
and cheerful Ventana label. These are standard varieties, but include Pinot
Blanc, Gewurztraminer (usually off-dry), and dry Riesling, varieties at which
the vineyard often excels.

San Luis Obispo County

Unless otherwise indicated, the area code for the wineries listed is 805.

Adelaida ☆☆→☆☆☆☆

5805 Adelaida Rd, Paso Robles, CA 93446.
Tel: 239 8980. Fax: 239 4671. adelaida.com
75 acres. 10,000 cases. Tasting room.

Owned by the Van Steenwyk family, Adelaida includes among its Westside
vineyards part of the historic Hoffmann Ranch, where Pinot Noir had been
planted as long ago as 1967. These old vines deliver an unusually rich,
dense, smoky wine with a marked personality. Indeed, all the Adelaida
wines have abundant character, none more so than "Pavanne", a powerful,
barrel-fermented Chenin Blanc. The full-bodied Riesling comes from
Paraiso Springs (*qv*) and the Cabernet Sauvignon is made in a rich, hefty,
minty style. John Munch was the winemaker until 1999, when he was
replaced by Steve Glossner.

Alban ☆☆☆☆→☆☆☆☆☆

8575 Orcutt Rd, Arroyo Grande, CA 93420. Tel: 546 0305. Fax: 546 9879.
65 acres. 8,000 cases. No visits.

All it took was a taste of Condrieu to persuade John Alban that he wanted
to produce wines from Rhône varieties. In 1990, he began planting his
vineyards with nothing but, and he was shrewd enough to realize that they
would thrive best in a relatively cool site. He has always sold much of the
fruit to other wineries, but in 1992 made his first Syrah, subsequently
supplemented with Viognier, Roussanne, and Grenache. He goes easy on
the new oak, and the intense fruit comes shining through. His top Syrah is
called Lorraine but often the regular Reva bottling is almost as fine. Alban
has also experimented with straw wines, a Rhône speciality, and a TBA-style
Roussanne, produced in some kind of collaboration with Austrian sweet-
wine guru Alois Kracher.

Arciero ☆☆

5625 Highway 46 East, Paso Robles, CA 93447.

Tel: 239 2562. Fax: 239 2317.

625 acres. 200,000 cases. Tasting room.

The Italian-born Arciero brothers came to the United States in 1939 and built up a successful construction business. In 1983, they started planting vineyards here, but much of the fruit is sold to other wineries. The range of wines consists of standard varietals and some Italian-style blends. Quality is average, but some of the wines can be good value, and there is some charming Muscat Canelli.

(*See also* Eos.)

Baileyana ☆☆

4915 Orcutt Rd, San Luis Obispo, CA 93401.

Tel: 597 8200. Fax: 546 0413. baileyana.com

1,000 acres. 18,000 cases. No visits.

The Niven family are the owners of the large Paragon Vineyard in Edna Valley. Since the mid-1990s, some of the fruit has been used to supply the family's own label. The winery has enjoyed a resurgence under winemaker Christian Roguenant, who joined it in 1999. In addition to Chardonnay, Sauvignon Blanc, and Pinot Noir, Baileyana is producing Syrah as well. The Nivens' Firepeak Vineyard is planted with new clones of Pinot Noir, Chardonnay, and Syrah, and some of these wines are given separate bottlings.

Carmody McKnight ☆☆☆

11249 Chimney Rock Rd, Paso Robles, CA 93446.

Tel: 238 9392. Fax: 238 3975.

100 acres. 3,500 cases. Tasting room.

Formerly known as Silver Canyon, this westside estate has enjoyed a recent makeover. Actor Gary Conway bought the property in the 1960s but only planted vines in 1985. Greg Cropper is the winemaker. The reds are typical "mountain" wines with deep colour, firm tannins, and tones of chocolate and liquorice. The Chardonnay is fresh and citric. The only failures are the jammy, late harvest Cabernet Sauvignon and Cabernet Franc!

Casa de Caballos *NR*

2225 Templeton Ave, Templeton, CA 93465.

Tel: 434 1687. Fax: 434 1560.

3 acres. 300 cases. No visits.

As the name suggests, Dr Tom Morgan's first love is raising horses, but since 1995 his family has been raising vines, too, producing tiny quantities of Pinot Noir, Merlot, and other varieties from their 1,200-foot-high vineyards. The wines are named after Morgan's Arabian mares, lending a whimsical air to the operation.

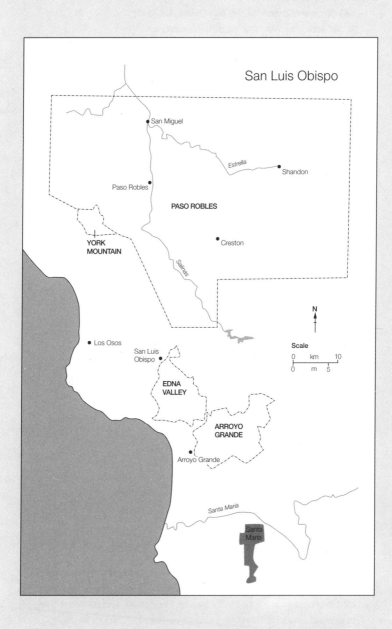

San Luis Obispo

Claiborne & Churchill ☆☆

2649 Carpenter Canyon Rd, San Luis Obispo, CA 93401.
Tel: 544 4066. Fax: 544 7012. claibornechurchill.com
No vineyards. 5,000 cases. Tasting room.

This husband-and-wife team enterprisingly specializes in Alsatian varieties, which they supplement with Pinot Noir and Chardonnay from McGregor Vineyard in Edna Valley.

Creston *NR*

679 Calf Canyon Highway, Creston, CA 93432. Tel: 434 1399. Fax: 434 2426.
155 acres. 12,000 cases. No visits.

Under owner Alex Trebek, this large property developed a good reputation for robust reds, but it was put on the market in 2000.

Dark Star *NR*

2985 Anderson Rd, Paso Robles, CA 93446.
Tel: 237 2389. Fax: 237 2589. darkstarcellars.com
No vineyards. 4,000 cases. No visits.

Norm Benson has the intention of producing small lots of high-quality red wines from Cabernet, Merlot, and Zinfandel.

Domaine Alfred *NR*

7525 Orcutt Rd, San Luis Obispo, CA 93401.
Tel: 541 9463. Fax: 546 2744. domainealfred.com
82 acres. 15,000 cases. No visits.

Originally founded as an outlet for the Chamisal Vineyard, the property was bought by electronics tycoon Terry Speizer after the death of the founder, Norman Goss. The only wines made are Chardonnay and Pinot Noir, and the reserve bottling carries the Califa label.

Dover Canyon ☆☆☆

4520 Vineyard Dr, Paso Robles, CA 93446.
Tel: 237 0101. Fax: 237 9191. dovercanyon.com
5 acres. 2,000 cases. Tasting room (weekends only).

Dan Panico, a former winemaker at Eberle (*qv*), set up Dover Canyon in 1997 and produces small lots of wines from various local vineyards, with excellent Zinfandel and assertive Viognier among the early releases.

WESTSIDE WINERIES

Some of the most exciting developments in the Paso Robles wine scene are taking place in the mountainous westside region. Here, most of the wineries have grouped together under the name of the Far Out Wineries. Many are very small but tend to open to visitors at weekends. Participating wineries are: Adelaida, Carmody McKnight, Le Cuvier, Dover Canyon, Dunning, HMR, Justin, Nadeau, Norman, and Paolillo.

Dunning *NR*

1953 Niderer Rd, Paso Robles, CA 93446.

Tel/fax: 238 4763. dunningvineyards.com

46 acres. 2,000 cases. Tasting room (weekends).

Robert Dunning's westside property dates from the early 1990s, and up until now has focused on Cabernet, Merlot, and Chardonnay. Syrah and Zinfandel were planted in 1999.

Eberle ☆☆→☆☆☆☆

Highway 46 East, Paso Robles, CA 93447.

Tel: 238 9607. Fax: 237 0344. eberlewinery.com

40 acres. 24,000 cases. Tasting room.

Gary Eberle is a veteran of Paso Robles winemaking. He was the winemaker at the now-defunct Estrella River winery, and planted 500 acres, including some exceptional Syrah, which later succumbed to phylloxera. In 1982, Gary Eberle founded his own winery, and has produced a series of elegant long-lived Cabernets, and more recently has specialized in Rhône varietals, releasing some delicious single-vineyard Syrah and Viognier. Eberle's influence has been considerable, as a significant number of Paso Robles winemakers began their careers working with him.

Edna Valley Vineyards ☆☆☆

2585 Biddle Ranch Rd, San Luis Obispo, CA 93401.

Tel: 544 5855. Fax: 544 0112. ednavalley.com

1,000 acres. 102,000 cases. Tasting room.

This large winery draws on the capacious resources of the Paragon Vineyards. The Niven family owns the vineyard, but Edna Valley Vineyards, part of the Chalone Group, vinifies and markets the wines. This is a cool region, marginally warmer than Santa Maria Valley in Santa Barbara, but the wines are quite rich.

Eighty per cent of production is Chardonnay. The rest is Pinot Noir, and small lots of Viognier, Syrah, and, when conditions permit, late harvest Riesling. Steve Dooley was the winemaker for many years; the current winemaker is Harry Hansen.

Eos ☆☆

Highway 46 East, Paso Robles, CA 93447.

Tel: 239 2562. Fax: 239 2317. eosvintage.com

625 acres. 60,000 cases. Tasting room.

Eos is an offshoot of Arciero, and the two wineries share facilities. Indeed, Stephen Felten is the winemaker for both. Certain blocks of the Arciero vineyards are reserved for Eos wines, but despite extensive tastings, I find it hard to see the rationale behind this new marketing venture. Overall, the wide range of varietals are medium-bodied and somewhat bland. The Petite Sirah is the best wine, and the Chardonnay is attractive.

Garretson ☆☆→☆☆☆

2323 Tuley Court, Paso Robles, CA 93446. Tel: 239 2074. Fax: 239 2057. mrviognier.com
No vineyards. 3,000 cases. No visits.

The website address says it all. Mat Garretson is devoted to Viognier
and a driving force behind the annual Hospices du Rhône celebration.
A former marketing man, he began making wine in 1997 and opened
his winery in 2001. As well as Viogniers, he makes Syrah and Roussanne
from single vineyards.

Grey Wolf Cellars *NR*

2174 Highway 46 West, Paso Robles, CA 93446. Tel: 237 0771. Fax: 237 9866.
10 acres. 3,000 cases. Tasting room.

Founded in 1994, this new winery, run by Joseph Barton, is specializing
in Meritage, Zinfandel, Syrah, and Chardonnay.

Hunt Cellars ☆

2875 Oakdale Rd, Paso Robles, CA 93446.
Tel: 818 237 1600. Fax: 818 718 8048. huntwinecellars.com
52 acres. 15,000 cases. Tasting room.

David Hunt produces a range of wines from locally grown fruit, as well as
from Sauvignon bought from Edna Valley and Chardonnay from Santa
Maria Valley. The wines receive prolonged oak-ageing, with the unhappy
consequence that many of the reds are attenuated and dry.

Tobin James Cellars ☆☆→☆☆☆

8950 Union Rd, Paso Robles, CA 93446. Tel: 239 2204. Fax: 239 4471.
40 acres. 27,000 cases. Tasting room.

Toby Shumrick sells his wines from the funkiest tasting room in eastside
Paso Robles. Some of his wines, the Cabernet and Sangiovese, are fairly
simple, but his real passion is evidently Zinfandel, and as many as ten
different bottlings may be produced in some years. The James Gang
Reserve Zinfandel is consistently exuberant.

Jan Kris ☆

Route 2, Bethel Road, Templeton, CA 94365. Tel: 434 0319.
50 acres. 3,000 cases. Tasting room.

Founded in 1991, Mark Jendron's family winery has few pretensions,
offering a range of easy-going, fruity varietal wines that are sold only
at the welcoming tasting room.

Justin ☆☆☆☆

11680 Chimney Rock Rd, Paso Robles, CA 93446.
Tel: 238 6932. Fax: 238 7382. justinwine.com
72 acres. 40,000 cases. Tasting room.

Justin Baldwin, a former investment banker, and his wife Deborah came
to this beautiful but remote spot in the mountains in 1982. Here they have
created a fine estate and small resort. Viticulture has to be adapted to the

microclimate, about which little was known until the vineyards were established. All wines are estate-grown. There have been many winemakers (Jeff Branco being the present one) and unavoidable changes of style, but quality has remained high. The white wines include a delicious, zesty Sauvignon Blanc and an intense, well-balanced Chardonnay, but the reds are more remarkable. There is powerful Cabernet, a delicious Bordeaux blend called Isosceles, and an immensely promising Syrah. Other wines include a softer Bordeaux blend called Justification, and a port-style wine, aged in oak puncheons, called Obtuse. Wines not deemed up to the mark for the Justin label are sold under the Epoch label. The winery seems to be going from strength to strength, but the proliferation of names and styles can be confusing, suggesting a lack of clear focus.

Laetitia *NR*

453 Tower Grove Dr, Arroyo Grande, CA 93420.
Tel: 481 1772. Fax: 481 6920. laetitiawine.com
390 acres. 15,000 cases. Tasting room.

The Champagne house Deutz set up shop in Arroyo Grande in the early 1980s, but the anticipated market for sparkling wine never materialized. Maison Deutz had a refit and emerged as Laetitia, using its vineyards to produce mostly still wines from Burgundian varieties, as well as a handful of single-vineyard wines. A little sparkling wine is still being made.

Laura's Vineyard ☆

3620 Highway 46 East, Paso Robles, CA 93446. Tel: 238 6300.
50 acres. 2,000 cases. Tasting room.

Patrick O'Dell, who owns Turnbull (*qv*) in Napa, is also the proprietor of this eastside estate. The wines are made at Turnbull. There's a gamey Syrah and a succulent Semillon, but overall, the wines are dull. Unsurprisingly, O'Dell has put the property up for sale.

Live Oak Vineyards *NR*

1480 North Bethel Rd, Templeton, CA 93465. Tel: 227 4766. Fax: 227 4968.
93 acres. 2,500 cases. No visits.

Bill and Janie Alberts planted a Chardonnay vineyard in 1981, but only started releasing wines under their own label in 1995.

Martin & Weyrich ☆→☆☆☆

2610 Buena Vista, Paso Robles, CA 93447. Tel: 238 2881. Fax: 238 3950.
180 acres. 30,000 cases. Tasting room.

The Martin brothers launched themselves with enthusiasm into the production of Italian varietal wines, bravely attempting to make the trickiest of all varieties, Nebbiolo. Results were very patchy. In the late 1990s, the brothers were bought out by their brother-in-law, which led to the change of name. Craig Reed and Alan LeBlanc-Kinne are the winemakers, and have continued with Tom Martin's Italian bent.

Quality remains variable: lacklustre Edna Valley Chardonnay, fresh Pinot Grigio, powerful Viognier, fairly thin Nebbiolo and Sangiovese, good Zinfandel, and some full-bodied, Super-Tuscan-style blends.

Mastantuono ☆

2720 Oak View Rd, Templeton, CA 93465.
Tel: 238 0676. Fax: 238 9257.
17 acres. 5,000 cases. Tasting room.

For twenty years, Pasquale Mastantuono has been producing rough-hewn wines, mostly from Italian varieties, at this westside property. Much of the wine is made from purchased fruit, and there is a strong local following for these rather burly old-fashioned wines.

Meridian ☆☆☆

7000 Highway 46 East, Paso Robles, CA 93447.
Tel: 237 6000. Fax: 239 9624. meridianvineyards.com
7,000 acres. 900,000 cases. Tasting room.

Veteran winemaker Chuck Ortman founded this large estate in 1984, a few years later it became part of the Beringer empire, and it is now owned by Beringer Blass. Ortman draws on Beringer's large vineyard holdings in the Central Coast to produce a range of cleanly made varietal wines.

Overall quality is much higher than the modest prices suggest, and some of the reserve bottlings – such as the Edna Valley Chardonnay and Santa Barbara Pinot Noir – can be very fine indeed. Paso Robles fruit is reflected in the spicy Syrah and dense, plummy Petite Sirah.

Norman ☆

7470 Vineyard Dr, Paso Robles, CA 93446l.
Tel 227 0138. Fax: 227 6733. normanvineyards.com
40 acres. 15,000 cases. Tasting room.

Art Norman and his winemaker, Robert Nadeau, have specialized in Zinfandels, such as the Old Vine Zinfandel from Cucamonga, and the dense, sweetish, alcoholic Monster Zin. Neither is for the faint-hearted. Other wines, such as Pinot Noir, Barbera, and Cabernet, can be thin or coarse.

Peachy Canyon ☆☆☆→☆☆☆☆

2025 Nacimiento Lake Dr, Paso Robles, CA 93446.
Tel: 237 1577. Fax: 237 2248. peachycanyonwinery.com
40 acres. 30,000 cases. Tasting room.

Doug and Nancy Beckett founded this property in 1988, drawing on estate-grown fruit and on grapes bought in from top vineyards such as the Dusi Ranch. They are deservedly well known for their range of Zinfandels, which have not only richness and weight, but an invigorating freshness and vigour. The Dusi Zinfandel is an especially impressive wine.

HOSPICES DU RHÔNE

In 1993, a group of Rhône-variety enthusiasts founded the Hospices du Rhône, a celebration of this style of wines. Although based on the celebrated Hospices de Beaune, this event is far more laid-back than its Burgundian model. It consists of workshops, food and wine events, tastings, barbecues, and an auction, and takes place in late May or early June each year. For further details, contact the organization at 2175 Biddle Ranch Rd., San Luis Obispo, CA 94301. Tel: 805 784 9543. Fax: 805 784 9546.

Pesenti *NR*

2900 Vineyard Dr, Templeton, CA 93465. Tel/fax: 434 1030.
45 acres. Tasting room.

This old family winery, established in 1934, has produced a range of very thin table wines, robust fortified wines, and Zinfandel in gallon jugs! In 2000, Pesenti was bought by Turley, presumably to gain access to its old vineyards.

Piedra Creek ☆

6238 Orcutt Road, San Luis Obispo, CA 93401. Tel: 541 1281.
No vineyards. 50 cases. No visits.

This is Edna Valley's smallest winery, founded in 1994 and run with zest by retired aerospace engineer Meo Zuech. He delights in fat, oaky Chardonnay from the MacGregor Vineyard, and also produces a little Zinfandel.

Stephen Ross *NR*

4910 Edna Valley Rd, San Luis Obispo, CA 93401. Tel: 594 1318. Fax: 594 0178.
9 acres. 2,800 cases. No visits.

Stephen Ross Dooley was for many years the winemaker at Edna Valley Vineyards (*qv*) and now works as a consultant winemaker. In 1994, he created this small operation specializing in wines from purchased fruit from local vineyards, as well as from remote Napa and Sonoma.

Saucelito Canyon ☆☆→☆☆☆☆

1600 Saucelito Canyon Rd, Arroyo Grande, CA 93420.
Tel/fax: 543 2111. saucelitocanyon.com
10 acres. 2,000 cases. No visits.

In 1974, Bill and Nancy Greenough bought this very isolated property, and to their surprise discovered a few ancient Zinfandel vines, planted in 1879, still clinging to life. They revived the old vines, replanted a few parcels, and added some Cabernet Sauvignon. The Zinfandel is harvested over many weeks, and the result is a dense, sometimes alcoholic wine; there are also small quantities of old-fashioned and very sweet, late harvest Zinfandel. Quality varies considerably according to the vintage.

Seven Peaks ☆☆→☆☆☆

5828 Orcutt Rd, San Luis Obispo, CA 93401.

Tel: 805 781 0777. Fax: 831 655 0904. 7peaks.com

1,000 acres. Tasting room..

Seven Peaks is a division of the large Australian Southcorp wine company. Southcorp formed a partnership with the Niven family of Paragon Vineyards and Baileyana (*qv*) to produce wines from Central Coast grapes, often from Paragon. With the exception of the Paso Robles Shiraz, all the wines are released under the Central Coast appellation. The range includes that Australian standby, Cabernet/Shiraz, and the wines are soundly made. The Chardonnay, Pinot Noir, and Shiraz are crowd-pleasers but the Cabernet is very good.

Stephan Vineyards *NR*

2815 Live Oak Rd, Paso Robles, CA 93446.

Tel: 227 6888. Fax: 227 6988. aventurewines.com

35 acres. 3,000 cases. No visits.

French winemaker Stephan Asseo and his partner, Frank Benedict, launched this ambitious project in 1997, planting vineyards with Cabernet and southern French varieties. The first three vintages were made from purchased grapes. The main label is L'Aventure; the second wines are released under the Stephan Ridge label. The range consists of Syrah, Zinfandel, Viognier, and new-oaked Chardonnay, and Optimus, a blend of Syrah, Cabernet, and Zinfandel. Prices are very high.

Tablas Creek ☆☆→☆☆☆

9339 Adelaida Rd, Paso Robles, CA 93446.

Tel: 237 1231. Fax: 237 1314. tablascreek.com

120 acres. 10,000 cases. No visits.

The Perrin brothers produce one of the great wines of France: Château de Beaucastel in Châteauneuf-du-Pape. They long dreamed of making Rhône-style wines in California, and formed a partnership with wine importer Robert Haas. After a long search, they settled on this site in the Santa Lucia Mountains. After many trials, they have now established a vineyard planted with healthy, high-quality French vines. The initial releases were a white blend (mostly Marsanne, Viognier, and Roussanne) and a red from Grenache, Syrah, Mourvedre, and Counoise. They seem somewhat ungainly, but the vines are still very young.

Talley ☆☆☆→☆☆☆☆

3031 Lopez Dr, Arroyo Grande, CA 93420.

Tel: 489 0446. Fax: 489 0996. Talleyvineyards.com

140 acres. 14,000 cases. Tasting room.

The Talleys were vegetable farmers in Arroyo Grande and suspected the land was well-suited to grapes. They began planting in 1982, eliminated varieties that didn't work (Cabernet Sauvignon) and located the best hillside sites, which they named Rosemary's Vineyard and Rincon. Brian Talley makes Pinot Noir and Chardonnay in a low-key, Burgundian style, emphasizing balance and complexity. Quality is impeccable. There is occasional, and superb, late harvest Riesling. Recently Talley has launched another label, Bishop's Peak, for good-value, early drinking Paso Robles wines.

Treana ☆☆

2175 Arbor Rd, Paso Robles, CA 93446. Tel: 238 6979. Fax: 238 4063.
140 acres. 11,000 cases. No visits.

There has been a long-standing and complex relationship between the Hope family of Hope Farms and Chuck Wagner of Caymus (*qv*) in Napa. The present outcome is a pair of wines under the Treana label: a soft, plump, overripe Viognier/Marsanne blend from the Mer Soleil (*qv*) vineyard in Monterey, and a fruity red from a blend of French and Italian varieties.

Vista del Rey *NR*

7340 Drake Rd, Paso Robles, CA 93446.
Tel: 467 2138. Fax: 467 2765.
26 acres. 700 cases. Tasting room (Sundays only).

An infant venture from Dave King, with winemaking assistance from the team at Wild Horse (*qv*). The winery will specialize in Zinfandel and Barbera.

Wild Horse ☆☆→☆☆☆☆

1437 Wild Horse Winery Court, Templeton, CA 93465.
Tel: 434 2541. Fax: 434 3516. wildhorsewinery.com
50 acres. 100,000 cases. Tasting room.

Ken Volk planted his vineyards in 1982, but most of his wines come from vineyards in various parts of the Central Coast. The long-term cellarmaster is Jon Priest, who has to cope with the dozens of varieties that have taken Volk's fancy. As well as sound Chardonnay and Pinot Noir, you can find Arneis, Malvasia Bianca, Negrette, and Trousseau. Volk's latest enthusiasm is for Rhône varieties, which he has planted near Tablas Creek (*qv*). There are other labels such as Rhône-varietal Equus (delicious Viognier and Syrah) and the upmarket Cheval Sauvage for their best Pinot Noir. Not surprisingly, quality is variable, but the wines from Wild Horse are never dull.

Windemere ☆☆

3482 Sacramento Dr, San Luis Obispo, CA 93403.
Tel: 542 0133. Fax: 545 8080. windemerewinery.com
25 acres. 3,000 cases. Tasting room (Thursday to Sunday).

Cathy MacGregor is the daughter of Edna Valley grower Andy MacGregor, and uses some of his Chardonnay grapes. She also produces Napa Cabernet and Paso Robles Zinfandel.

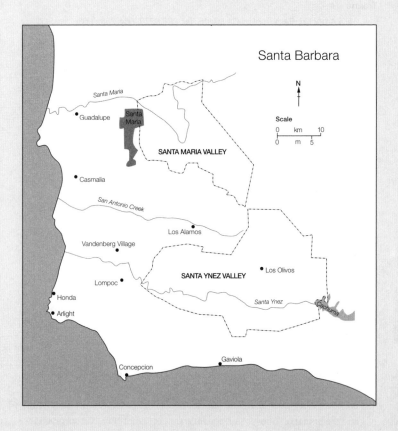

Windward Vineyard ☆☆

1380 Live Oak Rd, Paso Robles, CA 943446. Tel: 239 2565. Fax: 239 4005.
15 acres. 1,200 cases. No visits.

Marc Goldberg founded this property in 1990 with a view to producing high-quality and boldly structured Pinot Noir, with the aid of consultant winemaker Ken Volk of Wild Horse (*qv*).

York Mountain Winery ☆→☆☆

7505 York Mountain Rd, Templeton, CA 93465.
Tel: 895 238 3925. Fax: 895 238 0428. yorkmountainwinery.com
6,000 cases. Tasting room.

This is the major producer of wines from this cool, wet zone. An historic property, it was founded in 1882 and acquired by the Goldman family in 1970. The Pinot Noir is probably the best wine.

Santa Barbara County

Unless otherwise indicated, the area code for the wineries listed below is 805.

Au Bon Climat ☆☆☆☆

Santa Maria Mesa Dr, Santa Maria, CA 93454. Tel: 937 9801. Fax: 937 2539.
90 acres. 45,000 cases (26,000 Au Bon Climat). No visits.

Jim Clendenen may look as if he just emerged from a Neanderthal cave, but his shaggy locks should not disguise the fact that he has one of the most intelligent minds in the American wine industry. In 1981, he was bitten by the winemaking bug as a cellar rat in Burgundy, and took back techniques such as vinifying in open-top fermenters, punching down the cap during fermentation, and prolonged lees contact in barrel – techniques that were then unknown, or unpractised, in California.

From the beginning, Clendenen has focused on Burgundian varieties at Au Bon Climat. Although the winery has planted some vineyards, most of the grapes are bought in from the top vineyards of Santa Barbara, as well as a few from San Luis Obispo, such as Talley and Alban. He has also made Pinot from Oregon fruit (Ici/La Bas), and will in the future be sourcing grapes from North Coast regions such as the Russian River Valley.

Clendenen has always favoured finesse over power. Whether Pinot Noir or Chardonnay, the wine, he believes, should age and evolve in an interesting fashion. He has little time for the fat, oaky, alcoholic style that is so in vogue in California. One of his Chardonnay *cuvées*, Nuits Blanches, is deliberately made in an over-blown style just to prove that he can do it. It usually has fifteen degrees of alcohol, is entirely aged in new oak, and predictably wins high scores, even though Clendenen dislikes the wine and doesn't believe it will age as well as his more classic bottlings.

There has always been ample capacity at Au Bon Climat's hangar-like winery, so Clendenen has launched a number of other labels that demonstrate his versatility. Il Podere dell'Olivos, created in 1988, is devoted to 4,000 cases of Italian varietals, the more obscure the better. Vita Nova, a label he owns jointly with Bob Lindquist, specializes in Chardonnay, Sauvignon Blanc, Sangiovese, and a blend from Bordeaux varieties.

Babcock ☆☆→☆☆☆☆

5175 Highway 246, Lompoc, CA 93436. Tel: 736 1455. Fax: 736 3886.
85 acres. 20,000 cases. Tasting room.

Bryan Babcock produces a wide range of wines, of which the Eleven Oaks Sauvignon Blanc is probably the most consistent. The estate-grown wines are supplemented by wines from purchased grapes. The Chardonnays are widely admired but can be a touch heavy. More recently, he has started producing some interesting red wines: Sangiovese, Cabernet Franc, the splendid Black Label Syrah, and an unusually elegant Bordeaux blend called Fathom. The second label, mysteriously known as Troc, can offer excellent value.

Barnwood Vineyards *NR*

4250 Highway 33, Ventucopa, CA 93252.
Tel: 766 9199. Fax: 766 2949. barnwoodwine.com
380 acres. 8,000 cases. No visits.

These must be some of the highest vineyards in California, planted at 3,200 feet in the remote Cuyama Valley. The wines are mostly the Bordeaux varieties, but there are also some Rhône varieties and even Tempranillo. About one-third new oak is used for most of the wines. Owners Nebil Zarif and Selim Zilkha also own Laetitia (*qv*) in San Luis Obispo.

Beckmen ☆☆☆

2670 Ontiveros Rd, Los Olivos, CA 93441.
Tel: 688 8664. Fax: 688 9983. beckmenvineyards.com
175 acres. 20,000 cases. Tasting room.

Tom Beckmen, a pioneer of the electronic music business, has now turned his hand to grape farming. In addition to the home vineyards, new acreage is being planted on Purisima Mountain in Santa Ynez Valley. There is a strong emphasis on Rhône varieties, as well as Nebbiolo and a red Rhône blend: Cuvée Le Bec.

Bedford Thompson ☆→☆☆☆

9303 Alisos Canyon Rd, Los Alamos, CA 93440. Tel: 344 2107. Fax: 344 2047.
42 acres. 7,000 cases. Tasting room.

Stephan Bedford, former winemaker at Rancho Sisquoc, teamed up in 1993 with grape grower David Thompson. Part of the fruit is sold off. Bedford produces some spicy Chardonnay and lively Syrah and Cabernet Franc, but some of the other wines are unexciting.

Brander ☆☆

2401 Refugio Rd, Los Olivos, CA 93441. Tel: 688 2455. Fax: 688 8010. brander.com
43 acres. 8,000 cases. Tasting room.

Although Fred Brander produces Chardonnay, Merlot, and a Bordeaux blend called Bouchet, he is best known for his Sauvignon Blanc, which represents the majority of his production. One of them is called Au Naturel and is unoaked; the top Cuvée Nicolas is rich but too oaky for some tastes.

Brewer-Clifton *NR*

1502 Chapala St, Santa Barbara, CA 93101.
Tel: 963 2527. Fax: 963 2547. brewerclifton.com
No vineyards. 500 cases. No visits.

Greg Brewer is a rising star, buying in Chardonnay and Pinot Noir from low-yielding vineyards in Santa Barbara, making wines in a big, full-throttled style. In addition, there is a range of sparkling wines.

Buttonwood Farm ☆

1500 Alamo Pintado Rd, Solvang, CA 93463.
Tel: 688 3032. Fax: 688 6168. buttonwoodwinery.com
39 acres. 7,000 cases. Tasting room.

Australian-born Michael Brown makes the wines from these organic vineyards. As well as standard varietals, there are two proprietary blends: Devin (Sauvignon and Semillon), and Trevin from red Bordeaux grapes.

Byron ☆☆☆→☆☆☆☆

5230 Tepusquet Rd, Santa Maria, CA 93454.
Tel: 937 7288. Fax: 937 1246. byronwines.com
641 acres. 45,000 cases. Tasting room.

Ken Brown was the first winemaker at Zaca Mesa (*qv*) and left to start his own winery in 1983. After Mondavi bought the property in 1990, investments were made both in a new winery and in restructuring the vineyards; Burgundian varieties dominate, and some Rhône varieties are planted, too. Chardonnay is the most important wine. There are reserve bottlings of Pinot and Chardonnay, but often the regular *cuvées* have the freshness and elegance one looks for from Santa Maria fruit, whereas the Reserves can show a touch too much oak. Quality is highly consistent.

TOP SANTA BARBARA CHARDONNAYS

Any selection of producers of outstanding Chardonnay would almost certainly have to include the following wineries: Arcadian, Au Bon Climat, Babcock, Bedford Thompson, Byron, Cambria, Foxen, Koehler, Longoria, Meridian, Qupé, Sanford, and Sunstone.

Cambria ☆☆☆

5475 Chardonnay Lane, Santa Maria, CA 93454.

Tel: 937 8091. Fax: 934 3589. cambriawines.com

1405 acres. 100,000 cases. Tasting room (weekends only).

After Jess Jackson bought large sections of the former Tepusquet Vineyard in 1987, he set up this winery to make use of its finest blocks. Although the Reserve Chardonnay is considered the best white wine from Cambria, the less opulent and confected Katherine's Vineyard is often more pleasurable. The Julia's Vineyard Pinot Noir can be delicious, and a sound Syrah has also joined the range. All the wines are well-made if not exactly memorable.

Chimère ☆☆

425 Bell St, Los Alamos, CA 93440.

Tel: 922 9097. Fax: 922 9143.

No vineyards. 5,000 cases. Tasting room (Friday to Monday).

Patrice Mosby, who used to work at Edna Valley Vineyards, produces small lots of wines from Bien Nacido and other leading vineyards. The red wines show a distinctive smokiness as a consequence of the long barrel-ageing that Mosby favours. The Merlot and Petite Sirah are ripe and vigorous, but the Pinot Noir and Nebbiolo lack freshness.

Clos Pepe *NR*

4777 Highway 246, Lompoc, CA 93436.

Tel: 735 2196. Fax: 736 5907. clospepe.com

28 acres. 250 cases. No visits.

Even though the vineyards are still young, Wes Hagen's Pinot Noir and Chardonnay grapes are eagerly sought after by the top wineries in Santa Barbara. In 2000, he began producing his own wines for the first time. They are sure to attract keen interest when they are eventually released.

Cold Heaven ☆☆

PO Box 717, Solvang, CA 93463.

Tel: 688 8630. Fax: 688 3593.

3 acres. 3,000 cases. No visits.

Jim Clendenen's wife, Morgan Toral Clendenen, makes a small quantity of Pinot Noir and Viognier under her own label at the Au Bon Climat winery.

Cottonwood Canyon ☆☆

3940 Dominion Rd, Santa Maria, CA 93454.

Tel: 937 9063. cottonwoodcanyon.com

76 acres. 5,000 cases. Tasting room.

Norman Beko founded this winery in 1988, initially specializing in Chardonnay and Pinot Noir. More recently, blends have been added to the range: Synergy from Merlot and Cabernet, Synthesis from the two Cabernets. Early vintages showed overripe fruit and premature oxidation.

Curtis ☆☆☆

5249 Foxen Canyon Rd, Los Olivos, CA 93441.
Tel: 686 8999. Fax: 686 8788. curtiswinery.com
65 acres. 14,000 cases. Tasting room.

This Santa Ynez winery belongs to its neighbour Firestone (*qv*), and the winemaker is Chuck Carlson. It specializes in Rhône varietals and blends, and recent tastings have impressed. There is aromatic Viognier, supple, elegant Syrah, and a delicious and inexpensive Heritage Cuvée, which pays homage to the southern Rhône.

Firestone ☆☆

5000 Zaca Station Rd, Los Olivos, CA 93441.
Tel:688 3940. Fax: 686 1256. firestonewine.com
535 acres. 240,000 cases. Tasting room.

Brooks Firestone left the tyre business in 1972 to establish this very successful Santa Ynez estate and winery, which is now owned by Suntory, although Brooks's son Adam still manages the property. It soon developed a good reputation for Riesling, Sauvignon Blanc, and Merlot. More recently, there have been some successful red blends, as Firestone realized early on that pure Cabernet did not always ripen here. Firestone has always aimed for sound wines at a fair price, and by and large it achieves this goal. Consequently, the wines never reach great heights, but they are well-made and usually good value.

Foley Estates *NR*

1711 Alamo Pintado Rd, Solvang, CA 93463.
Tel: 688 8554. Fax: 688 9327.
600 acres. 8,000 cases. Tasting room.

Originally founded as Carey Cellars in 1978, this property has been through many changes of ownership, and is now in the hands of William Foley, who appointed Alan Phillips as winemaker. A wide range of wines is produced, both from its own large vineyard and from Bien Nacido and other sites. There is also a Bordeaux blend called Arabesque.

Foxen ☆☆☆

7200 Foxen Canyon Rd, Santa Maria, CA 93454.
Tel: 937 4251. Fax: 937 0415.
10 acres. 12,000 cases. Tasting room (weekends only)

Dick Dore and (winemaker) Bill Wathen created this winery in 1987, and it has been going from strength to strength. Most of the fruit comes from prominent Santa Barbara vineyards, such as Tinaquaic for Chardonnay, and Bien Nacido and Julia's Vineyard for Pinot Noir. They do vary considerably depending on the vineyard source, so it's wise to taste before you buy. Overall, the Chardonnays are marked by good acidity, and the Pinot Noirs are silky in texture and spicy in flavour. Syrah has been patchy.

Gainey ☆→☆☆

3950 East Highway 246, Santa Ynez, CA 93460. Tel: 688 0558. Fax: 688 5864.
124 acres. 22,000 cases. Tasting room.

Gainey produces a sound range of varietal wines, but does not aim very high. Many of the wines are dilute, suggesting overcropping in the vineyards, but some of the reserve bottlings, known as Limited Selection, are marginally better. The reds, especially the Cabernet Sauvignon and Cabernet Franc, often show a green, herbaceous character. The Riesling, however, is fresh, crisp, and well-balanced.

Daniel Gehrs Wines ☆☆→☆☆☆

2939 Grand Ave, Los Olivos, CA 93441. Tel: 688 0694. Fax: 688 6121.
No vineyards. 7,500 cases. Tasting room.

Dan Gehrs was until recently the winemaker at Zaca Mesa, but since 1990, has also had his own label, producing wines from purchased grapes. Sources vary greatly, with Pinot Blanc and Chenin Blanc from Monterey, Barbera and Syrah from Santa Barbara. The white wines can be very good, with fresh acidity, but there can be something raw about the reds.

Hitching Post ☆☆☆

406 East Highway 246, Buellton, CA 93427.
Tel: 688 0676. Fax: 686 1353. hitchingpost2.com
No vineyards. 4,000 cases. No visits, but wines supply the eponymous restaurant.

Frank Ostini is a restaurateur who offers excellent BBQ. He also has a passion for wine, and for two decades has been producing mostly Pinot Noir, but also Syrah and a Cabernet/Merlot blend called Generation Red. Each year he makes up to five different Pinots and two Syrahs, from different vineyards sources.

IO ☆☆☆☆

See Byron.
2,000 cases.

This is a label reserved at Byron for a Rhône-style blend from Syrah, Grenache, and Mourvedre. The colour is deep, the fruit intense, the oak influence moderate.

Jaffurs ☆☆☆→☆☆☆☆

2319 Foothill Lane, Santa Barbara, CA 93105. Tel/fax: 962 7003. jaffurswine.com
No vineyards. 2,500 cases. No visits.

Craig Jaffurs has become one of Santa Barbara's leading Syrah specialists, using purchased grapes from top vineyards. These can be wonderfully fruity, supple, truffley wines. He also makes a little Chardonnay, Viognier, and Grenache; and there's an intriguing blend called Matilja Cuvée from Mourvedre, Syrah, and Cabernet Franc. Some of the wines show a sweetness on the palate that may be derived from the extensive use of American oak. The overall style is rich and lush.

Kahn ☆☆→☆☆☆

2990 Grand Ave, Los Olivos, CA 93441.

Tel: 805 686 2455. Fax: 877 868 8345. kahnwines.com

No vineyards. 2,500 cases. Tasting room.

Andrew Kahn began producing wine in 1996. Cuvée Jacques is a Rhône blend, and comes in red and white versions. In addition, there is pure Syrah, and a wildly overpriced Cabernet Franc, dedicated to Frank Sinatra, and thus inevitably labelled Cab Frank. The wines are lively and vigorous, if not very complex.

Koehler ☆☆☆

5360 Zaca Station Rd, Los Olivos, CA 93441.

Tel: 686 8484. Fax: 686 8474. koehlerwinery.com

100 acres. 12,000 cases. Tasting room.

The Koehlers have been growing grapes in Santa Ynez for many years, but only began producing their own wines in 1999. Chris Curran was the winemaker, and the first releases – Sauvignon, Chardonnay, Riesling – were fresh, vigorous, and charming. In 2001, a new winemaker, Doug Scott, was appointed, so the style may change.

LinCourt ☆☆→☆☆☆

343 North Refugio Rd, Santa Ynez, CA 93460.

Tel: 688 8381. Fax: 688 3764.

300 acres. 12,000 cases. Tasting room.

Since 1996, LinCourt has had the same owner and winemaker as Foley (*qv*), and is in effect a second label. The winery specializes in Chardonnay, Pinot Noir, and Syrah, all aged in French oak, but there is also some Viognier and Cabernet Franc. The Reserve Pinot Noir is excellent.

Richard Longoria ☆☆☆→☆☆☆☆

2935 Grand Ave, Los Olivos, CA 93441.

Tel: 688 0305. Fax: 688 2767. longoriawine.com

8 acres. 5,000 cases. Tasting room.

Richard Longoria is a Santa Barbara veteran, having made wine in the past for Carey and Gainey. He has had his own label for many years, but only built a winery in 1997. There is a wide range of wines made in a bright, vibrant style, emphasizing fruit rather than oak or tannin. The Pinot Gris, Pinot Noir, Cabernet Franc, Merlot, and Syrah are all of high quality.

Los Olivos Vintners ☆

2923 Grand Ave, Los Olivos, CA 93441.

Tel: 688 9665. Fax: 824 8584.

No vineyards. 2,500 cases. Tasting room.

Founded in 1982 as Austin Cellars, the business was bought in 1992 by Hart White. The wines are standard varietals, made in a lush, somewhat confected style. Austin Cellars has been retained as a second label.

Melville ☆

5185 East Highway 246, Lompoc, CA 93436.
Tel: 735 7030. Fax: 735 5310. melvillewinery.com
82 acres. 4,000 cases. Tasting room.

The Melville family planted vineyards in 1994, and the grapes are much sought after by other wineries. They began producing wines in 1999, with Greg Brewer of Brewer-Clifton (*qv*) as the winemaker. Yields are very low, and quality potential is clearly excellent, but the Chardonnay is made in a blowsy, over-alcoholic style, and the Pinot Noir is disappointing (in addition, the 1999 was cloudy thanks to a perverse refusal to filter).

Mosby *NR*

9496 Santa Rosa Rd, Buellton, CA 93427.
Tel: 688 2415. Fax: 686 4288. mosbywines.com
74 acres. 9,500 cases. Tasting room.

Bill Mosby specializes in Italian varieties, all estate-grown. Sangiovese is the principal wine, but you can also find Freisa, Nebbiolo, Cortese, Primitivo, and Teroldego.

Andrew J Murray ☆☆☆☆

6701 Foxen Canyon Rd, Los Olivos, CA 93441. Tel: 686 9604. Fax: 686 9704.
50 acres. 7,000 cases. Tasting room: 2901 Grand Ave, Los Olivos, CA 93441.

Los Angeles restaurateur James Murray took his teenage son Andrew on gastronomic tours of France, where they first became acquainted with the great wines of the Rhône. When James retired to Santa Ynez in 1990, he began planting Rhône varieties, and Andrew became the winemaker. There are four different *cuvées* of Syrah, based on different vineyard parcels and blends, as well as delicious Viogniers and sound Marsanne. There are also red and white Rhône blends, known respectively as Esperance and Enchanté. The Syrahs are quite exotic, with tones of cloves and black olives. Yields are kept low, so all the wines show fine concentration and length of flavour.

Fess Parker ☆→☆☆☆

6200 Foxen Canyon Rd, Los Olivos, CA 93441.
Tel: 688 1545. Fax: 686 1130. fessparker.com
660 acres. 50,000 cases. Tasting room.

Visitors flock to this spacious winery hoping for a glimpse of Mr Parker, known to older Americans for his portrayal of Davy Crockett in the movies. Often they are rewarded. This is very much a family business and Fess's son Eli is the winemaker.

There is a large range of wines, with a number of cheaper bottlings produced from fruit purchased in various parts of California. The Chardonnays are made in a crowd-pleasing, tropical-fruit style, and the Pinot Noir is a touch sweet and broad. There are Rhône-style blends, red

TASTING ROOM ETIQUETTE

Most large wineries in California have tasting rooms, but in Napa and Sonoma it is increasingly common to find a charge, usually around $5, levied per person, presumably to deter daytrippers from getting drunk at a winery's expense. This charge is usually refunded if any wine is purchased, and often tasters are allowed to keep the logo-inscribed glass. Where no charge is made, you are not under any obligation to buy any wine, although a modest purchase in return for an extensive and hospitable tasting is always appreciated. Some wineries offer limited releases of wines only at the winery, and these are often from unusual grape varieties and worth looking out for.

and white, and a newcomer to the range, Cabernet Franc. The reserves are patriotically known as American Tradition Reserve, and are almost always aged exclusively in new oak.

Podere dell'Olivos.

See Au Bon Climat

Qupé ☆☆☆→☆☆☆☆

4665 Santa Maria Mesa Rd, Santa Maria, CA 93454. Tel: 937 9801. Fax: 686 4470.
12 acres. 20,000 cases. No visits.

Bob Lindquist mystifyingly describes Qupé as "a modern stone-age winery." Although he makes good Chardonnay, Lindquist is best known for his fine Rhône-style wines. His Syrah has always been exemplary, especially the single-vineyard bottlings. The Marsanne/Roussanne is creamy and rich, and more recently he has released good Marsanne, delicious Alban Vineyard Roussanne and what may be the only Albariño in California.

Rancho Sisquoc ☆→☆☆

6600 Foxen Canyon Rd, Santa Maria, CA 93454.
Tel: 934 4332. Fax: 937 6601. ranchosisquoc.com
320 acres. 12,000 cases. Tasting room.

This long-established vineyard/winery dates from 1968, and produces a range of standard varietals, together with a little Marsanne. Whites have usually been the best wines, and a small quantity of Sylvaner, possibly the only example in California, is also made. Alec Franks is the winemaker.

Rusack Vineyards *NR*

1825 Ballard Canyon Rd, Solvang, CA 93463. Tel: 688 1278. rusackvineyards.com
37 acres. 5,000 cases. Tasting room.

Geoff Rusack bought the defunct Ballard Canyon Winery in 1995 and produces Chardonnay, Riesling, Cabernet Sauvignon, Cabernet Franc, Merlot, and Syrah.

Sanford ☆☆→☆☆☆☆

7250 Santa Rosa Rd, Buellton, CA 93427. Tel: 688 3300. Fax: 688 7381.
16 acres. 40,000 cases. Tasting room.

Richard Sanford is a pioneer of Pinot Noir production in Santa Barbara. He first planted the variety in 1971, at what soon became the most famous Pinot Noir vineyard in southern California: Sanford & Benedict. That original partnership split, and in 1981 Sanford started his own winery.

He has focused on Sauvignon Blanc, Chardonnay, and Pinot Noir, all made in a rich, ripe, succulent style. The stylish Estate Chardonnay is often preferable to the costlier but less vigorous Barrel Select. In 1999 Sanford added a delicious new Pinot Noir to the range, La Rinconada, produced from a newly acquired vineyard in Santa Rita.

Santa Barbara Winery ☆☆→☆☆☆☆

202 Anacapa St, Santa Barbara, CA 93101.
Tel: 963 3633. Fax: 962 4981. sbwinery.com
96 acres. 35,000 cases. Tasting room.

Pierre Lafond founded the county's first winery in 1962, and in 1972 began planting vineyards in Santa Ynez. Bruce McGuire has been the winemaker here for two decades, and over the years he has made some excellent Chardonnays and Pinot Noir, as well as some Syrah, barrel-fermented Sauvignon Blanc, and a series of late harvest wines from Riesling and Sauvignon Blanc.

Sunstone ☆→☆☆☆

126 Refugio Rd, Santa Ynez, CA 93460.
Tel: 688 9463. Fax: 686 1881. sunstonewinery.com
48 acres. 5,000 cases. Tasting room.

Fred Price began planting his organic vineyards in 1989, and first made wine in 1992. The present winemaker is Blair Fox. The range of wines is wide, and the highlights include a delicious, crisp Reserve Chardonnay, a peachy Estate Viognier, a delicate Merlot, and a supple Bordeaux blend called Eros. There are also some Rhône-style blends, however these can lack concentration.

Lane Tanner ☆☆☆

PO Box 286, Santa Maria, CA 93456. Tel/fax: 929 1826.
No vineyards. 2,200 cases. No visits.

This experienced winemaker specializes in vineyard-designated Pinot Noir and Syrah in a bright, fresh style.

Tantara ☆☆☆

15 acres. 2,000 cases. No visits.

Jeff Fink buys in fruit from well-known vineyards, such as Bien Nacido and Talley in Arroyo Grande, to produce a number of vineyard-designated Chardonnays and Pinot Noirs.

Vita Nova

See Au Bon Climat.

Whitcraft Wines *NR*

1861 Lewis St, Ballard, CA 93463. Tel: 963 0111. Fax: 688 4833.

No vineyards. 2,000 cases. No visits.

Chris Whitcraft specializes in single-vineyard Chardonnay and Pinot Noir, made in a non-interventionist style without pumping, fining, or filtration. Prices are high.

Zaca Mesa ☆☆☆

6905 Foxen Canyon Rd, Los Olivos, CA 93441.

Tel: 688 9339. Fax: 688 8796. zacamesa.com

450 acres. 45,000 cases. Tasting room.

This winery was founded in 1972, and since 1986, it has been owned by property tycoon John Cushman. Despite many changes in winemaker over the years (Clay Brock is the present one), Zaca Mesa has moved increasingly towards the production of Rhône-style wines. The Syrah is rich and plump, and marries well with the American oak in which it is usually aged. Viognier can be dull or excellent, and is very much at the mercy of vintage variation. Cuvée Z is a lush southern-Rhône blend, upfront and meaty. The Chardonnay is made with a light hand, and as a consequence is crisp and refreshing.

Other tasting rooms: The proliferation of small wineries in Santa Barbara means that it is not always practicable for such wineries to maintain tasting rooms. However, there are a number of cooperative tasting rooms along Grand Avenue in Los Olivos, where it is possible to taste wines from a number of wineries in one place. There are also a few tasting tooms devoted to single wineries. So if time is limited, Grand Avenue is the place to go for a rapid survey of Santa Barbara wineries.

Los Olivos Tasting Room and Wine Shop

2905 Grand Ave, Los Olivos, CA 93441. Tel: 688 7406. Fax: 688 0906.

Los Olivos Wine & Spirits Emporium

2531 Grand Ave, Los Olivos, CA 93441. Tel: 688 4409. Fax: 688 0025.

Other Wineries

With few exceptions, the wineries listed below are not attached to a particular region, but purchase grapes from various parts of California. The exceptions are the handful of wineries in southern California (such as Moraga in Bel Air or Ojai in Ventura) and the Central Valley (such as Ficklin and Quady). One significant wine-producing region in southern California, Temecula, is in decline after being ravaged by Pierce's disease. The hot Central Valley is not ideally suited to grape farming, but with the help of irrigation, night-harvesting, and other techniques, it is possible to make clean, simple wines form this vast region. Nonetheless, very few wineries are based here, and those that are, such as Gallo, buy grapes from all parts of the state.

Ancien *NR*

PO Box 10667, Napa, CA 94581.
Tel: 707 255 3908. Fax: 707 255 6104. ancienwines.com
No vineyards. 2,400 cases. No visits.

Ken and Teresa Bernards, both winemakers of long experience, set up Ancien in 1992 to specialize in Pinot Noir from top vineyards in Carneros, Sonoma Mountain, and the Russian River Valley. The wines are usually aged in fifty per cent new French oak.

Arcadian ☆☆☆☆

PO Box 1395 Santa Ynez, CA 93460.
Tel: 805 688 1876. Fax: 805 686 5501. arcadianwinery.com
No vineyards. 8,000 cases. No visits.

Joseph Davis is a Burgundy admirer who dislikes the current trend in California towards high-alcohol, over-ripe wines. He leases blocks within celebrated vineyards such as Bien Nacido in Santa Barbara and Sleepy Hollow in Monterey so that he can control yields and pick at the ideal moment. The result is a range of elegant, perfectly balanced Chardonnay, Pinot Noir, and, since 1999, Syrah.

Baywood ☆

381 Cannery Row, Monterey, CA 93940.
Tel: 831 645 9035. Fax: 831 645 9345. baywood-cellars.com
2,000 acres. 30,000 cases. Tasting room.

Baywood is the label for grape growers John and James Cotta, who farm in Lodi and Monterey. These are simple wines, pleasant enough, but of little distinction. The top Grand Reserve range is overpriced for the quality. However, there is an appealing Tempranillo from Yolo County.

Blackstone Winery *NR*

9060 Graton Rd, Graton, CA 95444.
Tel: 707 824 2401. Fax: 707 824 2592. blackstone-winery.com
No vineyards. Tasting room.

Owned since 2001 by Pacific Wine Partners, a joint venture between Constellation and BRL hardy of Australia, this winery specializes in Merlot, although it also produces Chardonnay and Cabernet. With the exception of a Napa Merlot, the grapes come from all over the state.

Bogle ☆→☆☆☆

37783 County Road 144, Clarksburg, CA 95612.

Tel: 916 744 1139. Fax: 916 744 1187. Boglewinery.com

1,200 acres. 200,000 cases. Tasting room.

Although the Bogle family own large vineyards in the Sacramento Delta, they also buy in grapes for blending. Thus, all their wines appear under the California appellation. They have kept up with the times by downplaying varieties such as Chenin in favour of Chardonnay and Cabernet. The wines are very sound, and the Petite Sirah consistently good.

Bronco Wine Company

6342 Bystrum Rd, Ceres, CA 95307. Tel: 209 535 3131. Fax: 209 538 4634.

This is one of a handful of corporations that pump out enormous (if undisclosed) quantities of usually mediocre though inexpensive wines under brand names that include the following: Rutherford Vintners, Hacienda, Grand Cru, Laurier, Domaine Napa, Napa Creek, Napa Ridge, Estrella, JJJ, Charles Shaw, and Antares.

Calera ☆→☆☆☆☆

11300 Cienega Rd, Hollister, CA 95023. Tel: 408 637 9170. Fax: 408 637 9070.

47 acres. 30,000 cases. No visits.

Josh Jensen became addicted to Pinot Noir when working in Burgundy in the early 1970s and concluded that the region owed its supremacy to its limestone soils. So he sought after a similar *terroir* in California and found it in a remote spot high in the Gavilan Mountains. Here he planted vineyards with Pinot Noir and Viognier, but supplemented production by purchasing Chardonnay and Pinot Noir from the Central Coast. The estate Pinots have been very inconsistent: sometimes powerful and long-lived, in other years earthy, volatile, and raw. The Viognier, on the other hand, is among the finest in California.

Callaway ☆→☆☆

32720 Rancho California Rd, Temecula, CA 92589.

Tel: 909 676 4001. Fax: 909 676 5209. callawaycoastal.com

750 acres. 250,000 cases. Tasting room.

Ely Callaway, who died in 2001, was a golf tycoon who developed Temecula vineyards in 1969 and became the region's leading producer, specializing in mostly unoaked wines from Chardonnay and Chenin Blanc, both dry and sweet. When, in the late 1990s, Pierce's disease gravely affected the vineyards, Callaway was deftly repositioned as Callaway Coastal, buying in grapes from all over California and using more oak-ageing.

Constellation Brands

The corporation, previously known as Canandaigua, has given itself a glitzy rebranding. It was previously known for brands that exploited once-famous winery names, even though the wines were mediocre. These included

NEGOCIANT WINERIES

Every ambitious American winemaker wants to set up shop in California, but the soaring cost of vineyards and of winery construction makes it impossible for all but the wealthy. So many top winemakers operate out of rented or shared facilities (or the basement of their home), often located in unprepossessing industrial estates. But these offer them inexpensive and clean premises in which to vinify and age wines made from grapes bought in from some of the top vineyards in California. The best of these wineries include: Ancien, Arcadian, Dashe, Edmunds St John, Kalin, Littorai, Patz & Hall, Ramey, Siduri, Testarossa, and Sean Thackrey.

Inglenook, Almaden, Paul Masson, Dunnewood, and Taylor. More recently Constellation has acquired leading wineries such as Franciscan, Simi, most of Sebastiani, and Ravenswood; fortunately, there is no evidence as yet that these distinguished names will be downgraded by their new owner.

Delicato ☆→☆☆☆

12001 South Highway 99, Manteca, CA 95336.
Tel: 209 824 3501. Fax: 209 824 3510. delicato.com
9,000 acres. Tasting room.

Delicato was founded in 1924, when Gaspare Indelicato planted a few vineyards. The company grew into one of the largest bulk-wine producers in California and became proprietor of the state's largest vineyard, San Bernabe in Monterey County. By the early 1990s, Delicato was said to be producing some two million cases of wine. Now it has cosily refashioned itself as Delicato Family Vineyards, itself divided into various ranges. The Blue Label series is of standard varietals, while Monterra (*qv*) is devoted to Monterey fruit, as is the more exclusive Monterey Vine Select.

Edmunds St John ☆☆☆→☆☆☆☆

1331 Walnut St, Berkeley, CA 94709.
Tel: 510 981 1510. Fax: 510 981 1610, edmundsstjohn.com
No vineyards. 4,000 cases. No visits.

Steve Edmunds was one of the original "Rhône Rangers" in California and is even said to have coined the term. Since 1985, he has made a series of wines from Syrah and Mourvedre, as well as blends. He has hunted down his fruit sources: Syrah from Sonoma, Mount Veeder in Napa, and El Dorado County; and Mourvedre from the old vines in Oakley and from Mount Veeder. New oak influence is minimal so as to preserve the intense, wild fruitiness of Syrah especially. He also makes small quantities of Pinot Grigio and Sangiovese, and has found new sources of grapes that should permit the winery to expand.

Estancia ☆☆☆

See Franciscan.

1,800 acres. 160,000 cases. No visits.

This label is used by owner Franciscan for wines from Monterey and Paso Robles, which are mostly aged in American oak. As well as Merlot and Cabernet, there is a Cabernet/Sangiovese blend called Duo and a Meritage, all of which are reasonably priced.

Ficklin ☆☆☆→☆☆☆☆

30246 Avenue 7.5, Madera, CA 93637. Tel: 559 674 4598. ficklin.com

35 acres. 11,000 cases. Tasting room.

Walter Ficklin planted vineyards in one of the hottest parts of the Central Valley in 1911, but it wasn't until 1946 that his sons planted the Portuguese varieties that are now the source for some of California's finest port-style wines. Their principal product is a non-vintage Tinta port made by a kind of *solera* method. In exceptional years, they release a vintage wine, and have recently produced a ten-year-old tawny, planning in due course to make a twenty-year-old. Quality is consistent.

Fiddlehead Cellars ☆☆→☆☆☆

1667 Oak Ave, Davis, CA 95616. Tel: 916 756 4550. Fax: 916 756 4558.

25 acres. 2,000 cases. No visits.

Kathy Joseph has earned a good reputation by producing rather odd wines: Sauvignon Blanc from Santa Ynez, Santa Barbara Pinot Noir, and another Pinot Noir from the Willamette Valley in Oregon. The Sauvignon can lack vigour, but the Pinots have been good. In the late 1990s, she bought land near the Sanford & Benedict Vineyard in Santa Ynez, where she planted Pinot Noir of her own.

E & J Gallo ☆→☆☆☆

600 Yosemite Blvd., Modesto, CA 95354. Tel: 209 341 3111.

6,000 acres. 75,000,000 cases. No visits.

What can one say about a winery that produces more volume than the whole of Australia? Only a small part of that volume appears under the Gallo name; other brands include Livingston Cellars, Carlo Rossi, Turning Leaf, Anapamu, Indigo Hills, and Zabaco. Most of the wines are mediocre.

Back in the 1960s, about half the production of Napa Valley was vinified by a local cooperative and dispatched to Gallo in the Central Valley, so there was a time when even jug wines such as Hearty Burgundy had some decent grapes in them. In the 1980s, the Gallos realized it made better sense to secure their own vineyards, which is when they created Gallo Sonoma (*qv*), both as a source of fruit for their various brands and as an opportunity, eagerly seized, for them to improve their image. The standard Gallo wines are aggressively marketed at enormous cost, and are essentially bland. Many of the brands play down or don't mention the Gallo name at all, so they are exercises in marketing.

The Gallos are a highly secretive bunch – requests to visit their Modesto winery over the years have simply been ignored – but they are up-to-date and competent in their viticultural and winemaking techniques. Decades ago, they were encouraging their regular growers to grub up the poor-quality varieties with which Central Valley vineyards were planted (Flame Tokay, even Thompson Seedless table grapes) and to replace them with the international varieties that would soon be in great demand from the consumer.

They are also ruthless in defence of their name, dispatching writs and lawyers to see off anyone other than themselves who tries, with however much legitimacy, to put the name of Gallo on a bottle of wine.

Guenoc ☆☆

21000 Butts Canyon Rd, Middletown,CA 95461.

Tel: 707 987 2385. Fax: 707 987 9351. guenoc.com

270 acres. 100,000 cases. No visits.

This large Lake County estate is owned by the Magoon family, and much is made of the fact that Lillie Langtry lived here in the late nineteenth century. There was a vineyard here in 1854, and the modern vineyard is planted with standard varietals. Both red and white Bordeaux blends are produced, as well as good Chardonnay and Petite Sirah.

Hart ☆

413909 Avenida Biona, Temecula, CA 92593. Tel: 714 676 6300.

12 acres. 6,000 cases. Tasting room.

Joe Travis Hart specializes in Merlot and Zinfandel and southern French varieties such as Grenache and Mourvedre, these latter wines being produced from purchased fruit. There used to be Cabernet here, but the vines have been grafted over to Syrah and Viognier.

Paul Hobbs ☆☆☆→☆☆☆☆

3355 Gravenstein Highway N, Sebastopol, CA 95472.

Tel: 707 824 9879. Fax: 707 824 5843. paulhobbs.com

14 acres. 8,000 cases. No visits.

Paul Hobbs is an experienced wine consultant who set up his own company in 1991, buying in fruit from top vineyards in the Napa Valley and Sonoma County. His Sonoma Chardonnays are his best wines: rich but not overbearing, and full of flavour. His own vineyard of Pinot Noir will come on stream in 2003.

JC Cellars *NR*

Alameda. Tel: 510 435 6357.

No vineyards. 1,000 cases. No visits.

The initials stand for Jeff Cohn, the winemaker at Rosenblum (*qv*). Like his boss, he specializes in single-vineyard Zinfandels, but has also released small quantities of Syrah and Petite Sirah.

Kalin Cellars *NR*

61 Galli Dr, Novato, CA 94949.
Tel: 415 883 3543. Fax: 925 283 2909. kalincellars.com
No vineyards. 7,000 cases. No visits.

Terrance Leighton buys in fruit from various parts of the state: Semillon and Chardonnay from Livermore and Sonoma, and Pinot Noir from Sonoma and Mendocino. The white wines are barrel-fermented in a good deal of new oak, and there is also a high proportion of new oak used to age the red wines, which are bottled without fining or filtration. Leighton also makes a range of sparkling wines. The rich Chardonnays are the most admired wines in the range. Kalin is unusual in only releasing wines for sale after they have had many years of bottle age.

Kendall-Jackson ☆☆→☆☆☆☆

421 Aviation Blvd, Santa Rosa, CA 95403.
Tel: 707 544 4000. Fax: 707 544 4013. kj.com
12,500 acres. 4,000,000 cases.
Tasting room at 5007 Fulton Rd, Santa Rosa, CA 95439.

Jess Jackson, a lawyer, only started producing wines from his small Lake County vineyards in 1982. His Chardonnay was an instant hit from 1983, Jackson has never looked back, and must be one of the very few self-made billionaires in the American wine industry. From the start, he focused on coastal fruit, buying or planting large vineyards in the Central Coast as well as in Alexander Valley and the Sonoma Coast. Jackson's winemaking team blended wines to create their consistent Vintners Reserve range; a dollop of residual sugar in the Chardonnay did no harm to its commercial success.

In the 1990s, Jackson started acquiring other wineries, though he retained their separate identities under the umbrella organization of Jackson Family Vineyards, now renamed Kendall-Jackson Wine Estates. These wineries are owned by Jackson and his wife and not formally associated with Kendall-Jackson. These includes Edmeades, Hartford Court, Lokoya, Pepi, La Crema, Stonestreet, Cambria, and Matanzas Creek (*qv*). He also created new labels for very expensive wines with a specific identity, such as those originating from mountain vineyards. These labels include Cardinale, Atalon, Verité, and Carmel Road.

The Kendall-Jackson style, whether for Vintners Reserve or its more limited Grand Reserve or Great Estates, is that of a fruit-driven blend. Jackson created what he calls "flavor domaines", which are styles of wine derived from local microclimates and easily identifiable by his winemakers as blending components. The high-priced wines, such as Carmel Road and Verité, are heavily oaked and opulent.

By 2000, Jess Jackson, entering his seventies, began to step back from direct control of his companies, although he retains personal ownership of many of the vineyards. His empire was in negotiation with other companies with a view to a merger or takeover, but by mid-2001, Kendall-Jackson seemed to have been withdrawn from the market.

Leeward *NR*

2784 Johnson Dr, Ventura, CA 93003. Tel: 805 656 5054.

4 acres. 15,000 cases. No visits.

This winery is best known for its Chardonnay, bought in from Edna Valley and other Central Coast locations. Yet the range can vary according to grape availability: at various times there has been Cabernet and Merlot from Napa and from Alexander Valley, and Pinot Noir from the Bien Nacido vineyard in Santa Maria.

Littorai ☆☆☆→☆☆☆☆

1985 Vineyard Ave, St Helena, CA 94574. Tel: 707 963 4762. Fax: 707 963 7332.

No vineyards. 2,000 cases. No visits.

As the first American to make the wine at a major Burgundian estate – Domaine Roulot in Meursault in the early 1980s – Ted Lemon has a more instinctive grasp of authentic Burgundian style than most. After many years working for Chateau Woltner (*qv*) and as a consultant, he set up this small *négociant* business in the mid-1990s. He argues for the importance of low yields, clonal selection, and minimal intervention in the winery. Always searching for the finesse that is the elusive hallmark of great Burgundy, he has sought out cool vineyards, mainly from the Sonoma Coast, but also from Anderson Valley in Mendocino and the Russian River Valley. The style is lean and elegant and a far cry from the overblown Chardonnays and jammy Pinot Noirs that more usually find favour with American wine-lovers.

Moraga ☆☆☆☆

650 Sepulveda Blvd, Los Angeles, CA 90031.

Tel: 310 471 8560. Fax: 310 471 6435.

15 acres. 500 cases. No visits.

There are few more unlikely locations for a vineyard in California than this deep canyon in Bel-Air, close to Beverly Hills. Aviation executive Tom Jones soon realized that his hobby vineyard had different microclimates and enjoyed higher rainfall than most of southern California. With advice from consultant winemaker Tony Soter, he began in the late 1980s to produce a series of sumptuous and oaky Cabernet Sauvignons, aged mostly in new French oak.

Ojai ☆☆☆→☆☆☆☆

10540 Encino, Oak View, CA 93022. Tel: 805 649 1674. Fax: 805 649 4651.

No vineyards. 6,000 cases. No visits.

Adam Tolmach, the winemaking partner of Jim Clendenen at Au Bon Climat (*qv*) until the early 1990s, began creating his own label at his family property north of Los Angeles in 1984. Until 1995, there were vineyards here, but they

PIERCE'S DISEASE

If the resurgence of phylloxera in the 1980s weren't bad enough, there was more to come in the form of an airborne bacterial infection called Pierce's disease. It is spread by a creature called the glassy-winged sharpshooter. This insect is often active near watercourses, so vineyards close to streams and rivers are vulnerable. The disease, for which there is no cure, has long proved troublesome on Spring Mountain in Napa, and has destroyed hundreds of acres in the southern Californian region of Temecula. Insecticides are ineffectual, but recent suggestions that genetically modified vines could keep the disease at bay have led to considerable controversy.

succumbed to Pierce's disease. He buys Syrah and Viognier from Roll Ranch, the only surviving vineyard in Ventura County. Even better is the spicy Bien Nacido Syrah, and the same vineyard, as well as Pisoni in Monterey, provides him with Pinot Noir. Vin de Soleil is a white Rhône blend, and there is also pure Roussanne from Santa Barbara. There is a rich white Bordeaux blend, and an occasional late harvest Viognier. Tolmach knows that quality originates in the vineyard, and stipulates precise yields to the growers he works with.

Patz & Hall ☆☆
PO Box 518, Rutherford, CA 94573. Tel: 707 963 4142. Fax: 707 963 9713. patzhall.com. No vineyards. 12,000 cases. No visits.

This *négociant* winery is run by two winery executives and oenologist Ann Moses. They select top-quality Pinot Noir and Chardonnay from vineyards throughout the North Coast. The wines are aged in mostly new oak, and can be marred by excessive oakiness and high alcohol. This appears to be a stylistic choice rather than clumsy winemaking, as the winery proudly describes its own wines as "full-blown". However, high alcohol can disguise vineyard characteristics, which is regrettable, since grapes are sourced from outstanding North Coast vineyards such as Hyde, Dutton Ranch, and Caldwell.

RH Phillips ☆→☆☆☆
26836 Country Road 12A, Esparto, CA 95627.
Tel: 530 662 3215. Fax: 530 662 2880. rhphillips.com
1,600 acres. 500,000 cases. Tasting room.

This large Yolo County estate was founded in 1981 and run by the Giguiere family, until its sale in 2000 to the Vincor group of Canada. It employs a number of labels: EXP is dedicated to Rhône varieties (the Viognier can be very good), "Toasted Head" to oaky Cabernet, Merlot, and Cabernet/Syrah, and the winery name is used for sensibly priced varietals.

Quady ☆☆→☆☆☆

13181 Road 24, Madera, CA 93639.
Tel: 559 673 8068. Fax: 559 673 0744. quadywinery.com
13 acres. 22,000 cases. Tasting room.

When Andrew Quady set up shop in 1981, fortified wines had a dreadful reputation in California. But fortified wines were what Madera, in the hot Central Valley, did best. Quady's inspiration was to create new wine styles from Orange and Black Muscat, and package them brilliantly in half-bottles with inventive labels. His Essensia, Elysium, and Electra recognize the delicacy of Muscat, and are light in alcohol and bright in their fruit quality and aroma. They have been enormously successful. At the same time, Quady makes good port-style wines, fruitier than those of his neighbour Ficklin (*qv*). A recent innovation has been the introduction of two Vermouth-style wines.

Ramey ☆☆☆☆

1784 Warm Springs Rd, Glen Ellen, CA 95442. Tel: 707 833 4650. Fax: 707 833 5620.
No vineyards. 1,000 cases. No visits.

David Ramey, the celebrated winemaker for Matanzas Creek, Dominus, and now Rudd, also has his own label, which allows him to make wines without consulting employers. The Chardonnays come from Carneros, with the Hyde Vineyard bottling usually having a slight edge over the Hudson Vineyard. Ramey has plans to produce a Bordeaux blend from Diamond Mountain fruit, and a Syrah.

Rosenblum ☆☆→☆☆☆☆

2900 Main St, Alameda, CA 94801.
Tel: 510 865 7081. Fax: 510 865 9225. rosenblumcellars.com
32 acres. 70,000 cases. Tasting room.

Kent Rosenblum, a vet, founded this *négociant* winery in 1978, aided by his brother Roger and now by winemaker Jeff Cohn. He is justly celebrated for his Zinfandels: up to ten different bottlings each vintage, each one sourced from a different vineyard. But there are many more wines on offer: Merlot and Petite Sirah from Napa, a Bordeaux blend called Holbrook Mitchell Trio, and occasional Viognier, Chardonnay, and Black Muscat. As befits a vet, Rosenblum has also invented a line of inexpensive but characterful blends under the whimsical Chateau La Paws label. But the Zin's the thing, and Rosenblum's are richly fruity and well-balanced.

Siduri ☆☆☆→☆☆☆☆

980 Airway Court, Santa Rosa, CA 95403.
Tel: 707 578 3882. Fax: 707 578 3884. siduri.com
No vineyards. 5,000 cases. No visits.

Since 1994, Adam Lee has bought in top-quality Pinot Noir from leading vineyards in Sonoma Coast, Sonoma Mountain, Santa Lucia Highlands, and Oregon. Very rapidly, he has gained an enviable reputation for his hard-to-find wines, which are produced with minimal intervention, and without fining or filtration. In addition, from vineyards belonging to Lee's wife, Dianne, Siduri produces a few thousand cases of Bordeaux varieties and blends under the Novy label.

Sine Qua Non

Ventura.

No vineyards. 1,500 cases. No visits.

This eccentric winery was founded and operated by Austrian restaurateur Manfred Krankl, who owns Campanile in Los Angeles. His wines are one-offs, produced from purchased fruit and sold in weirdly shaped bottles at high prices to avid collectors on his mailing list.

Many of the wines are from Rhône varieties and are made in a very oaky style. His most interesting venture was a collaboration with Austrian sweet-wine supremo Alois Kracher to produce a range of sweet wines under the "Mr K" label: a Viognier Trockenbeerenauslese, a straw wine from Semillon, and an icewine from Traminer.

Steele ☆☆→☆☆☆

4793 Cole Creek Rd, Kelseyville, CA 95451.

Tel: 707 279 9475. Fax: 707 279 9633.

65 acres. 30,000 cases. No visits.

Jed Steele spent much of the 1980s as winemaker for Kendall-Jackson (*qv*), but after a falling-out with Jess Jackson, he left to set up his own winery in Lake County. Although he buys Pinot Noir from leading vineyards throughout the state, Steele retains a fondness for the vineyards of Lake County and Mendocino, which supply much of the Syrah and Zinfandel he produces. The style of his wines is ripe and fleshy, and they can sometimes lack finesse. The second label is Shooting Star.

Testarossa ☆☆☆→☆☆☆☆

330A College Ave, Los Gatos, CA 95030.

Tel: 408 354 6150. Fax: 408 354 8250. testarossa.com

No vineyards. 9,000 cases. No visits.

Since 1994, Rob and Diana Jensen have established Testarossa as one of the best *négociant* wineries in California. Although based in part of a former winery in Los Gatos, they buy most of their fruit from further south: from Chalone, the Santa Lucia Highlands, and Santa Maria. Winemaker Ed Kurtzman uses a fair amount of new French oak for both the Chardonnay and the Pinor Noir, but the wines have sufficient structure and concentration for the oak not to dominate.

The wines have different personalities, too, and the Michaud Chardonnay from Chalone has a mineral quality and tight texture that are rare in California. There is also some highly promising Syrah from Gary's Vineyard in the Santa Lucia Highlands.

Sean Thackrey ☆☆→☆☆☆☆

240 Overlook Dr, Bolinas, CA. Tel: 415 868 1781. Fax: 415 868 9290.
No vineyards. 3,000 cases. No visits.

A small town on the chilly Pacific coastline north of San Francisco is usually regarded as a great place to watch whales but a poor choice for a winery. Sean Thackrey has led a double life, as an art dealer in the city, and as a winemaker who has the freedom to do exactly as he pleases. His best-known wine is Orion, a magnificent Syrah, although production has been dogged by the disappearance or sale of successive vineyard sources. No sooner does Thackrey make them famous than a rich buyer snaps them up.

Pleiades is as close as Thackrey gets to an easy-drinking style, being a blend of Grenache, Syrah, and Zinfandel, and combining the efforts of various vintages in a non-vintage bottling. He has also bought Viognier and Roussanne from Alban in Arroyo Grande, and there is no telling what he will do from one year to the next. Only one thing is certain: it's bound to be interesting.

Acknowledgments

I particularly wish to thank the Wine Institute of California for helping to organize my travels in order to research this book. John McLaren and Venla Freeman in London, and Diane Berardi in San Francisco, were all extremely helpful and efficient. John Enquist of the Mendocino Winegrowers Alliance organized a tasting of Rhône varieties for me in Hopland, and Mat Garretson did the same many hundreds of miles further south, in Paso Robles. Eric Wente helped to clarify some of the regulations governing the labelling of California wines.

I also wish to thank the wine merchants and importers who provided me with samples of wines I might not otherwise have had an opportunity to taste: Berry Bros & Rudd, Joseph Berkmann, Corney & Barrow, Hatch Mansfield, and Southcorp. Patricia Parnell also arranged for me to taste the IO wines.

Index

Directory entries for wineries are in bold.